David Bade

Integrational Linguistics for Library & Information Science
Linguistics, Philosophy, Rhetoric and Technology

International Association for the Integrational Study of Language and Communication

International Association for the Integrational Study of Language and Communication

2015

David Bade, Rita Harris, Charlotte Conrad. *Roy Harris and Integrational Semiology 1956-2015: A bibliography.*

2020

Sinfree Makoni. *Language in Africa. Selected papers*, vol. 1
David Bade. *Efficiencies and Deficiencies: Essays on Cataloging and Communication in Libraries.*
Sinfree Makoni. *African Applied Linguistics. Selected Papers*, vol. 2
David Bade. *Integrational Linguistics for Library & Information Science: Linguistics, Philosophy, Rhetoric and Technology*

In preparation:

Sinfree Makoni. *Linguistic Ideologies, Sociolinguistic Myths and Discourse Strategies in Africa. Selected Papers*, vol. 3
Cristine Severo and Sinfree Makoni. *Language in Lusophonia: Perspectives from Bakhtin, Southern Theory and Integrational Linguistics*
David Bade. *Epistemologies of Rape and Revelation*
David Bade. *Making Mongolians: Linguistics, Historiography, Fiction*

The International Association for the Integrational Study of Language and Communication

The IAISLC was founded in 1998. It is managed by an international Executive Committee, whose members are:

Adrian Pablé (University of Hong Kong), Secretary
David Bade (University of Chicago, retired)
Charlotte Conrad (Dubai)
Stephen J. Cowley (University of Southern Denmark)
Daniel R. Davis (University of Michigan)
Dorthe Duncker (University of Copenhagen)
Jesper Hermann (University of Copenhagen)
Christopher Hutton (University of Hong Kong)
Peter Jones (Sheffield Hallam University)
Nigel Love (University of Cape Town)
Sinfree Makoni (Penn State University)
Rukmini Bhaya Nair (Indian Institute of Technology)
Jon Orman (Brighton)
Talbot J. Taylor (College of William & Mary)
Michael Toolan (University of Birmingham)

Anyone wishing to join the Association can do so by email apable@hku.hk or by sending their name and address to the Secretary:

Dr Adrian Pablé
School of English
Run Run Shaw Tower
Centennial Campus
The University of Hong Kong
Hong Kong S.A.R

For my parents
Philip (1929-2020) and Margaret Bade

©2020 David Bade.
Corrected printing

Acknowledgements

The Semantics of Science ©2006 Originally published in *Journal of Documentation*, v. 62, no. 1, p.145-153

Definition in Theory and Practice ©2007 Originally published in *Journal of Documentation*, v.63, nr.6, p.987-992

Of Minds and Language ©2009 Originally published in *Journal of Documentation*, v.65, nr.6, p.1027-1036

After Epistemology ©2011 Originally published in *Journal of Documentation*, v.67, nr. 1, p.194-200

Was ist Information? ©2008 Originally published in *Journal of Documentation*, v.64, nr.1, p.172-174

Language, Meaning and the Law ©2011 Originally published in *Journal of Documentation*, v.67, nr.4, p.731-738

Principia Rhetorica ©2009 Originally published in *Journal of Documentation*, v.65, nr.3, p.515-522

Media and New Capitalism in the Digital Age: The Spirit of Networks ©2011 Originally published in *Journal of Documentation,* Vol. 67 No. 5, pp. 878-892

Ethos, Logos, Pathos or Sender, Message, Receiver? A Problematological Rhetoric For Information Technologies ©2009 Originally published in. *Cataloging & Classification Quarterly*, v. 47, nr.7, p.612-630

The Zheng He Dilemma ©2006 Originally published in *Language & Communication* v. 26, nr. 2, p. 193-199

Relevance Ranking Is Not Relevance Ranking ©2007 Originally published in *Online Information Review*, 2007, v. 31, nr. 6, p.831-844.

It's About Time! Temporal aspects of metadata management in the work of Isabelle Boydens. ©2011 Originally published in *Cataloging & Classification Quarterly*, v.49, nr.4, p.328-338

IT, That Obscure Object of Desire ©2012 Originally published in *Cataloging & Classification Quarterly*, v.50, nr.4 p.316-334

What Happened to Politics and Ethics? Seven 21st Century Library Philosophers on the Epistemological and Ontological Foundations of Library Science ©2013 *Journal of Information Ethics* v. 22, nr.1, p. 80-108.

Thinking About Efficiency in Libraries ©2010 Originally published in *Journal of Documentation*, v. 66, nr.1, p.154-170.

Cover painting by Khaliun

Contents

Preface
Part One
Integrational Linguistics for Information Science
I. *The Semantics of Science*....................5
II. *Definition in Theory and Practice*....................22
III. *Of Minds and Language*....................37
IV. *After Epistemology*....................57
V. *Was ist Information?*....................71
VI. *Language, Meaning and the Law*....................77
VII. *Principia Rhetorica*....................91
VIII. *Media and New Capitalism in the Digital Age*....................105
Part Two
Integrational Linguistics and Information Technology
IX. *Ethos, Logos, Pathos or Sender, Message, Receiver? A Problematological Rhetoric For Information Technologies*........119
X. *The Zheng He Dilemma*....................147
XI. *Relevance Ranking Is Not Relevance Ranking*....................157
XII. *It's About Time!*....................183
XIII. *IT, That Obscure Object of Desire*....................199
XIV. *Technology waits for no one?*....................231
Part Three
Library Science:
Ethics, Language, Management, Philosophy
XV. *What Happened to Politics and Ethics? Seven 21st Century Library Philosophers on the Epistemological and Ontological Foundations of Library Science*....................251
XVI. *Se vogliamo che tutto rimanga com'è, bisogna che tutto deva essere scritto in inglese* (English version)....................295
XVII. *Thinking About Efficiency in Libraries.*....................307
XVIII. *Outsourcing and Cooperation: Questions of Flexibility and Responsibility.*....................339
XIX. *The Content of Journals Published by Nova Science Publishers, Inc*....................365
XX. *Nullum crimen sine lege*....................373
XXI. *I Know Where I Am Going, Do You?*....................387

Preface

Much of my writing since discovering the work of Roy Harris has been devoted to communication in libraries, in particular the practice of cataloging. As a library employee and library cataloger during most of the past 40 years, I felt both a personal need and a professional responsibility to understand what I was doing and what I saw happening around me. A number of those papers were published in a previous volume, *Efficiencies and Deficiencies*. The papers reprinted here focus upon how Harris's theoretical explorations are relevant to other aspects of library related activities, in particular to the fields of information science and the discourses of library science and management.

Part One contains reviews of several books by Harris, as well as books by Eran Fischer, Chris Hutton, Peter Janich and Michel Meyer, these latter all reviewed in light of integrational linguistics, and all written for the *Journal of Documentation* with an intended readership of information scientists. What I strove to do in each of these lengthy reviews was to argue for the relevance and importance of these works (and integrational semiology in general) for information science. The papers in Part Two directly address certain questions arising from the theories, design and use of information technologies, and do so from a perspective informed by integrational linguistics and semiology. The papers reprinted in Part Three examine the language of library science and of library management, with particular emphasis on issues of professional ethics and responsibility in a world that remains ours to make or to break.

David Bade
Rachel's Farm
4 April 2020

Part One

Integrational Linguistics for Information Science

I

The Semantics of Science[1]

The use of the literature of linguistics in information science was the topic of a dissertation by Amy Warner (Warner, A., 1987) in which the author described her finding that there was no significant use of linguistics literature in the literature of information science. An occasional uncritical nod to the 'standard authorities' was found, but little more. While the lack of influence of linguistics may be deserved and perhaps even a blessing, nevertheless there are some linguists developing ideas which should be not only of great interest to librarians and information scientists, but which ought to provoke a serious critical examination of some of the most cherished assumptions upon which our theories and practices are based.

---

[1] A review of Roy Harris' *The semantics of science.* (London: Continuum, 2005)

In the literature of information science the references to linguistics which appear most frequently are to Chomsky and his followers working in what was originally (but not so originally) called The Standard Theory, a name which was modified with a following publication becoming The Extended Standard Theory and then shortly thereafter The Revised Extended Standard Theory. Numerous changes in the theory since the 1970's have had different names, leading many linguists now to write simply of The Standard Theory meaning by that 'whatever Chomsky believes today.' Chomsky's genius lay not so much in his understanding of language as in calling his theory The Standard Theory, an appellation which at the same time established all competing theories as Non-Standard.

In contrast to Chomsky's political writings, the Standard Theory has been described by the author of the book under review here as 'a fascist concept of languages if ever there was one' (Harris, 1983). A similar judgement was put forward by George Steiner in a recent interview:

> It could be that, by an irony of history, the future may view Chomsky not as the anarchist and extreme leftist radical but rather as the proponent of a vision of grand linguistic capital, of the monopoly of power of a single language. A world of Chomskian universality would be the world of an anglo-american *patois*. (Quoted in Duch, 2004, p. 109)

While this anglo-americentric Chomskian vision of the universe fits well with linguistic attitudes commonly held by non-linguists (including many librarians and information scientists) such non-standard views as those represented by Harris and Steiner are inimical to and probably for that very reason rarely cited in the literature of information science, the only exception that I know of being Julian Warner's use of Harris' work, including his review of two of Harris' earlier books in this journal (Warner, J., 1997).

Among linguists Roy Harris is well known but not always appreciated and almost as rarely cited in linguistics as he is in the literature of information science. He has been described as a linguistic anarchist, an accusation no one could ever lay on Chomsky *qua* linguist. In the words of one of the contributors to a festschrift for Harris

> The criticism of Roy Harris most frequently voiced by other linguists is that his work destroys without rebuilding. Nowhere in his writings does he articulate the kind of practical program on which the linguistics industry could continue to survive, let alone expand. As if his relentlessly trenchant judgements on other theoreticians of language from the beginning of history to the present day didn't do damage enough, he casts them in a lucid and elegant prose style that can actually be read by people outside the field. Hence he is a threat to linguistics not only from within—where he can be safely ignored—but from without, where his scepticism over the possibility of any scientific linguistics puts the general reputation of the discipline into peril.
> The failure to establish a practical programme is indeed a problem that Harris should confront... (Joseph, 1997, p. 9)

There are good reasons for this cool reception. To follow Harris entails accepting severe criticisms of the current profession of linguistics and all existing theories of language, an insistence upon situating any theory of language within a wider theory of communication, the admission that linguistics should be prescriptive and not merely descriptive, and even questioning the existence of 'languages'. For most linguists trained under Chomsky (and his predecessors and his followers), this is simply too much to accept, even conditionally. Yet in spite of my being among that crowd (University of Illinois, MA, 1977), my experiences as a librarian prepared me to greet Harris' books and their heretical ideas with excitement and great expectation. And Harris's latest book is a book that I think many other librarians ought to read as well, at least all those librarians whose minds are engaged in thinking about information technologies, information retrieval, subject searching, natural vs. controlled subject vocabularies and multilingual or cross-language information seeking.

With the 1980 publication of his second book *The language makers* Harris initiated what has come to be known as *Integrational linguistics,* a theory of language which makes a radical break with all previous western theories of language. In the years which followed *The language makers* Harris published a number of monographs on the history of linguistics, tracing the legacy of myths about language from the Biblical Tower of Babel and Plato to Saussure, Wittgenstein, Chomsky and Pinker, demonstrating how certain ideas about language have influenced the way we think, speak and write about everything else. He also published a number of books on the signs of writing and semiology in general, argueing for a wider theory of communication as essential to an adequate understanding of the varied expressions of language. By insisting on the communicative nature of language, Harris put himself at odds with the Chomskians, for whom language is simply an innate mental device which was perhaps accidentally put into the service of communication. In the aforementioned festschrift, two of Chomsky's faithful (Borsley and Newmeyer) insist that communication is irrelevant to linguistics and The Standard Theory makes no claims nor attempts to explain linguistic communication:

> Chomsky has missed few opportunities to stress that language is only incidentally an instrument of communication; its 'design features' do not manifest any signs of communicative ends ... The following passage, from Chomsky (1979), is typical:

There is no reason to believe—to repeat myself once again—that language 'essentially' serves communicative ends, or that the 'essential purpose' of language is 'communication', as is often said, at least if we mean by 'communication' something like transmitting information or inducing belief. (p. 87)

Lately, Chomsky has taken to claiming that the organization of grammar makes it ill-designed for communication and that only a series of 'computational tricks' allow it to be used to these ends at all (see for example Chomsky 1991).
The goal of generative grammar is not now and never has been to explain linguistic communication. (Borsley and Newmeyer, 1997, pp. 46-47)

Perhaps in response to the complaints of Joseph and other linguists noted above, during these first years of the new millenium Harris has been taking his analysis abroad, investigating the role that language plays in the creation and maintenance of a number of cultural and academic 'supercategories': first Art (*The necessity of artspeak* (2003)), then History (*History, science and the limits of language* (2003); *The linguistics of history* (2004)), and now with the volume under review, Science. In each of these books his topic is not the supercategory itself, but the ideas about language which ground and fashion the speaking and writing of the practitioners of these cultural activities: artists, art critics, and lovers of art; historians and all those who speak of the past; scientists, philosophers of science and all those working in, as he puts it, "Laboratories and Libraries". This larger project of investigating language is not, of course, what Joseph and other linguists had in mind; what they really wanted was a new manner of writing grammars so that the linguistics industry could renew itself with an improved model and once again redescribe 6000+ languages with all the opportunities for employment, publication and fame that this would provide.

The Semantics of science is not about the language of science as that topic is ordinarily conceived; it is about the ideas and theories (lay or professional) *about* language that are presupposed by those people who write about science, whether scientists, philosophers, journalists or laymen. When people speak and write of the linguistic character of scientific discourse, of the language of science, what do they think that language is? What does language do and how does it do what it does? When a physicist speaks of *mesons* or *gravity* or *space-time*, does she assume that there is 'really' something called a *meson* or a 'thing' called *gravity* or *space-time* which can be discovered, described and known once and for all? May they not also end up like ether and polywater? And if people writing in other languages use different words, are they referring to the same things? Harris introduces the problem thus:

> I think that for most of its history science has subscribed to an erroneous theory of language, originally propagated in antiquity, which I call the 'language myth'. It still flourishes today, not only in Laboratories and Libraries. According to this myth, language 'works' as follows. Words are items belonging to a conventionally agreed linguistic code, shared by all members of a linguistic community. This code allegedly functions as a system enabling one member of the community to exchange thoughts with any other member who understands the code. Thanks to this, A can know what B thinks (provided B has used the code correctly to express those thoughts). (*The Semantics of Science*, p. 2-3)

This process of thought transference differs from telepathy in that it requires the mediation of public signs (which the code provides). Harris calls this *telementation*. Harris claims that this theory of language and its assumptions underlie the whole enterprise of Western science and scientific education, including mathematics. They provide the basis for believing that there is such a body as 'the scientific community', whose members, although divided into various subcommunities with their own technical dialects, nevertheless have access to a common language of science. (ibid. p. 3)

If these assumptions are not credible, Harris suggests, 'the impressive edifice of scientific thinking is itself based on linguistic foundations of sand' (ibid.).

Why should librarians and information scientists read such a book, especially since the author is an advocate of a non-standard theory of language? It is precisely Harris's insistence upon situating the study of language within a larger more comprehensive theory of communication that makes his entire project (and not simply this latest volume) of interest to everyone in LIS. We all know the model of communication set forth by Shannon and Weaver so many years ago: sender—message—receiver. This is the same model which Saussure proposed nearly 100 years ago and which remains the foundation for linguistics as well as information science. At the heart of this model two principles are established: Harris calls these telementation and a fixed code.

> Communication must not be confused (although it often is) with the successful use of a shared system of signs. And one of the prime reasons for the neglect of communication in semantics is *nothing other than that confusion*. This point has important implications for the study of science ... The traditional philosophy of language, shared by humanists and scientists alike, has at its core a 'fixed-code' semantics. Languages are regarded as providing their users with a vocabulary in which words have—or should have—fixed forms and fixed meanings.

> For this is the linguistic property *par excellence* which, according to the Western language myth, enables speaker and hearer, writer and reader, to understand each other, and allows truth to be established. In the eyes of those who accept this position, a language in which words had no fixed meanings would be as absurd as a currency in which the coins had no determinate values. Under such conditions, consistent and reliable verbal communication would be impossible. Hence science would be impossible, unless it could be carried on without reliance on verbal communication at all. (ibid. p. 109)

This model Harris completely rejects, and in its place he offers the integrational model:

> Integrationism is a philosophy of language which rejects fixed-code semantics lock, stock and barrel. Instead it adopts a different approach to communication altogether. In this approach, meaning is treated as being radically indeterminate, whether expressed by words or by non-verbal signs. But integrationism is not just a philosophy of language. The indeterminacy of meaning is, for integrationists, one of the basic features of the human condition, and is intrinsic not only to language but to the development of all human institutions, social and political. ...
>
> The integrationist alternative to fixed codes construes communication as a continuum of creative activities in which the participants strive to integrate their own actions and objectives with those of others, as best they may, in particular circumstances. The communicational continuum is open-ended and that is why there is no determinacy of meaning. Nor is there any guarantee in advance that a satisfactory integration is possible. In

integrational semiology, signs are not prerequisites of communication, but its products. (ibid. p. 109-110.)

The implications of this alternative theory of language are far reaching for any project involving automated language processing, the use of restricted indexing language, subject analysis, international shared databases and cross language information retrieval; in short, for librarians and information scientists.

****

The structure of *The semantics of science* is straightforward and loosely historical. The first three chapters ('Language and the Aristotelian scientist', 'Before and after Aristotle' and 'Semantics and the Royal Society') discuss the origins of reocentric theories of language in Aristotle, as well as all anachronistic modern attempts to trace 'science' back to the Greeks (or even beyond) and most importantly the development of a language of science, this last project being ultimately the center of Harris's interest. 'How do words relate to the real world?' was the matter solved by Aristotle with a reocentric theory of language and much later by Wilkins in his *Essay towards a Real Character and a Philosophical Language* (1668), a book which should be familiar to any student of the history of classification and nomenclature in the sciences. Harris describes the reocentric ideal thus:

> The model offered is one in which Nature's stall is already laid out with her genera and species neatly arranged upon it. All that scientists have to do is come along and, by means of careful observation and experiment, affix the right verbal labels to the right items. Getting it right is the foundation of good science. (ibid. p.14)

The problem encountered by Wilkins (and others) in setting up a language of science is that such a vocabulary presuppose the results of scientific knowledge:

> In the first place, drawing up a definitive universal language on this basis of a comprehensive classificatory scheme such as Wilkins proposed presupposes that a complete knowledge of the world of Nature is already available. ... In the second place, if the proposed language is to allow in due course for the acquisition of *new* knowledge, it must be so constructed as to admit additions. But these additions must not be such as to upset the basic classification: otherwise the whole language has to be restructured every time such an upheaval occurs. (ibid. p.61)
>
> To see this is to see that there is no way out of Wilkins' reocentric dilemma. He cannot put the cart before the horse: a classification system that purports to reflect the 'real' organization of the world of Nature cannot be proposed *in advance of* the experimental investigations necessary to determine that organization. That would be to risk prematurely adopting an 'incompleat' language. And an 'incompleat' language might be a positive hindrance to 'real Knowledge' rather than a means to attaining it. ... (ibid. p. 62)

He notes that in the matter of biological classification, biologists are even now

> forced to fall back on quite un-Aristotelian 'polytypic' terms and classifications. Why? Because they now recognize that in Nature 'things are not so clear-cut'. In brief, when it comes to establishing a comprehensive isomorphic correlation between words and the possible classifications of living organisms, that scientific basis is lacking, or has not yet been discovered. (ibid., p.62)

There are some who have claimed that these perennial problems are no longer problems in the age of the Internet. The possibility of full-text searching eliminates the need for any classification, order, and even any description at all. Yet this assumption is also founded upon the reocentric notion that words have fixed meanings and have no necessary relation to their use or context (temporal, geographical, disciplinary, etc.). Most importantly, the entire dimension of time is eliminated and impossible to incorporate into the simultaneity which the Internet requires. Harris notes that one of the basic tenets of integrational linguistics is "the 'principle of cotemporality', which treats it as axiomatic that all signs are time-bound. Communication is a matter of integrating past experience with present experience and anticipated future experience." (ibid., p. 115) Many readers of this journal will be familiar with the similar claim made by Hjørland that the provision of subject description (of existing materials) must be made (by us now) with potential future users in mind, this being one of the many points of intersection between Harris' integrational linguistics and the practices of documentation and librarianship.

Chapter 4 'Science in the kitchen' takes up the problem of the relationship between the language of science and the language of the community, a matter reflected in the LIS literature in the debate between the use of a restricted thesaurus of subject terms and the use of 'natural language.' He looks at a number of controversies in the modern history of science and philosophy of science concerning this relation. The question was asked at the end of the Introduction:

> Is it possible for science to construct a semantics on scientific principles that is independent of the non-scientific language that most of us speak and write for the purpose of conducting our everyday affairs? (ibid., p. 4)

In Chapter 4 the question is rephrased:

> Wherever and whenever specialists embark on developing a language of their own, the question will inevitably arise at some posing: 'How does the specialized language relate to the general language of the community?'. (ibid., p. 71)

The problem lies, according to Harris, in the preponderance of reocentric approaches to definition:

> If and when the ghost of 'real definitions' is finally exorcised, where does that leave the discourse of science? Perhaps in a position where many scientists would not like it to be: namely, as a form of discourse like any other. And therefore language-dependent, subject to all the defects and fallibilities that words are heir to. (ibid., pp. 68-69)

At the conclusion of this chapter Harris points to a problem which is exactly the problem of documentation in all its forms. All of the controversies discussed in the chapter, Harris claims,

> are not about the *validation* of what the scientist says. Nor are they about problems of scientific method. They are controversies, rather, about whether and how what the scientist says can be linguisticaly integrated into other (non-scientific) forms of discourse. This integration is the ultimate locus of dispute. (ibid., p. 81)

In academic libraries, one of the principle loci of that integrational activity is the library catalog, and bibliographical description, subject analysis and indexing are all founded on one or another solution to disputes of exactly this nature.

Chapter 5 'The Rhetoric of linguistic science' discusses the history of linguistics, and among the many revealing and relevant comments he makes, his remarks on some 19th century attitudes towards comparative philology are sure to catch the attention of readers of this journal:

> The corollary of Müller's strategy is to treat the viewpoint of the language user as totally irrelevant to the scientific investigation of language. ... The scientific method that Müller espouses requires the linguist to abstract from the speakers altogether, to ignore the communicational activity of the language community and to treat 'the language' simply as a set of forms and combinations of forms. Only then is there any basis for the operation of a scientific method which equates the collection, classification and comparison of words with the collection, classification and comparison of rocks and plants.
>
> Thus Müller's claim for the scientific status of comparative philology was ultimately based on a misleading metaphor. The metaphor removes language from its natural embedding in the communicational practices of a living community and reduces it to a static inventory of discrete, collectable items. These items, recorded one by one in the notebooks of grammarians and lexicographers, are available for inspection, analysis and classification on whatever principle the linguist may decide. (ibid., p. 88)

In chapter 6 'Mathematics and the language of science' Harris provides a radically original interpretation of the meaning of numbers and a criticism of the notion of the 'language of number'.

> If reocentrism [is] to yield fixity of meanings, it can only do so on the supposition that this world of external things, from which words derive their meanings, remains constant. Otherwise, meanings would be changing all the time. In the case of numerals, however, reocentric

semantics encounters a problem; namely, that there are no obvious 'real world' entities which stand as their meanings in the way that *butter* can be regarded as designating a certain fatty substance, or *melts* as designating a certain kind of process. (ibid., p. 120)

The integrational approach to number does not tie the meanings of numbers to any specific abstract meanings, timeless eternities or Platonic ideal forms. The search for a language of science which more and more closely approaches the mathematical ideal presumes that such a language would be more and more perfect, 'an ideal fixed-code in which misunderstanding is impossible ... somehow able to override all linguistic diversity, because its definitions are based on universal truths that brook no denial.' (ibid., p. 111). Instead, Harris claims, numbers are like all other words:

Their value depends on the context. When 554256 functions as a telephone number, it has no arithmetic value at all. But when integrated into certain types of operation it does. The basic types of operation involved are calculation and measurement (to be considered in Chapter 7); and the reason why numerical signs then acquire specific contextual values is that this is required in order that the integration of activities can proceed and be successfully completed. The social utility of these activities is thus the ultimate reason for the apparent semiological stability of this type of sign and its incorporation into pedagogic programmes of instruction and other traditional practices. (ibid., pp. 127-128)

The seventh chapter 'Science and common sense' discusses measurement and operationalism in science, and, as one would expect, Harris focuses on how scientists write about the results of science which run counter to all common sense, i.e. the 'communication barrier' in science. How does one translate mathematical statements into English (or Navaho, Silozi, Buginese) prose? The theory and mathematics behind Galileo's famous 'Eppur si muove' was incomprehensible to his audience, but what he meant was understood in spite of that; had his comments been restricted to a mathematical formula, he would have had no trial in the first place.

Kuhn and Carnap get their due in chapter 8 'Supercategory semantics' where the issue is 'What is science?' At the heart of this chapter is an investigation into how it is that sciences get to be Science. Some, like Library Science and Information Science, simply appropriate the term into the name of their discipline in order to win the battle before it starts: given Library Science, one asks only 'In what does it consist?' not 'Really? Since when?'. Harris himself is not worried about whether or not linguistics or library science or any other science actually is or is not a science. Nor does he think that this should concern scientists any more than the possibility or impossibility of a perfect language of science.

> Those who regard themselves as scientists need not be unduly worried about this. unless, perchance, they attach as much—or more—importance to being called 'scientists' than to the work they actually do. If there be any such, I do not think it will hinder their work, or make it less valuable, to rid themselves of the illusion that the language of science has a more scientific basis than the language of the home or the street; or to concede that it is subject to the same semantic indeterminacy and the same context-dependence as all forms of human communication that have so far been devised. That realization might even be a scientific step forward? (ibid., p. 175)

In the concluding chapter 'Integrating science' Harris states clearly the basis of the problem for any unified semantics of science, the reason that there can be none:

Why not? Because human experience does not reduce to the quantifiable, and human experience as a whole is what underwrites language. (ibid., p. 180)

This understanding alone puts Harris in a class almost by himself, at least among linguists. It is this understanding which allows Harris to ask questions where nearly everyone else rests comfortably in myths, whether those myths come from the Bible, Plato or Chomsky. And the difference which Harris brings to linguistics is what makes his work, virtually alone in the literature of linguistics, not only worthwhile for everyone outside the discipline of linguistics, but absolutely exciting for anyone in LIS.

In his 1997 review mentioned above, Warner warned that "Neither work is easy, nor fully comprehended here" and I would have to add that Harris's books are perhaps more difficult books for linguists to read than for others precisely because they require the reader to rethink some of the linguists' "deeply ingrained notions" (Warner, J., 1997, p.194). Yet stylistically all of Harris' writings are consistently as clear as any academic writing one could ever hope to read. Having read some thirty volumes of the writings of Harris and other linguists working from the perspective of integrational linguistics, I am convinced that this theory presents a departure from previous linguistic theories as radical as Copernicus's astronomical theory differed from the cosmology of the ancient Greeks. Neither a short review nor a much longer review would suffice to argue the case for integrational linguistics (that argument has been carried out in a few dozen books and many articles), let alone prove its relevance to librarianship and information science.

Throughout this review I have quoted extensively and limited my own comments; Harris' own words are clearer and more concise than any summary that I could provide. The quotations should suggest—to some readers at least—the relevance of

Harris's book—in fact many of his books—to the principle problems confronting those working in the various areas of documentation and information retrieval, from catalogers in libraries and software designers working on web search engines to researchers involved in cross-language information retrieval and automatic translation and indexing.

References

Borsley, R. D. and Newmeyer, F.J. (1997), "The language muddle: Roy Harris and Generative Grammar". In: Wolf and Love (eds.), *Linguistics Inside Out: Roy Harris and His Critics*, Amsterdam: John Benjamins.

Duch, L. (2004), "Notas para una antropología de la comunicación". In his: *Estaciones del Laberinto*, Barcelona, Herder.

Harris, R. (1983), "Literary translating: theoretical ideas", *Times Literary Supplement*, 14 Oct., p. 119.

Harris, R. (2003), *The Necessity of Artspeak*, London: Continuum.

Harris, R. (2003b), *History, Science and the Limits of Language*, Shimla: Indian Institute of Advanced Study.

Harris, R. (2004), *The Linguistics of History*, Edinburgh: Edinburgh University Press.

Joseph, J.E. (1997), "The "Language Myth" myth: or, Roy Harris's red herrings". In: Wolf and Love (eds.), *Linguistics Inside Out: Roy Harris and His Critics*, Amsterdam: John Benjamins.

Warner, A. (1987), *Quantitative and Qualitative Assessments of the Impact of Linguistic Theory on Information Science*. PhD dissertation, University of Illinois at Urbana-Champaign.

Warner, J. (1997), "Studying writing: two books by Roy Harris", *Journal of Documentation*, v. 53, No. 2 (March), pp. 185-195.

II

Definition in Theory and Practice[1]

Despite the title, this book is not just for linguists, lexicographers and lawyers. Roy Harris has steamed up with University of Hong Kong Professor of English Christopher Hutton to produce a book that is as interesting and relevant to LIS as Harris's earlier books. Anyone interested in the problems of meaning and context in information retrieval and especially those focussing on the construction and use of thesauri, ontologies and the dream of the "semantic web" will find much thought for food here. The problem of reference (in the philosophical and lexicographical sense) is central to the authors' arguments and provides an unexpected illumination of problems of reference work in libraries as well. Rather than review the book in detail, my intention is to discuss certain parts of the authors' methodology and arguments as these relate to various aspects of meaning in current discussions within LIS.

---

[1] Review of Roy Harris and Christopher Hutton. *Definition in Theory and Practice: Language, Lexicography and the Law*. London and New York: Continuum, 2007.

The most significant barrier to the appropriation and use of the literature and theory of linguistics in librarianship and information science is the former's long-standing rejection of communication as the foundation of language, the claim that communication is irrelevant to the study of language. From Saussure to Pinker the language of "linguistics proper" has not been Saussure's "parole"—the empirical facts of the actual linguistic activity of human beings—but his "langue"—the linguist's model of the system underlying "parole." Lyons (1977) specifically noted this disjunction as something non-linguists do not realize:

> It is not generally realized by non-linguists how indirect is the relationship between observed (or observable) utterances and the set of grammatical sentences postulated (and cited by way of example) by the linguist in his description of any particular language. ...
> What the linguist does when he describes a language, English for example, is to construct what is commonly referred to by scientists as a model, not of actual language-behaviour, but of the regularities manifest in that behaviour (more precisely of that part of language-behaviour which the linguist defines, by methodological decision, to fall within the scope of linguistics): he constructs a model of the language-system. (Lyons (1977), v. 1, p. 26, 29)

Since librarians, library users and the information technologies which they use have to deal entirely and only with actual usage and that "actual usage in its totality is chaos" (*Definition in Theory and Practice*, p. 79), the librarian's and information system designer's task is exactly like the task of the lexicographer as Harris and Hutton describe it: "to reduce chaos to order." No lexicographer, they insist, has "ever undertook to document chaos"; rather the task of the lexicographer, like the librarian, is to bring some order to that chaos, to engage in interpretation and sense-making.

The authors of *Definition in Theory and Practice* (hereafter, DTP) are not interested in constructing a model of any in-your-head language-system. They assume the basic tenets of integrational linguistics, including the assumption that linguistic signs are not the prerequisite for communication but are instead the products of communicational activity, this activity requiring the making of signs. One of the consequences of that theoretical presupposition is that language must be studied within the context of that communicative activity. How that presupposition affects linguistic research and theorizing can be demonstrated by contrasting a remark by Chomsky in *Syntactic Structures* (1957) with remarks in the book under review.

> Syntax is the study of the principles and processes by which sentences are constructed in particular languages. Syntactic investigation of a given language has as its goal the construction of a grammar that can be viewed as a device of some sort for producing the sentences of the language under analysis. More generally, linguists must be concerned with the problem of determining the fundamental underlying properties of successful grammars. The ultimate outcome of these investigations should be a theory of linguistic structure in which the descriptive devices utilized in particular grammars are presented and studied abstractly, with no specific reference to particular languages. (Chomsky (1957) p. 11)

> [T]here is no more need for postulating invariant collective codes that allegedly make it possible for one individual to exchange thoughts with another. ... Communication in all its forms is permanently at the mercy of circumstances and human reactions that are, in the final analysis, unpredictable. Which amounts to saying

that the serious student of human communication cannot expect that study to be a 'science'. (DTP, p.69)

We can profitably compare the differences between these approaches with the differences in LIS between Shannon and Weaver's mathematical approach and Brenda Dervin's "Communication, not information" approach. We know that much has been accomplished along the lines of Shannon and Weaver's mathematical theory of communication, and the usefulness of current information systems are to a large extent testimony to the value of the mathematical theory for developing communication technologies. Yet Dervin's work (among others) suggests that the theoretical assumptions of the mathematical theory and the interpretations which they impose do not do justice to the actual facts of human communicative behaviour in spite of their usefullness. If we wish to understand actual human communicative activity in the context of information production, seeking and use, we must seek a different theory.

The search for an abstract system in linguistics is pursued with a reliance on "intuitions" of grammaticalness and decontextualized bits of text that Lyons referred to as "system-sentences":

> [S]ystem-sentences are sequences of words in a one-to-one order-preserving correspondence with what would be judged, intuitively by native speakers, to be grammatically complete text-sentences. ...
> [S]ystem-sentences never occur as the products of ordinary language-behaviour. Representations of system-sentences may of course be used in metalinguistic discussions of the structure and functions of language; and it is such representations that are customarily cited in grammatical descriptions of particular languages. (Lyons (1977), p.30-31)

This issue is at the heart of the difference between Harris and Hutton's approach in DTP on the one hand and theoretical linguistics not oriented toward the integrational approach on the other. Harris and Hutton look at definition not only as theorized by philosophers, linguists, lexicographers (Hutton himself having published a dictionary of Hong Kong Chinese slang) and lawyers, but also as practiced, examining the definitions found in writings of all of the above, in dictionaries, court cases and legislation. Again, a conparison with Chomsky is illuminating. Four pages after the passage from *Syntactic Structures* quoted above, Chomsky's first and most famous example appears as a demonstration that grammatical sentences of English need not be meaningful:

> Second, the notion "grammatical" cannot be identified with "meaningful" or "significant" in any semantic sense. Sentences (1) and (2) are equally nonsensical, but any speaker of English will recognize that only the former is grammatical.
> (1) Colorless green ideas sleep furiously.
> (2) Furiously sleep ideas green colorless.
> (Chomsky (1957), p. 15)

With these examples, we are a long way from English, and even further from communication.

In contrast, Harris and Hutton offer no hypothetical definitions, no imaginary scenarios, no abstract systems of defining, and no nonsense. What they offer instead is a careful presentation and critical analysis of four types of theories of definition as these are found in the literature on definition (stipulative definition, common usage, real definition and ostensive definition) on pages 1-74, followed by an examination of various lexicographers' understandings of their task and their practices as they are evident in their dictionaries (p. 75-130) and a discussion of how words are defined, contested, argued and redefined in the practice of law (including the use of "authoritative" dictionaries in court), basing their discussion on about fifty actual cases from *Partridge v. Strange & Coker* (1553) to an uncited case reported in the *Daily Telegraph* in 2005 (p. 131-195). In Part Four, the Conclusion, the authors discuss indeterminacy, reference and deconstruction in linguistics, philosophy, literary theory and law, distinguishing their position from that of deconstructionists, Legal realism and Critical Legal Studies. Stanley Fish gets a careful critical reading ("his more general argument about the nature of texts and interpretative communities seems to rely on the very distinction between 'inside' and 'outside' that he rejects in law" (DTP, p. 219), while Popper's belief that "we never know what we are talking about" is dealt with briefly: "For one who never knew what he was talking about, Popper talked a great deal, and convinced many naive scientists to the contrary." (DTP p. 222).

The authors' decision to study the theory and practice of definition in the construction and interpretation of law was due to their recognition that while all of what they call the "supercategories" of our time (such as History, Science and Art)

> are, at least to some extent, linguistic constructs, ... the law is unique among them in the extent to which it relies overtly upon the possibility of determining verbal meanings. Appeal to the dictionary has become one of the features of contemporary jurisprudence. This presupposes the possibility of integrating lexicographical practice with legal practice. Second, the law is in any case a practical, institutionalized attempt to implement one particular type of integrational procedure; namely, integrating (1) the past verbal activities of legislators and testators with (2) the present and future activities (verbal or non-verbal) of all those affected or potentially affected by (1). The form such integration will take, or should take, it is the function of judges and courts to decide. Without that integrational function, the law would have no *raison d'être*. (DTP, p. viii)

By describing the function of the law as the integration of past, present and future activities relying upon the creation and integration of linguistic signs, the authors have sought to understand communication in law in the same manner as Hjørland has insisted that librarians must approach communication in the world of information and information users. Without the need to integrate the world of information with the present, future, and potential users of that information, LIS would also have no *raison d'être*.

The integration of information, information users, information professionals, information technologies and social agent technologies on the Web is itself an interesting enough research area begging to be approached from the perspective of integrational linguistics. Where it gets really interesting—and where this particular book has so much to offer—is in the context of the conceptualization, construction and perhaps realization of the Semantic Web, a vision first articulated by Berners-Lee et al. in their 2001 article in *Scientific American*. Since this Semantic Web relies primarily on a system of definitions and interpretive rules (called "ontologies") to make the meaning of everything on the Web (!) precise (!!) and unambiguous (!!!), one might expect to find amongst the vast literature on ontologies and the Semantic Web some careful discussion of definition informed by the philosophical, linguistic and lexicographical literature. Yet Alas! and Alack! Thou mayest Seek, but Thou shalt not find. All the more reason, then, for researchers in LIS to welcome Harris and Hutton's contribution to the conceptualization and articulation of the Semantic Web (even though they never mention it).

The easiest manner of demonstrating the pertinence of DTP to some of the most current and urgent issues in LIS—like controlled vocabularies, ontologies and the Semantic Web—is simply to juxtapose passages from that book with passages from recent articles like the Berners-Lee piece mentioned in the preceding paragraph. Here we go:

The Semantic Web is not a separate Web but an extension of the current one, in which information is given well-defined meaning... (Berners-Lee et al. 2001)

[A]ll signs (not only linguistic signs) are semantically indeterminate. In this perspective, semantics is the study and practice of human attempts to impose some degree of communicational determinacy on signs. The successes, failures and limitations of such efforts are, in our view, central to the enterprise of definition. (DTP, p. viii)

Ontologies furnish the vocabulary necessary for communication between social agents and Web pages, defining relations between concepts ... in practice, an ontology defines terms associated with the texts it describes, what they mean themselves, and the formal axioms that restrict the interpretation and use of those terms. (Pickler, 2007, p.72)

A definition can only be as effective as the context allows it to be, and the context includes the situation of the person seeking to understand the meaning. The notion of a definition adequate to all occasions and all demands is a semantic *ignis fatuus*." (DTP, p. 49)

An ontology defines the classes and concepts of an area of knowledge or of a process, offering the definition, the characteristics and attributes, and the relations that are established as well as the functions that complete the elements. Ontologies codify the knowledge of a domain and are made to be reusable. (Romaní, 2006, p. 9)

The problem for the general lexicographer, who purports to be giving definitions for the total inventory of words in languages like English and French, is that the technique so successfully deployed in restricted domains such as physics and chemistry cannot be extended to general vocabulary. ... The reason is that words have no *general* referential focus, nor even anything that approximates to one: the very idea is self-contradictory. Focus implies the deliberate exclusion, from a particular communicational context or type of context, of all facts deemed irrelevant thereto. ... That is why those who compile general dictionaries are forced to assume, whether they like it or not, that certain facts about the world are of more interest than others ... Their definitions are tailored to those assumptions of referential focus, whether they realize that consciously or not. (DTP, p.212-213)

A program that wants to compare or combine information across the two databases has to know that these two terms are being used to mean the same thing. Ideally, the program must have a way to discover such common meanings for whatever databases it encounters. (Berners-Lee et al. 2001)

The postulated semantic consensus underlying everyday talk about cats and dogs is a theoretical illusion conjured up by generalizing across separate, individual decisions to call Fido a dog and Tibbles a cat for the communicational purposes to hand. But it is an idle cog in the explanatory wheel. For *even if* it were true that all members of a linguistic community had reached an agreement in advance on what to call Fido and Tibbles, their implementation of that agreement would still require an individual decision by each of them on each occasion. (DTP, p. 202)

Ontologies, as "explicit representations of shared understanding" can also be used to codify the terminology's semantics. For example, it must be assumed in using XML that the author and reader of <foo>7</foo> have the same understanding of what "foo" means. (Kim, 2002, p. 52)

[N]o form of definition can render the meaning of a sign determinate, i.e. can guarantee that those who have either formulated or understood the definition have thereby grasped the same meaning. Definition, in short, *always* allows room for semantic divergence and hence misunderstanding. It may, depending on the circumstances, *reduce uncertainty* but cannot *eliminate* it." (DTP, p.65)

At the heart of the semantic web, ontologies are used to add a semantic layer to the actual web. They are references for communication between machines but also between machines and humans by defining consensually the meaning of objects firstly through symbols (words or phrases) that designate and characterize them, and then through a structured or formal representation of their role in the domain. (Hernandez et al., 2007, p.144)

[T]here is no particular underlying consensus about the meanings of words, because the routines of everyday interaction do not require it. (DTP, p. 173)

An ontology is not a taxonomy, a classification scheme or a dictionary. It is, in fact, a unique representational system that integrates within a single structure the characteristics of more traditional approaches such as nested hierarchies, faceted thesauri and controlled vocabularies. An ontology provides the semantic bases for metadata schemes and facilitates communication among systems and agents by enforcing a standardized conceptual model for a community of users. (Jacob, 2003)

All definitions purporting to capture orthodox or "good" linguistic practice are inherently stipulative: in effect, they instruct the reader "This is how the word *should* be used and understood". They are stipulative in just the same respect as the *Highway Code* is stipulative. It tells one how people *should* behave on the road, not how they actually do behave. It proposes a model to be followed, just as a dictionary does. ... Linguistic "standardization" is an inherently prescriptive notion. (DTP p. 91-92)

If we are going to have programs that understand language, we will have to encode what words mean. Since words refer to the world, their definitions will have to be in terms of some underlying theory of the world. We will therefore have to construct that theory, and do so in a way that reflects the ontology that is implicit in natural language. (Hobbs, 1995, p. 819)

An integrationist theory of reference ... has no room for the idea of static relations between words and the world. (DTP, p. 208)

A linguistically-based ontology corresponds to the way people think about objects. It is a useful way to predict their thinking about the knowledge in structured databases. (Dahlgren, 1995, p.810)

Thus the postulate of semantic determinacy makes it possible to transfer the responsibility for making meaning from the individual to the collectivity, and from the circumstantial to the macrosocial level. ... Words come to be construed as autonomous signs that can and do function semantically without support from any other semiological source, providing the essential self-sustaining mechanisms for the facilitation and regulation not only of human interactions but of human thought itself. (DTP, p.203-204)

Librarians and other users and designers of information technologies should be especially challenged by that last quotation for at least two reasons. If indeed words do not regulate "human thought itself" then we can expect a measure of indeterminacy of meaning and mismatches between the language of the user and both the information we deal with and the metadata associated with that information. Furthermore, although the metadata we create cannot be understood to be "enforcing" interpretations on the library users/information searchers, the manner and context of its creation will significantly determine its communicational value. Since the objects with which we deal—printed texts, recorded sound, visual materials, digital objects of all sorts—must all be interpreted, the first question is who will do that interpretation for its present, future and potential users and uses? The author/creator of that information? An alive and engaged human being with a stake in the consequences of interpretation? An information professional with an eye on profit? An information proletariat counting the piece-work or watching the clock? Software written by a programmer who believed that disagreement, debate, disinformation and misunderstanding do not exist or are irrelevant? Using their examination of the practice of definition in lexicography and law Harris and Hutton have argued and demonstrated that "signs do not 'have meanings' but are 'made to mean'." (DTP p. 223). This, they conclude, "points to the only basis on which human communication can—and does—proceed." (DTP p. 223). And that points us to the basis for a theory of communication for LIS.

Read this book and rejoice.

References

Berners-Lee, Tim; Hendler, James; Lassila, Ora (2001). "The Semantic Web" *Scientific American* v. 284, iss. 5 (May) p. 34-43.

Chomsky, Noam (1957). *Syntactic Structures*. The Hague: Mouton.

Dahlgren, Kathleen (1995). "A linguistic ontology" *International Journal of Human-Computer Studies* v.43 p.809-818.

Hernandez, Nathalie; Mothe, Josiane; Chrisment, Claude; Egret, Daniel (2007). "Modeling context through domain ontologies" *Information Retrieval* (2007) v.10 p.143-172.

Hobbs, Jerry R. (1995). "Sketch of an ontology underlying the way we talk about the world" *International Journal of Human-Computer Studies* v.43 p.819-830.

Jacob, Elin K. (2003). "Ontologies and the Semantic Web" *Bulletin of the American Society for Information Science and Technology* v.29 no. 4(April/May)

Kim, Henry (2002). "Predicting how ontologies for the Semantic Web will evolve," *Communications of the ACM* v. 45 no. 2 (February) p. 48-54.

Lyons, John (1977). *Semantics*. Cambridge: Cambridge University Press.

Pickler, Maria Elisa Velentim (2007). "Web Semântica: ontologias como ferramentas de representação do conhecimento." *Perspectivas em Ciência da Informação* v.12 n. 1 (jan/abr) p.65-83

Romaní, Mar (2006). "Webs semàntiques, les webs de segona generació" *Item: Revista de Biblioteconomia i Documentació*, v.42 (Jan-Apr), p.7-19.

III

Of Minds and Language: A Comparative Review[1]

Linguistic theorizing in the United States has long been based on the belief that language provides a "window into the mind," that linguistic structures reveal brain and/or mental structures. In a lecture first given in 1967 Chomsky argued that "the study of language may very well, as was traditionally supposed, provide a remarkably favorable perspective for the study of human mental processes" (Chomsky, 2006, p.86). Linguists have made many bold claims about the mind on the basis of dangling participles, left versus right branching syntactic notations, vowel movements, and, in the first of the books under review here, "Merge", i.e. "a primitive operation that takes objects already constructed, and constructs from them a new object" (from Chomsky's "Opening Remarks" on p. 25). We are informed that

---

[1] Review of: Massimo Piattelli-Palmarini, Juan Uriagereka, and Pello Salaburu (editors). *Of Minds and Language: a Dialogue with Noam Chomsky in the Basque Country*. Oxford: Oxford University Press, 2009; Roy Harris. *Mindboggling: Preliminaries to a Science of the Mind.* Luton: The Pantaneto Press, 2008; Roy Harris. *Rationality and the Literate Mind.* New York and London: Routledge, 2009.

most of the linguistic-biological organs discovered during the 1960s-1980s have been replaced by an organ called Merge, and that this was an evolution of theory rather than of brains. Of Merge we read

> Emergence of unbounded Merge in human evolutionary history provides what has been called a "language of thought," an internal generative system that constructs thoughts of arbitrary richness and complexity, exploiting conceptual resources that are already available or may develop with the availability of structured expressions. ... The core principle of language, unbounded Merge, must have arisen from some rewiring of the brain, presumably the effect of some small mutation. Such changes take place in an individual, not a group. The individual so endowed would have had many advantages: capacities for complex thought, planning, interpretation, and so on. The capacity would be transmitted to offspring, coming to dominate a small breeding group. At that stage, there would be an advantage to externalization, so the capacity would be linked as a secondary process to the sensorimotor system for externalization and interaction, including communication. (p. 29).

Chomsky then argues that "there seems little reason to postulate precursors to unbounded Merge" (referring to the assumed biological organ, not the theoretical imagination): the appearance of Merge is at one and the same time the appearance of language and thought, "a language of thought". The mind and all things mental are "emergent properties of brains" (Chomsky, quoting Vernon Mountcastle on p. 17). As "reflective creatures" Chomsky argues, "we go on to seek a deeper understanding of the phenomena of experience... In principle these questions are subject to empirical inquiry into what we might call 'the science-forming faculty,' another 'mental organ'" (ibid. p. 18). If I understand this correctly, language and thought are properties of biological systems, specifically those we call brains. For Chomsky, "the term 'language' means internal language, a state of the computational system of the mind/brain that generates structured expressions, each of which can be taken to be a set of instructions for the interface systems within which the faculty of language is embedded" (p. 18-19). The study of "the genetic endowment for language" he calls "Universal Grammar" and this he studies within "the biolinguistic framework ... the study of language as part of biology" (p. 19).

Anyone who can buy into a theory which takes "the perceived sentence (7) What did John eat?" (p. 28), analyzes it semantically and synactically, postulates a computational system in the brain that will "generate" this structure (but why?), claims that this system arose as a mutation (ah, that's why) and that is why human beings are capable of complex thought will find this book fascinating. It is, as its proponents never cease to repeat, the standard theory and a rational, empirically based, scientific theory at that. The papers which follow Chomsky's Opening Remarks treat of foundational abstractions, Merge, evolution, epigenesis and brain wiring in Part I (Overtures), Merge, universals, interfaces, movement, uninterpretable features and probabilistic grammars in Part 2 (On Language), language acquisition in Part 3 and biological variation, innateness, perception and the brain in Part 4 (Open talks on Open Inquiries).

While most of the papers in this collection follow the Chomskyan paradigm, not all do, or rather, one does not. Gallistel's chapter "The Foundational Abstractions" presents a brief argument against the view that "language is the (or, perhaps, a) medium of thought," claiming that birds compute elapsed time, make cognitive maps, search those maps for records of food, perform operations of subtraction and numerical comparison and recognize the intentions of those observing them. This all suggests to Gallistel that it is unlikely that "these abstractions arose either from the language faculty itself or from whatever the evolutionary development was that made language possible in humans" (p. 68). His arguments suggest something rather different to this reviewer, namely that he has engaged in extensive anthropomorphization when interpreting the findings he has reported.

If one wishes to look at language as people use it rather than as arbitrary structures that the brain generates, there is very little relevant material in this volume other than some of the discussions of language acquisition in Part 2. There are discussions of the measurements of brain activity while engaged in some linguistic task, but that is a look at neurology, not language. An explanation for this lacuna is ready to hand in Hinzen's paper "Hierarchy, Merge, and Truth". There we read that "Today's 'standard' theory of the architecture of the human language faculty" has been developed in response to what "this faculty has to have if it is to be usable" (p. 125). Those must have features are:

> (i) a computational, combinatorial system that combines expressions from a lexicon, LEX (i.e., a syntax) and employs a basic structure-building operation, Merge;
> (ii) a realm of "meanings" or "thoughts" that this combinatorial system has to express or "interface with";
> (iii) a realm of sound, or gesture (as in sign languages), that the system has to equally interface with, else language could not be externalized (or be heard/seen). (p. 125-126)

That is, everything is as easy as i, ii, and iii, or ABC, except that neither numeracy nor literacy play any role in the theory. In the case of numeracy this is evident in Chomsky's brief remark "it means that the numbering system might just be a trivial case of language" (p. 33). (In other papers in this collection—those of Gallistel, Gelman, and Hauser—numbers and counting are discussed briefly.) In the case of literacy, this volume contains no discussion at all. Astonishingly, there is no theory of signs, just an "interface" between the combinatorial system and "meanings" or "thoughts" (which is it? or are these terms synonymous?) and another interface between the combinatorial system and the mechanics of making and perceiving noises and gestures. A theory of signs would have to address the relation between the sign made and its meaning but in this model no such relationship is possible as the "interfaces" are elsewhere. Language is a biological system and its description is exhausted in treating of (i) syntax, (ii) semantics, and (iii) physiology of speech, understood here as being limited to sound or gesture. Language is not an activity arising from social interaction but simply a biological "organ" (the scare quotes used by Chomsky apparently mean that he is hedging his bets) whose properties—accidentally, Chomsky insists—allow it to be utilized for communicative purposes. One suspects that both language and thought as depicted in these papers would look much different were we to regard them as emerging from the social life of creatures with bodies and brains, much like fashion shows, gourmet cooking, mass transit, house building, football and internet surfing emerged.

The two recent works by Roy Harris discussed here are as far removed from the biolinguistics framework as one could imagine. For one thing, Harris offers no just-so stories as the contributors to *Of Minds & Language* do whenever one might expect evidence: neither "some small mutation" nor "rewiring" are brought in as *deus ex machina*. Harris does draw on recent neurological research, but in a very different way and with a decidedly careful attitude about what we may actually conclude from that research after we have stripped it of its questionable assumptions and the conclusions following from them.

Perhaps the clearest expression of the main difference between Harris's approach to "language and the mind" and that of *Of Minds & Language* appears in his discussion of the "mereological fallacy" in *Mindboggling*. The term mereological fallacy refers to "attributing to parts of a human being (or animal) features and functions that logically belong only to the whole creature" (*Mindboggling*, p. 141). He quotes Bennett and Hacker:

> Human beings, but not their brains, can be said to be thoughtful or thoughtless; animals, but not their brains, let alone the hemisphere of their brains, can be said to see, hear, smell and taste things; people, but not their brains, can be said to make decisions or to be indecisive. (Bennett and Hacker, 2003, p. 73)

While Chomsky and the contributors to *Of Minds & Language* equivocate and excuse themselves with "huge promissory notes left to pay" (Chomsky on p. 32), they are nevertheless confident that mind is an emergent property of brain. The "unresolved problem" of "how properties 'termed mental' relate to 'the organical structure of the brain'" (Chomsky, quoting Joseph Priestly, p. 32) remains. This problem of mind and matter is related to "The basic problem" of linguistic research, which is, Chomsky writes, "that even the simplest words and concepts of human language and thought lack the relation to mind-independent entities" (p. 27).

These basic and unresolved problems for the study of language and mind have a different status for Harris. The connection between mind, language and world he conceives in very different terms, since he does not seek the "essential nature of language" (Chomsky, ibid.) or of mind in neurology. Their is no equivocation in *Mindboggling*:

> I do not think that my mind is my brain (or any part of my brain) under a different description. Nor do I think it is related to my brain as one organ to another. But I do not think it could function without my brain any more than I think I could see without eyes. ... But, having said that, I admit that the mind I think I have is largely a linguistic construct. In other words, I can imagine that, if I had been brought up to speak a quite different language, I might have learnt quite different ways of talking about my inner and my outer world—perhaps it might have been a language in which there was no word for

mind at all. But I think I would have needed some way of articulating verbally the connexions and differences between those two worlds. (p. 157-158)

And why would he or any of us talk "about my inner and my outer world ... articulating verbally the connexions and differences between those two worlds"? Because

> The primary function of mindspeak is nothing other than to integrate two kinds of experience that we all have: experience of an 'inner' world and experience of an 'outer' world. ... [T]he fact remains—and it is a fact of first-order experience, not a product of 'theory'—that the conduct of our daily lives constantly requires us to distinguish between thinking that something is the case and finding that it is—or is not—the case. ... But if we cannot manage this thinking-it-is-the-case-versus-finding-that-it-is/isn't-the-case distinction at all, we are likely to find ourselves in deep trouble with our fellow human beings. (p. 145-146)

Mindboggling is a series of twenty-seven short chapters (all but three of them exactly five pages long, the others four and six) on the various ways that human beings have thought (or at least written) about mind: "The vulgar mind," "The ghostly mind," "The well-behaved mind," "The other mind," and so on all the way to "My mind." The questions, problems and positions discussed in these chapters are each examined with Harris' sharp mind, clear prose and wonderful humour. For example Chapter 11 "The mind located" closes with the following paragraph:

> The fuss about the location of the mind (including whether it has a location at all) is symptomatic of a failure to grasp something important—the role of vulgar mindspeak in our understanding of experience. The mis-

> take of those who insist on a location for the mind is on a par with supposing that it ought to be possible to find the exact place on (or off) the football pitch where the match was won. The mistake of those who deny that the mind has any location is on a par with supposing that winning the match had nothing to do with what happened on the pitch at all. (p. 64-65)

His references to the "vulgar mind" and "mindspeak" are crucial to understanding his arguments throughout the book, and thus the book begins with the chapter "The vulgar mind."

> I propose to start from the question itself as presented here, "Do you have a mind?": that is, a question formulated in English and addressed to readers whose acquaintance with English is sufficient to enable them to grasp the relevant vocabulary and syntax. ...
> Where did you get the idea that you even might have a mind? I suggest it came from one or both of two sources. One is whatever you might happen to have read about the mind. But even if you have never read anything on the subject, there remains the other source, which I will call for convenience "vulgar mindspeak". (p. 1-2)

Vulgar mindspeak is Harris's term for "the language of what is sometimes called 'presystematic' or 'commonsense intuitions' about the mind" (p. 3). It is the language of "I think", "I have an idea", and mind your "baby, the step, the consequences and your Ps and Qs" (p. 2). We are using Harris's vulgar mindspeak when we speak or write of intentions, opinions, reasons and recollections. It is not a theoretical or scientific language, but one rooted in personal inner experience. Vulgar mindspeak "does not encapsulate some kind of transcendental wisdom about mental activities" Harris writes, adding "I think it harbours the roots of those widespread confusions about human communication that I labelled the language myth" (p. 148).

Mindboggling is neither a textbook on philosophy of mind, nor an exposition of any particular theory of mind. The book was, Harris writes, "a self-imposed project" which forced him "to address certain questions I had previously thought about only vaguely, and obliged me to 'think them through'" (p. 160). My suspicion is that this "self-imposed project" was a necessary "thinking through" that was intimately bound up with the writing of *Rationality and the Literate Mind*.

In *Rationality and the Literate Mind* Harris sets out to argue two theses: 1) "conceptions of human rationality vary according to the view of language adopted," and 2) "the view of language adopted by the literate mind is not the same as the view of language adopted by the preliterate mind" (p. xiv). His point of departure is "the 'plasticity' or 'malleability' of the human brain as established in contemporary neuroscience," a matter of great importance for Harris as "it means there is no reason to believe that human rationality (whatever that may amount to) is somehow already built into the structures of the brain *ab initio*" (ibid.). The recognition of this plasticity of the brain (not of the mind) has led to the "concern that changes in language-related technologies may, over the course of time, change the way human beings think. ... concerns about whether current information technologies are not already bringing such changes about." He notes that "Worries are voiced about the dangers here of 'blurring the cyber-world and 'reality'" (p. xi), quoting from recent works by Maryanne Wolf and Susan Greenfield, but Harris offers a few words of caution:

> Valuable as the results of contemporary neuroscience are, it is impossible to ignore the fact that the way these results are presented by neuroscientists often bears the mark of cultural *idées fixes* about literacy itself. From the examples mentioned above, for instance, it is clear that literacy is unquestionably accepted as a Good Thing, while anything that threatens to undermine the achievements of the literate mind is a Bad Thing. But this is a

value judgment: it is not a factual conclusion delivered by the results of neuroscientific research." (p. xii)

His second caveat concerns the mereological fallacy mentioned above:

> The brain no doubt plays an essential role in coordinating various separate processes that are involved in the act of reading. But it is nevertheless the child—not the child's brain—who learns to read, just as it is the child—not the child's brain—who learns to eat with a knife and fork, play hide-and-seek, and do many other things that children learn to do. (p. xiii)

The third caveat concerns the distinction between brain and mind:

> For some neuroscientists, evidently, the mind just is the brain under another description, or when considered as operating in a certain way (especially when 'thinking'). According to Greenfield, "challenging the old dichotomy of mind versus brain, or mental versus physical, is one of the most important achievements of current neuroscience" (Greenfield 2008: 50). But, again, this is to confuse the factual deliverances of neurological research with their culturally slanted interpretation. Whatever Greenfield or like-minded neuroscientists may claim for their own discipline, there is no translation available which will convert the neurophysiological predicates of English (or any other language) into corresponding mental predicates. So it would save a lot of needless embranglement to keep the two separate from the start. (p. xiii)

In the first chapter, "On Rationality, the Mind and Scriptism," Harris discusses various views on the nature of rationality and its relation to writing. To avoid the many problems associated with the different ways people think about rationality, Harris makes it clear that the rationality he is discussing "has to do strictly with establishing the validity of conclusions. ... Unless attention remains focussed upon valid inference ... the discussion of rationality easily slides into a free-for-all about the psychology of belief and its relation to human behaviour" (p. 15).

The second through fifth chapters are largely devoted to the anthropological literature on the primitive or "prelogical" mind: Evans-Pritchard, Frazer, Lévy-Bruhl, Boas, Tylor, Durkheim and Mauss, with the fifth chapter ("The Great Divide") tackling the writings of Millman Perry, Eric Havelock, Walter Ong, Jack Goody and Marshall McLuhan on the effects of writing and mediated communication on the mind. This is all material that Harris has not previously discussed in much detail and a welcome addition to his previous discussions of the literatures of linguistics and philosophy. A couple of passages critiquing "Jack Goody's argument that 'writing gives a permanent form to speech'"especially caught my eye:

> First, the survival of of a text is entirely dependent on the materials used and the way they are used by the user. Second, regardless of the materials, the survival of a text also depends on the survival of a population of readers. Writing that cannot be read is not a text but a collection of marks. Furthermore, even under conditions of near-universal literacy such as prevail in modern Western societies, very little of what is written is destined to function as an everlasting record for future generations. (p. 72)

> In speech, an item cannot just be "shifted" from one place to another, or held in abeyance pending a reorganization of the whole sequence. These points that Goody makes are well made and well taken. But what Goody seems reluctant to admit is that examples of this kind

> (written lists and tables), which support his case best, are actually those which show up most clearly the misconception involved in regarded writing as just a "representation" of speech. For the (physiological) fact is that speech affords no room for structures that rely on two-dimensional relations, as do writing and all forms of drawing. It is that—and not the sensory shift to "the visual domain" as such—which makes writing structurally different from speech. (p. 72-73)

Harris follows his critique of Goody with short sections on McLuhan and Lévi-Strauss and then sums up some of the literature critical of the champions of the "writing restructures consciousness" school in a section entitled "Technological Determinism," concluding with "The Great Divide Reconsidered."

> For present purposes what emerges as important is that, neurophysiologically, the literate brain is different from the preliterate brain. That difference cannot be dismissed as a theoretical fiction or cultural illusion. ... What has to be recognized is that, just as the literate brain is variously configured as between different individuals and communities, so too is the literate mind.
> If even this much is admitted as the contribution of neuroscience, there is no ground for dismissing out of hand the thesis that literate and preliterate communities tend to produce typically different mental habits, insofar as these are favoured by the brain's development of new patterns of circuitry....
> On the other hand, as far as rationality is concerned, brain research offers no positive evidence to suggest that reasoning processes are in some way independent of other mental abilities (including linguistic and language-related abilities). Just as there is no brain "centre" for reading and writing, there seems to be no brain "centre" for reasoning either. (p. 77-78)

And with this much established and disestablished, Harris returns to the "question of exactly how rationality relates to literacy." We go back to Aristotle, dialectic, the syllogism, and the principle of non-contradiction.

> When we examine the *Organon*, it is evident that there is one pivotal piece of thinking that bears the hallmark of a literate mind above all else. That is Aristotle's invention of the seemingly simple device which is crucial to his syllogistic. The device in question is nowadays known as the variable ... The idea of allowing a single arbitrary letter of the alphabet to "stand for" a whole class of items cannot, for obvious reasons, be entertained in a preliterate society. Here we see literacy leaving its indelible mark on Western thinking about reasoning... (p. 87)

His discussion of Aristotle's variables, the syllogism and definitions throughout chapters six and seven have much of interest for anyone working with ontology development. The discussion of the homonymy problem is marvelously clear:

> [T]here is no natural "reason" why the same name should—or should not—be given by convention to two quite different individuals or things or classes thereof. Nor is the existence of synonyms a problem: nothing prevents the same person or thing from having two (or more) different names. Linguistic convention appears to be tolerant of both states of affairs. There is no overriding linguistic principle that decrees a universal one-to-one correspondence between a name and what is thereby named. ... [I]f there are no general critieria for homonymy, every proposed definition (*logos*) is potentially ambiguous. ... So we find Aristotle maintaining through thick and thin that "correct" definitions can be given. ... Be that as it may, before the work of syllogistic

reasoning can begin there seems to be a prior obligation on the logician to establish that the terms in question are free of homonymy. (p. 97-98)

Aristotle attempts to solve his problem by defining a definition as "a statement of 'essence'" (p. 99). And here, ontologists take note:

> [W]hat Aristotle takes for granted is that an essence is what is defined by a definition. A definition is given in a form of words. No form of words is self-defining. So the form of words has to capture something else other than its own image. This something else ... is—precisely—the essence of the thing to be defined. But this is where the muddle takes off. For what has not been explained is how the essence can be both (i) what makes the form of words interpretable as a definition (i.e. supplies its meaning) and, at the same time, (ii) whatever it is that makes the thing what it "essentially" is, i.e. "in itself". The gap between (i) and (ii) tends to go unnoticed by the literate mind. For writing encourages the illusion of being able to deal with thought, or the abstractions involved in thinking, "directly", i.e. at a level where the abstractions in question can dispense with any communicational anchorage other than that of the signs visually present before the reader. ... What is in fact being bypassed is speech; but consciousness of bypassing speech is easily construed subjectively by the reader as bypassing words altogether and thus gaining immediate access to the processes of thought. (p. 100)

Harris's discussion of propositions, the syllogism and the principle of non-contradiction fascinated me as Michel Meyer has also seen in these the source of a long-lasting philosophical malaise in the Western tradition. The critiques of Harris and Meyer are not identical, but reading them one after the other was quite an experience for this reviewer. Since the Semantic Web is simply the technological instantiation of the world as propositions (triplets) related syllogistically, at least chapters seven and eight should be required reading for everyone seriously engaged in thinking about the foundations of the Semantic Web.

For this reviewer, Chapter 9, "Interlude: Constructing a Language-Game" was the most spectacular. In previous books Harris has discussed Wittgenstein's imaginary primitive language of a group of builders and those discussions impressed me greatly. Here, the analysis and discussion go way beyond anything Wittgenstein attempted, and reveals Harris to be a far more profound thinker. Harris concludes:

> According to the integrational account, A's actions anticipate B's, which in turn presuppose A's. That is what makes their signs part of an integrated language-game. What each of the participants does is contextually and systematically relevant to what the other does within the same temporal continuum and the same programme of activities. It has nothing to do with truth. It is a conception of communication which lies beyond the reach of Aristotelian logic altogether. It proposes an account of meaningful human interaction that is radically different, in theoretical basics, from any other account that has been proposed in the Western tradition. (p. 132-133)

In the final three chapters Harris brings out the key consequence of literacy: the decontextualization of the word. With Aristotle's introduction of variables

> The first steps are being taken towards divorcing "logical relations" from "social relations", i.e. removing the concept of rationality from the everyday activities of human beings dealing as best they can with everyday situations, and relocating it in a hypothetical realm of possibilties. Recognizing actual causes and effects, together with the

practical connexions between them, thus becomes of secondary importance. (p. 151-152)

Literacy "sponsors the conception of words as decontextualized bearers of meanings. That makes it feasible to identify 'propositions' as unsponsored combinations of words. The sentence 'All men are mortal' does not need a sponsor: it just 'exists' in its own right" (p. 152). And at this point Harris touches on the computer:

> The final steps in the relocation come with those extensions of symbolic logic which make it possible to award the accolade of rationality to complex operations far beyond the capacity of any normal human mind to execute. The burden of safeguarding rationality is thus transferred from human beings to machines, which do possess the requisite O[perational]D[escriptions]. The digital computer, as its developers proudly boasted, is the supreme 'logic machine'. It can tell you 'what follows from what' much faster and far more reliably than you can, or any fellow human being....
> What has been happening along the way in this long-term transfer of authority and responsibilities (from Aristotle, to the medieval scholastics, to the authors of *Principia Mathematica*, to the computer) is a gradual, progressive dehumanization of reason. ...
> What the computer can 'do with words' is a lot more than you can. Nowadays we cannot even ourselves judge whether the computer 'got it right'. We should have to employ another computer to check that. And perhaps a third computer to check the second...? A rationality regress looms. All this is an inevitable consequence of treating language and logic as if they could be divorced, by intellectual fiat, from social reality. ... (p. 152-153)

By decontextualizing language, meaning is assumed to reside in the text itself, the text is "intrinsically complete. ... An interpreter is surplus to requirements. The text needs neither the presence of the author nor the presence of a reader" (p. 157). This goes for information science as well as for Derrida, about whom these remarks were written.

In his "Epilogue: Rethinking Rationality" Harris begins with the statement "Rationality—or, at least, most of what we often try, overambitiously, to subsume under that generalization—is a product of the sign-making that supports it" (p. 160). This is followed by a sketch of an integrational view of meaning and an integrational semiology. Harris locates the difference between his and the Aristotelian and Western view of rationality at "the exact point at which human rationality is seen as linking up with language as social praxis" (p. 176). The Western view has always taken language for granted, beginning the "analysis of reason at a level where 'propositions' can be identified simply by citing" sentences and systematizing them. The integrationist view "sees rationality as being based in the first instance in the ways that human beings attribute meanings to signs of any kind in the pursuit of integrated activities" (p. 177).

That last remark suggests that Harris's integrational semiology has as much to offer researchers on graphical interfaces and web design as to those engaged in ontology development. Both of the Harris books reviewed here discuss issues of importance in information science, and they approach these topics from a perspective not to be found anywhere else. They are as provocative and profound as they are clearly written. They are not books for everyone, however, as understanding them requires some pretty vigorous thinking and questioning much of what our literate culture takes for granted. On the other hand, *Of Minds & Language* is a book for a quite different reader. I do not think that anyone involved in any aspect of documentation would find anything of practical value in that book, and matters of theoretical interest are abundant only if you share the biolinguistics paradigm informing the papers therein.

I have reviewed these three books together because I recommend reading them together: the reader of *Of Minds & Language* who has previously read *Mindboggling* and *Rationality and the Literate Mind* will be reading with an awareness of the many assumptions, equivocations and careless language marring the papers edited by Piatelli-Palmarini. Most of the positions accepted, expounded or argued for in *Of Minds & Language* have been sharply criticized in one or the other of the Harris books. On the other hand, the reader of Harris' works who has also read *Of Minds & Language* will have a good background in the most current formulations of many of the ideas that Harris critiques.

As one who deals all day everyday with language in use, particularly in the context of libraries and the use of information technologies, I have found Harris's writings more interesting and more fruitful than those of any other writer on linguistics. Perhaps if I were a biologist or a neuroscientist I would have a greater appreciation for *Of Minds & Language*, but as a student of language and linguistics, I found *Of Minds & Language* to be totally confused. The confusions arise in part from the reification of theoretical entities, turning them into objects of natural science, and in part because of the near complete disregard for actual linguistic behaviour (linguistic examples are always made up and such pitifull examples of language at that).

If language is an organ in the brain, then we need to find it, but the neurosciences have found no such language organ or centre. So Chomsky puts "organ" in scare quotes. What does this mean? It can only mean that Chomsky recognizes the need for a biological basis if his ideas are not to be dismissed as theoretical fictions like the ether, but he has no such basis. His research and analysis are all based entirely upon not-so-arbitrary sentences which he himself has conjured up for the purpose of investigating language. He is in fact writing of a "spiritual organ" just like writers on the occult sciences do, perhaps hoping that sometime in the future his "organ" will be discovered by real biologists (among whom he cannot be counted). In spite of the linguistic facts all around us (spoken and written), in spite of all the references to scientific writers from Priestly to Lewontin and Carroll and the promisory notes to be paid, the language "organ" as Chomsky presents it is on a par with the "Third Eye" and ESP, i.e. it is offered as an hypothetical biological explanation for which there is no biological evidence. This is the price he pays for trying to investigate language as something existing entirely and only within us, a matter of an inaccessible and invisible (occult) "organical structure," while ignoring the ubiquitous phenomena of language around us.

While Chomsky can develop an entire theory of language and mind based on his analysis of made-up texts such as "Colorless green ideas sleep furiously" and "John is easy to please," Roy Harris is not so easy to please. Harris has thought long and hard about actual linguistic behaviour, about speech, writing, sign language, art and cricket as biomechanical, macro-social and meaningful activities. That attention to the empirical facts of language use, of human and animal communication in the real world, shows in everything he has written, nowhere more than in these two latest volumes.

The language and style of *Of Minds & Language* is one of science, knowledge and confidence. With the exception of the paper by Gallistel, there is nowhere any critical examination of ideas, assumptions, terminology or the interpretation of research. This is in stark contrast with the two books by Harris which are almost entirely devoted to the relentless examination of presuppositions and their consequences for theory as language and practice. *Rationality and the Literate Mind* is the culmination of a lifetime of thinking about language by one of the most important philosophers of the past century. *Mindboggling* is, as Richard Gregory wrote in his review, "valuable in asking questions and throwing down the gauntlet" (Gregory, 2008). So exercise your mind—I assume you have one—and read these three books. There is far more to be gained by reading them each against the other than just choosing the one or two that might suit our habitual way of thinking about minds and language.

References

Bennett, Maxwell R. and P.M.S. Hacker (2003). *Philosophical Foundations of Neuroscience*. Oxford: B lackwell.

Chomsky, Noam (2006). *Language and Mind*, 3rd ed. Cambridge: Cambridge University Press.

Gregory, Richard (2008). Review of *Mindboggling: Preliminaries to a Science of the Mind*, in *Times Higher Education*, 13 November 2008 (viewed online 9 April 2009).

IV

After Epistemology[1]

Ten minutes ago I finished reading *After Epistemology* (in one sitting) and after the thrilling experience of all one hundred and eighty seven pages (I even read the bibliography and index item by item) I have already asked myself if I am not entirely lacking in critical intelligence, for my only criticism is that it was only 187 pages long. I would have liked to read 187 or 1870 pages more. Perhaps an apology is in order for yet another rave review of a book by Professor Harris, but I have none to offer.

After Epistemology was even more of a surprise and even more enjoyable that I expected—and I always expect to be pleased and surprised by Harris—for some very personal reasons. First, some of the main arguments Harris makes and the conclusions he draws recalls those made—albeit in much less clear and concise a manner—between fifty and one hundred years ago by two nearly unknown philosophers (Owen Barfield and Eugen Rosenstock-Huessy) whom I have long admired but from whose ideas I was never able to discern "what next?" Until now. Secondly, I have for a long time wished—and with my reviews secretly hoped to inspire—a book by Professor Harris on information science from the perspective of his philosophy of

---

[1] Review of: Roy Harris. *After Epistemology*. Gamlingay: Bright Pen, 2009.

language. I assumed that to ask him directly would draw his response "Isn't that your task?" But here we have that book, and as I should have expected, he treats the topic with an entirely unexpected approach. And finally, there is page 172 on dancing. Why that matters so much to me will, however, remain personal.

Traditional epistemology, Harris writes in his Preface, "allows no scope for recognizing that the forms of knowledge recognized and valued in any society depend on the forms of communication practiced in that society" and that "Forms of communication make a crucial difference not only to what is known, but to what is knowable" (p. 2). McLuhan, Harris notes on p. 118, did see this, but, as Harris argued in *Rationality and the Literate Mind*, he drew the wrong conclusions. So the book begins where Harris left off in that book also published last year (2009).

The first eight chapters of the book (Part I: Epistemology in the Western Tradition) discuss the challenges to the ancient Greek philosophy of language underpinning epistemology as discussed in the West, beginning with Bacon's 'idols of the market'. Those idols were, for Bacon, "names of things which do not exist ... [and] names of things which exist, but yet confused and ill-defined" (p. 24-25, quoting from the *Novum Organum*). Harris then proceeds to Wilkins, Locke and Hume, and then surprisingly, Darwin. In his altogether unexpected discussion of Darwin it is not the influence of early 19th century theories of linguistic evolution on his theory of evolution that Harris focuses, but Darwin's reluctance to define two key terms: species and instinct. Here he quotes Darwin's remark in *The Origin of Species*:

> in determining whether a form should be ranked as a species or a variety, the opinion of naturalists having sound judgment and wide experience seems the only guide to follow. We must, however, in many cases, decide by a majority of naturalists, for few well-marked and well-known varieties can be named which have not

been ranked as species by at least some competent judges. (Darwin, quoted by Harris on p. 50)

To this Harris responds "Leaving aside the question of how 'competence' in such a matter is to be determined, counting heads hardly seems to be a shining example of scientific method." I single out this passage not only because it is a marvelous example of Harris' critical perspicacity, nor because his wit sometimes makes me double up in laughter, but more importantly for readers of this journal because of the implications of this witticism for the notion so prevalent these days of "the wisdom of the crowd." Harris goes on to quote Darwin's concluding remarks on the term species as being a term "arbitrarily given, for the sake of convenience" (p. 53) and asks "why, if Darwin believes this to be so, he does not declare species to be worthless as a scientific term and reject it" (p. 53).

Part One concludes with three 20th century challenges to traditional epistemology, those of A.J. Ayer, Saussure and Harris's own approach, integrationism. He sums up his discussion of classical epistemology by remarking that it

> treats knowledge as dealing with matters that are public, communicable and debatable. This move rests ultimately on the assumption that a public language is or can be put in place, on which discussion of these matters can be based. So Classical thinking in practice imposes an epistemological hierarchy, in which linguistic knowledge takes priority over non-linguistic knowledge" (p. 78).

While critical of this view of knowledge, he acknowledges that this is "a great advance on the more primitive view of knowledge as dealing with ineffable mysteries" (p. 79). Western ideas about that public language, whether imagined as being imposed on us from without (as prior consensus) or from within (some innate linguistic program in the brain) have always "ignored or marginalized the overriding role of the communicational context" (p. 80).

In Harris's view—the integrationist perspective—"there is no such thing as a decontextualized sign. What a dictionary lists as 'words' are decontextualized abstractions. Signs exist only in the particular circumstances in which they function as signs. Consequently the theoretical focus of linguistic inquiry shifts from using signs to the making of signs" (p. 80). The implications of this for epistemology are far-reaching:

> Just as every sign presupposes a context, every item of knowledge presupposes a context. There are no free-floating, contextless items of knowledge. There are no processes of knowing that exist independently of what is known. Knowledge, thus understood, is a form of activity. Most importantly of all, this activity is seen as a constructive, creative process. It is not a passive accumulation or residue of any kind. The creative process requires an active engagement of the self. It is not 'triggered' automatically. It cannot be undertaken by the collectivity on behalf of the individual. (p. 80-81)

And with this reconception of knowledge and what it means to know, Harris launches into Part II: Integrating Knowledge, which is in large part a critique of that understanding of knowledge which reduces, confuses or identifies it with information, this latter being, he writes, "the static, inert residue to which knowledge dwindles when subjected to persistent and systematic reification" (p. 116). That description of the relation between knowledge and information is 'from the top down' so to speak. He also gives a description 'from the bottom up':

> [M]aking use of information usually demands of the user (i) the interpretation of some static form in which the information appears, and (ii) that this interpretation be integrated into some further process of knowledge-

making in an appropriate context. Appreciating the potential utility of information is no more excuse for confusing information with knowledge than for confusing a symphony score with an orchestral performance. Information, of its own accord, does not somehow convert automatically into knowledge. Knowledge, like music, is made and in the making of knowledge, as in the making of music, the systematic integration of activities lies at the heart of the creative process" (p. 141-142)

Harris' discussion of information as opposed to knowledge runs throughout Part Two, but is most directly treated in chapter 13 ("Knowledge and Information"). In that chapter he clarifies that he is referring not to "the technical term information as used in mathematical 'information theory'" (p. 116, referring to Colin Cherry's 1957 *On Human Communication*) nor to the same term used in linguistics (referring to Halliday's 'systemic linguistics'), but to "information in the lay sense in which one consults a train timetable ... or a telephone directory" (p. 116). He focuses first on the role of codes "in the reduction of knowledge to information" since these "'work' by imposing systematic simplifications on whatever is to be 'encoded'" (p. 116). Codification attempts, he writes "to split knowledge into conveniently small encodable items, determined not by what is known but by the structural requirements of whatever code is being used. The code, in other words, imposes its own analysis and organization upon any materials encoded" (p. 117) and thus "what began as knowledge then becomes mechanized: it is progressively divorced from the creative processes that brought it into being and the human values that presided over its creation. The systematic accumulation of mountains of codified items can safely be left to machines (or librarians), for it is a purely mechanical operation" (p. 118).

These remarks on codes and codification are followed by a discussion of a recent book on knowledge management which he refers to as "This little sermon for our times": Wenger, McDermott and Snyder's 2002 *Cultivating Communities of Practice: a Guide to Managing Knowledge*, published by the Harvard Business School. Harris quotes a couple passages, including the following in which the authors "rationalize the tricky connexion between knowledge and communication":

> You know that the earth is round and orbits the sun, but you did not create that knowledge yourself. It derives from centuries of understanding and practice developed by long-standing communities. Though our experience of knowing is individual, knowing is not (Wenger, McDermott and Snyder (2002), quoted by Harris on p. 120)

Harris then describes their epistemological presuppositions this way:

> You, as an individual, know nothing. Knowledge is something outside you, to which you can only gain access (if you are lucky). You gain that access by means of communication with an appropriate source. But that to which you might (with luck) gain access has been put in place not by you, but by a historical consensus in the past. It is already at one remove from 'the facts' (e.g. the shape and movement of the earth). Here we see *in vivo* what an integrationist would regard as the reduction of knowledge to information (p. 120)

The passage from Wenger et al. that Harris quotes leads him to ask "some obvious undergraduate questions":

> Presumably people in the past might have been wrong. So why rest content with that account of knowledge?

And if that account of knowledge were right, it is hard to see why knowledge has just not remained unchanged for centuries. If knowledge equates with 'the consensus of previous generations', how could we ever come to know something our ancestors did not? (p. 121)

Of this "knowledge management" view of knowledge Harris concludes that it "takes knowledge all the way from the laboratory to the market place without ever allowing one crucial question to be raised: has the journey had no effect on the knowledge itself? Is what ends up in the commercial market place any longer knowledge at all?" (p. 122).

Harris then turns to "theorists who speak as if a great deal of information were somehow already present externally in what is observable" (p. 122) such as Eysenck and Keane (1995) who write of the information in a photograph. Of this view Harris remarks that photographs are not "repositories of information, still less of knowledge. It is the human observer who creates knowledge by interpreting the photograph ... on the basis of certain assumptions about how" the photograph was produced. Perhaps, he suggests, this is a recent "misapplication of the ancient doctrine of natural signs" (p. 123). But "Smoke does not 'mean' fire. It is human beings who interpret smoke as a sign of fire" (p. 123).

It is in his discussions of metaphor, literal meaning and perception that Harris arrives at fundamentally the same claim that Owen Barfield made in various publications between 1926 and 1957: there is no literal meaning, and perception of a tree (for example) as a tree (rather than as some hitherto unknown object) involves an interpretation. In Harris' words "it is vain to look for an absolute distinction between the metaphorical and the non-metaphorical" (p. 144) and there are only more or less successful "attempts to establish fixed codes" (p. 133) and to communicate with others. Regarding sense perception Harris writes "sense perception as such is not knowledge. Saying 'I see a birch tree' already goes beyond sense perception. Knowledge in such cases begins by identifying what is seen, ... that already presupposes interpretation of sensory experience" (p. 94). The implications of this for any theory of signs is quite straightforward, a conclusion that Harris draws but Barfield did not: the identification of a sign as a sign is the act of contextualization and the making of the sign in one and the same act (p. 103).

At the end of the book Harris argues that we must "start thinking of words and meanings as spontaneous creations of the mind which function as tools for the contextualization of those activities in which you are engaged" and that this "requires abandoning the old idea that whereas knowledge may make a great deal of difference to the knower, it 'makes no difference to what is known'" (p. 176, quoting Price 1963:23). "That conception of knowledge" Harris insists, "must go" (p. 176). Here again I hear echoes of Rosenstock-Huessy and Barfield. (For me, the only intellectual pleasure greater than finding agreement among those who inspired my youth and those who inspire my old age would be to have them argue their disagreements face to face. That of couse is no longer possible.)

It is not just Barfield and Rosenstock-Huessy whose valuable ideas one can find here. In the notion of local knowledge Geertz is not far away, and his discussion of perception seems to present with an extraordinary concision the most valuable insights of Heinz von Foerster, Humberto Maturana and Francisco Varela. Integrationism itself could be understood as a more radical and more profound view of the world of living beings living together than that developed by von Bertalanffy, Bateson, Wiener and other figures in systems theory and cybernetics. Yet none of these authors appear anywhere in the book; Harris responds to Aristotle, Austin, Bacon and Black, Bruner and Darwin, Eysenck, Gombrich, Lakoff, Langer and Locke, and Vico, Vygotsky,Wenger and Wittgenstein—among many others—by seizing on some basic presupposition and making his judgements and remarks directly in response to that. Harris does not acquire his knowledge second-hand; he gets where he is going entirely through criticism—and boy does he go places!

One of the key conclusions that Harris draws is that "all communicable knowledge is local knowledge" because "signs do not exist independently of their integration into the particular activities that gave rise to their creation" (p. 97). If we accept this—or at least consider it—then the questions that epistemologists should be asking—but have not—are questions such as "What is the difference between knowing what time it is and not knowing?" ... What is the difference between knowing the date of the Battle of Hastings and not knowing?" (p. 98). The answer, Harris claims, is in knowing how to act. In the real world nothing "can be known without involving a knower, and knowledge makes a difference to people's lives" (p. 99). Here we see Harris' fundamental disagreement with Popper and his "third world" of objective knowledge (which he does mention), as well as with philosopher-librarian Gilbert Varet's notion of knowledge as being only that which is documented so well that it cannot be lost. (Harris does not mention it, but *Science et son information à l'heure d'Internet* (2001) is an interesting book and Varet an author to whom I am indebted. Unfortunately he developed a ludicrous epistemology that only a librarian could have arrived at.)

Harris gives four 'basic propositions' for the demythologization of knowledge, the last of which is "signs, and hence knowledge, arise from creative attempts to integrate the various activities of which human beings are capable" (p. 162). Reading this and many other passages in this book I could not help but think about Web2.0, tagging, the frequently expressed desire for more interactivity and user participation in the creation and management of information in libraries. Harris's discussion of art and photography are full of provocative discussions for anyone interested in graphic interfaces or the problems of searching and creating metadata for non-textual digital objects. The claims made for and hopes pinned upon techniques and technologies such as the LCSH, authority files, doi's and url's, the Semantic

Web, ontologies, data mining, and automated classification and subject analysis often came to mind as I read of the flaw in treating "knowledge as an aggregate of infinitely many separately knowable items, between which the only structure of organization recognized is the a priori structure imposed by the way we assign names and verbal descriptions to them" (p. 45-46). This book may be after epistemology but it also makes a strong case for "After Information Science."

We have all seen—some of us way too many times—the DIKW diagrams: data, information, knowledge, wisdom. We have read too many discussions of how data differs from information, and information from knowledge, etc. We have believed that the more information and the more metadata the more knowledge there is and the better the world will be. We have read that there is too much information and that there is not enough information and that everything is information and that everything is metadata and that everything is miscellaneous. We have even been told that information is a 'plastic word' that means anything and therefore nothing at all (Uwe Pörksen—and it is this view that has often seemed nearest the truth to me). What Harris has done in this book—whether he intended to or not—is to provide the rudiments of a coherent theory of information as a product of social activities. Instead of some metaphysical theory of platonic forms or some ontologically distinct form of entities alongside matter and energy, we have a notion of information as knowledge reduced to a sign awaiting its interpreter. Instead of definitional chaos we have information theoretically defined as that publicly available sign created for communicational purposes. The creation of knowledge and of information can be described in terms of a theory of signs, a semiology that is not limited to linguistic signs but that covers all manner of signs: gestures, silence, documents, road signs, signatures, advertising, painting, music, theater, propaganda, film, photography, clothing, nipple piercing, dance and even the archaic experience of nature "speaking." And this goes not only for the writer but the reader as well, not only for the web site designer but for the internet browser, not only for the cataloger but for the library catalog user. From perception to interpretation to knowledge to creating a sign for communication to information buried in the stacks or cyberspace to information discovered, interpreted and made knowledge anew in a different time and place. It is an understanding of information that takes account of time and circumstance, understanding and misunderstanding, normative practices and creative activity.

On pages 164-166 Harris offers a different scenario of actions involving perception, knowledge, information and communication, and his is not of levels as in the DIKW models, but rather a timeline of human activity. Taking the ideas from *After Epistemology* and ordering them for an information science we might arrive at something like this:

1) Perception—by creatures of a time and a place with a memory of interaction and engagement with other creatures of its own kind and others

2) Interpretation—perception being active rather than passive, the very things we notice being selected for their relevance to our situation and task as we already understand it prior to the perception

3) Knowledge—"we do have first-order knowledge of our own everyday experiences, because we actually create our own interpretations of those experiences" (p. 166)

4) Communication—if the knowledge we have is to be communicable knowledge we have first to initiate that communicative activity

5) Sign making—communication requires the making of publicly available signs

6) Information—those public signs which are recognized as signs (in the extreme case this would be "found art" where the art is in the eyes of the beholder, not the creator)

7) Libraries, documentation, archiving

8) Sign making by the reader, performer, audience, etc.—a text, painting, performance is informative only to someone who first understands it as a sign

9) Interpretation—having understood something as a sign—which is to say having made a sign of something—the sign must be interpreted, and this will be done in a manner appropriate to the reader/hearer/observer's current situation, interests and program of thought or action

10) Information again—having interpreted the sign as meaning something, that meaning is now available for intellectual and practical action

11) Knowledge—information that has been successfully incorporated into some individual's intellectual or practical project

12) Communication—the knower in his or her excitement sets out to write the book or book review to share her or his knowledge with the rest of the world

Knowledge comes before data and information because "reasoning about the world is based on knowledge of the world, not vice versa" (p. 47). Harris's understanding of communicable knowledge is not tied to any particular forms of knowledge—bicycle riding, the difference between Constable's knowledge of painting as revealed in his paintings as opposed to that found in his lectures on painting are two of his memorable examples—forms of communication or technical systems. Instead of an information science that often seems little more than an advertisement for some new technical development (or potential development), we have a broad view of human communicative activity through the use of signs of all sorts and any tools that we may use to make those signs.

One of the major differences between Harris's view of language and communication and other notable theories is his emphasis on time. In *The Semantics of Science* Harris stated "such knowledge as we have is always of change" (Harris, 2005,

p. 117). If fixity of meaning is to be sought in the external world (reocentrism) we "can only do so on the supposition that this world of external things, from which words derive their meaning, remains constant" (p. 120). Obviously such a solution is not only undesirable but impossible in LIS since we are constantly reminded that the only constant in libraries is change. Yet the recognition of change calls into question some of the techniques upon which our hopes for the future of libraries and information systems are pinned. Perhaps we should be asking ourselves how today's metadata and today's ontologies can be anything other than straitjackets for tomorrow's citizens?

Read *After Epistemology* and see what you think. Then let me know what you think, because I would love to get this discussion going.

V

Was ist Information?[1]

Last year I wrote Uwe Jochum asking for some references to recent German research and he responded to my request with a single citation: Peter Janich's *Was ist Information*? It was not what I was looking for, but it was definitely what I have been hoping for.

Janich is a philosopher who has written extensively on epistemological issues in science. At least since 1993 he has been looking at the use of the term "information" in scientific discourse, from Morris's theory of signs and its influence on cybernetics and communication theory to the influence of these latter on other sciences, especially molecular biology and genetics. Many of these themes were brought together in another volume published in 2006, his *Kultur und Methode: Philosophie in einer wissenschaftlich geprägten Welt*. While that book makes a good companion to *Was ist Information*, it is in the latter that Janich devotes all his attention to the discourse, concepts and theories in which information science is grounded.

---

[1] Review of Peter Janich. *Was ist Information? Kritik einer Legende.* Frankfurt am Main: Suhrkamp, 2006.

Unlike most other books on information, Janich does not attempt to describe, define or explain information; rather, he takes an historical-philosophical approach, showing how the everyday metaphorical discourse about information and communication was altered in the context of changing ideas about nature, science and the development of communication technologies. Information was transformed linguistically, metaphorically, into a natural object that could be studied according to the methods of the natural scienes. This linguistic adaptation to changing realities is typical of human communication, but when imported into scientific discourse such metaphors can lead to all manner of epistemological problems. Janich argues that the trap into which the concept of information got stuck in the 20th century was prepared by Hertz through his tripartite division of scientific knowledge as real in its object, mental in its method, and linguistic in its expression.

In connection with the inventions of Edison, Janich describes how communication was mechanized. With Edison's machines, "the spoken word turned into a lasting thing that could be transported through time and space" (p. 34) and "speech no longer comes from the speaker but what is communicated is detached from the normal pretechnical situation of personal presence and a place and time shared with the one communicating" (p. 35). Curiously at this point he does not discuss writing, and one would like to find here some discussion of why the mechanisation of communication and the thingification of information only happened in the 19th century and not with previous technological revolutions such as the invention of writing or printing. I suspect that the answer lies in the changing understanding of both nature and science from Galileo on, but the question does not arise. What Janich claims is that these technological developments led to misunderstandings revealed in everyday language: "the phonograph speaks, the calculator calculates, the camera sees, the teletype writes" (p. 36). What this language suggests is exactly what later information theorists assumed, namely that "human achievements such as speaking, calculating, seeing, thinking, writing etc. can be taken over and performed by machines" (p. 36). [2]

This is not a problem in everyday life; but when scientists adopt this understanding as the presupposition and starting point for theorizing, forgetting the human origin and intentions in which all communicative action is grounded, then the "legend" of information as natural object appears and gives birth to information science. The first two chapters of the book

---

[2] In an email (29 February 2008) Janich responded: "Noch eine kleine Bemerkung zu Ihrer Besprechung, leider, ein kleiner Einwand: im Absatz über Edison und die Mechanisierung schreiben Sie „Curiously at this point he does not discuss writing ..." Oh doch! Aber an einer anderen Stelle, weil ich Mechanisierung und Technisierung unterscheide. Auf S. 165 f. bespreche ich die Verschriftung von Rede, und genauer auf S. 168 f. das Schreiben und Lesen. Dabei kommt es auf folgende Unterscheidung an: Schreiben und Lesen sind menschliche Handlungen, die erlernt werden müssen, ge- und misslingen können sowie Erfolg oder Misserfolg haben können. In jedem Falle hängt der Erwerb dieser Fähigkeiten davon ab, dass der Mensch schon sprechen und Sprache verstehen kann. Schrift und Buchdruck sind Techniken, die menschliche Kommunikationsleistungen "leistungsgleich" substituieren.
Ganz anders die Mechanisierung. Edisons Phonograph funktioniert genauso für Musik, Lärm, für beliebige Geräusche. Für seine Funktion sind weder Semantik noch Geltung von Gesprochenem wichtig.
Sie haben zwar recht, dass sowohl Edisons Phonograph wie die Schrift dazu dienen, Rede über Raum und Zeit zu transportieren - aber eben sehr verschieden, was die dabei erhaltenen und die dabei verlorenen Qualitäten des Transportierten angeht. Deshalb war es auch richtig, die Schrift in einem anderen Kapitel zu besprechen als die Mechanisierung durch Nachrichtentechnik."

outline that history. Chapter three explores the history of that legend when it has become full-blown dogma: Morris's semiology, Wiener's cybernetics, and Shannon & Weaver's theory of communication.

In his extended critical examination of Morris's semiology Janich notes the "canonization and dogmatisation of the Syntax-Semantics-Pragmatics succession" (p. 47) and Morris's acceptance of the Vienna Circle's monological (rather than dialogical) understanding of communication and language. To this day, Janich claims, information theory and its concepts remain stuck in the dilemmas created by this philosophical foundation. The discussion of Wiener focuses on the dichotomy of communication and control and his use of metaphors. The confusion at the heart of Wiener's concept of information is "whether information is a real object of natural science or only a metaphor for model-building" (p. 55).

His discussion of Shannon and Weaver continues in the fourth chapter in the section entitled "The information-complex". His criticism cuts to the core: "The concept of a 'stock of possible messages' [quoting from *The mathematical theory of communication*] has nothing to do with the openness of human communication, but with the functional limitations of a technical system and the use of tools" (p. 72). On the following page he notes that "What a message 'is' or how one defines it remains unmentioned" (p. 73). In a section entitled "Have you understood me?" Janich returns to the monological views of communication in information science, noting that "the receiver's answer plays no role" in this view (p. 82). He gives a one sentence summary of his analysis of the "information-complex": "The dogmatic division of theoretical philosophy in the tradition of logical empiricism (through the amputation of pragmatics, separating it from the productive, constructive part) has assumed in its analytical, disintegrating manner only the ready-made (and assumed to be real) products of science and technology, not the human effort and reasons that give rise to them and allow their proper understanding. But this is a fundamental error" (p.

87). Information is already there, Why? and For whom? are questions never asked.

That section is followed by a discussion of the concept of information in molecular biology, chemistry and genetics and the anthropomorphisation of these theoretical/physical entities that accompanies that discourse. That discourse, of genetic information, codes, messages and their transcription, copying, sending and translating, he argues is "not only redundant but inadequate" (p. 106). Communication and information in these sciences are not human activities in any sense, but the descriptions in these literatures are more human (i.e. anthropomorphized) than in theories of human communication like those of Morris and Shannon and Weaver!

In the section "Das Geistlose in der Maschine" (wonderful!) Janich formulates in his terms what I have argued elsewhere: "meaningful or meaningless, true or false, useful or useless, understandable or incomprehensible play no role" in the functioning of communication technologies (p. 113). Reducing our understanding of communication to the technical, physical system in which these matters play no role is fatal for any theory of communication or information. And this, suprisingly enough, he discusses in the context of the age old "mind-body" problem of philosophy.

In the fifth chapter Janich discusses (among other matters) the purpose of communication. "The traditional theories of information and communication never ask why. Information and communication are always already there, and as natural facts at that" (p. 147). The description of nature according to science admits causality (in some theories at least) but not teleology. If, however, information and communication are products (and not the prerequisites) of human action as Janich argues, then they cannot be understood in terms of cause and effect but only in terms of purposes and intentions (i.e. teleologically, but Janich does not use that word).

A key theme of the book is that communication is a human activity arising from human purposes and intentions; it is not simply a technical process. And it is only within communicative activity that references to information can have any meaning; information is neither a natural object that is inserted into a communicative act, nor the explanation for communication. Those familiar with the works of Roy Harris will recognize this as the essence of his critique of linguistic theory: one can only understand language as a product of communicative activity, not as a prerequisite for communication or a preexistent tool/thing used in communication. These two criticisms converge precisely on the foundation which these two disciplines share: human linguistic communication. Janich is not the first to criticize theories of information through an investigation of the language, metaphors and philosophy of language informing those theories, but his discussion is one of the best. So good in fact, that if you cannot read German, it is time to learn. Don't wait for the translation.

VI

Language, Meaning and the Law[1]

In *Definition in Theory and Pratice* (reviewed by the present author in vol.63 nr.6 of this journal) Harris and Hutton wrote "semantics is the study and practice of human attempts to impose some degree of communicational determinacy on signs. The successes, failures and limitations of such efforts are, in our view, central to the enterprise of definition" (p. viii). Their object in that book was to look at the law and lexicography as two longstanding cultural attempts "to impose some degree of communicational determinacy on signs." In *Language, Meaning and the Law*, Hutton has continued his investigation into legal language, and this book is, like the earlier, full of observations and arguments that bear not only on the making and interpretation of law but on the theory, construction, use and understanding of ontologies, metadata and search engines. Those who are accustomed to thinking about information as something distinct from

---

[1] Review of: Chris Hutton. *Language, Meaning and the Law*. Edinburgh: Edinburgh University Press, 2009.

language and therefore presenting a separate set of facts and problems will find that assumption increasingly untenable as Hutton's discussion of language in the practice of law unfolds.

Reading the book with my eyes particularly on the lookout for discussions relevant to ontologies, the semantic web and cataloging in libraries—I am, after all, a cataloger—the introduction "Parables of language and law" got my attention immediately.

> Babel signifies that the human condition is one of perpetual linguistic and conceptual disorder, and that attempts to establish regimes of cooperation organised through language must struggle to master that disorder. (p. 2)

He immediately follows this statement with a discussion of Wittgenstein's hypothetical "complete primitive language." He reproduces Wittgenstein's description of that language:

> The language is meant to serve for communication between a builder A and an assistant B. A is building with building-stones: there are blocks, pillars, slabs and beams. B has to pass the stones, and that in the order in which A needs them. For this purpose they use a language consisting of the words 'block', 'pillar', 'slab', 'beam'. A calls them out; —B brings the stone which he has learnt to bring at such-and-such a call. — Conceive this as a complete primitive language. (Wittgenstein 1978:3, quoted by Hutton on p. 2)

Hutton remarks that "while it might be said to consist of a set of names" this language "is actually a set of commands" (p. 2). There is an unstated but obvious hierarchy and exercise of authority: A speaks, but B, a slave with no voice of her own, obeys. Think of this model in connection with the mechanical slave—the computer, which "knows" only those 'blocks', 'pillars', 'slabs' etc. programmed into it—and the computer user who commands the system only as well as s/he knows the language of the program.

> The builders' language is an endlessly recycled set of name-commands, and does not accrue a shared memory of past interactions: it has no history. The builders' world is a totalitarian one in which language, command and obedient act are perfectly coordinated. Therein may lie a clue to its hold over the builders: perhaps authority lies in the language itself and there is no need of law, since in the imaginary domain of this primitive language, there is no room to think outside its categories and therefore no escape from the compulsion it exercises. (p. 2)

"Coercion", Hutton argues, is the "element that ties the names to things, and that coercion is enacted through language as a system of commands" (p. 3). It is not language—whether ours or Wittgenstein's imaginary one—that enables communication and cooperation, the social system as a whole, to work, but the exercise of a coercive and effective authority. The moral Hutton takes from the myth of Babel is that

> on being expelled from the God-given domain of truth and representation, language entered the domain of human responsibility in which 'there is no connection between word and world unless we put it there' (Hogan 1996:9). Once it is no longer underwritten by divine authority, the ability of language to depict reality or provide points of shared orientation is constantly in question. There is no single authority which stands outside language and controls it, nor is there a consensus as to how to describe and characterise the world. This raises the question of whether human cooperation through language is only conceivable as a form of coercion, whether it is only through the exercise of power that

order can be imposed on the conceptual chaos of language and its relation to the world. (p. 5)

Recognizing that we have no gods to guarantee our linguistic cooperation, computer scientists in the 1980's decided that 'ontologies' can do the job for us. This soon led Hobbs to claim

> If we are going to have programs that understand language, we will have to encode what words mean. Since words refer to the world, their definitions will have to be in terms of some underlying theory of the world. We will therefore have to construct that theory, and do so in a way that reflects the ontology that is implicit in natural language. (Hobbs, 1995, p. 819)

Hobbs offered a brilliantly naive expression of that state of affairs which Hutton described thus: "In the global knowledge economy, the ultimate fetishised object is language itself" (p. 16). Instead of understanding language as an activity in and of the world and being meaningful only as an activity within the world, Hobbs insisted that we must understand the world as 'natural language' presents it. We can understand language without understanding or even dealing with the world at all. The reduction of a whole to one of its parts is the precise definition of 'fetish' and this fetishization (abstraction) of language (information) from world is the enabling fiction of information technology. Throughout the book Hutton presents the reader with this same enabling fiction as the basis of the operation of law. "The idea of meanings inhereing within texts" he remarks, is one of the fictions about language that allows the interpretation of law through restriction, but "once the processes of law are set in motion, the fictional nature of many of its elements falls from view" (p. 184).

Following the introduction Hutton continues with discussions of various legal issues involving language. Chapter one "Legal theory and Language" looks at discussions of language in theories of natural law, positivism, rule of law, Marxist and critical theories, law and economics and systems theories of law (Luhmann). The second chapter discusses law as descriptive of an autonomous system and as normative prescription, and from there Hutton proceeds through "Philosophy, law and language", "Issues in legal interpretation", "Literal meaning, the dictionary and the law", "Representation, reproduction and intention" and "Idols of the market" before turning, in Part III, Key Issues, to some particular cases. The relevance of chapter two—Systems theory, normativity and the 'realist dilemma'—to information science is particularly obvious, and his discussion of Luhmann pertinent as a bridge between information science, systems theory, social theory and law. In the conclusion, "The semiotics of law, language and money" Hutton returns to the themes of the introduction, this time with the reader prepared by 175 pages of detailed discussion of a number of divergent opinions on each of the issues addressed.

A description of the central chapters of the book which would link them to the pertinent issues in information science would be nice, but that would require more space that I intend to allow myself here. Instead, I will rejoin him in his conclusion at page 177, where I will follow his own method of misquoting a philosopher to reveal what I (and apparently he) believes to be a crucial similarity between some important social abstractions:

> There is no more striking symbol of the completely dynamic character of the world than that of information. The meaning of information lies in the fact that it will be addressed to someone. When information stands still, it is no longer information according to its specific value and significance. The effect that it occasionally exerts in a state of repose arises out of an anticipation of its further motion. Information is nothing but the vehicle for a movement in which everything else that is not in motion is completely extinguished. (p. 177)

Now everywhere I have written 'information', Hutton had written 'language'. But Hutton was misquoting Simmel (1990, p. 510-511), who had written 'money' everywhere Hutton wrote 'language'. Hutton continues with an exact quotation (actually an English translation) from the same page in Simmel's *The Philosophy of Money*:

> As a tangible item money is the most ephemeral thing in the economic-practical world; yet in its content it is the most stable, since it stands as a point of indifference and balance between all other phenomena in the world. The ideal purpose of money, as well as of the law, is to be the measure of all things without being measured itself, a purpose that can be realized only by an endless development.

To "the ideal purpose of money, as well as of the law", Hutton adds language, and I add information. The issue of time—change, movement, memory—looms large when we try to relate an abstraction—money, law, language, information—to social reality. These two issues, time and abstraction, Hutton brings together in a comment on the the history of law:

> From the point of view of autonomous legal history, the external, social history of law is 'chaos' or 'environmental noise', and is assimilated only with difficulty into the internal history of legal concepts. But even a systems theory of law, as we have seen, must include the dimension of time. The systems view of language as existing outside time is a further step up the ladder towards the Platonic heaven of pure and motionless concepts. (p. 181).

Hutton comments on the circulation or motion of signs (money, language, information) and how it comes to the fore in trademark law "since the commercial sign is understood as circulating in the market, a shared product of interaction between the creator-author, the consumer, media and the public sphere" and that the "law may be required to reduce this movement to a fixed yes-no determination ... but there is no immediate assumption that all consumers perceive the trademark alike, or that there is a uniformity of reception or meaning" (p. 182). The 'single meaning' that law sometimes attempts to determine is a heuristic fiction that the law recognizes as such.

Another issue that Hutton discusses in this context is Google:

> Linguistic memory is constantly in motion, utterances are recalled and recontextualised, or simply buried under unbounded layers of accumulated experienced utterances and their contexts. Just as the search engine Google is in a sense bigger than the internet (since it reputedly holds a record of all Google searches), so linguistic memory is bigger than language. More accurately, what we call language is an emergent property of individual and shared linguistic memory. ...
>
> If a book has millions of pages, an alphabetic index may be of little use. This leads to the conclusion that in relation to the worldwide web and 'cyberspace', what is fundamental not only to memory, but to the creation of a normative order in the present, is the search engine, and other means of tracking, evaluating and organising the massive corpus of information, searches and materials. This is not merely a commercial tool, but also a political and social form, which can reflexively reflect and create different orders of knowledge. (p. 180).

Reading this passage here, out of its original context (an extended discussion of the construction, interpretation and contestation of law), it is undoubtedly difficult to see how the passage came to appear in a book on law, what exactly its meaning is, and the implications that may be drawn from it. Yet I hope that readers of this review will recognize that if a book on language and the law leads to such a discussion in its conclusion, then it is relevant to those interested in Google, indexing, the World Wide Web, search engines "and other means of tracking, evaluating and organising the massive corpus of information" available on the internet.

Following these two discussions, Hutton remarks that "one way of understanding the relationship between legal language and ordinary language is to see that the latter is a fiction created by focusing on the former" (p. 182). To me, this was a relevation, and has an exact bearing on the issue that has been framed in information science as 'controlled vocabulary' versus 'natural language'. Consider Hutton's claim (actually a conclusion arising from many pages of evidence and argument) in light of the debate within LIS: 'natural language' is a fiction created in response to a focus on 'controlled vocabulary', a focus necessitated by the limits and possibilities of several generations of technical systems during the history of information technologies.

Having made this claim—that natural language is an abstraction, i.e. a fiction, made in a particular context—Hutton then proceeds to relate this linguistic matter to a similar abstraction made in law:

> When we talk of the autonomy of law, we are recognising its relative imperviousness to direct control by certain social forces, but this requires us to perform an initial conceptual separation between law and society. The autonomy of language is similarly only perceptible if we separate language as system from the totality of human behaviour. Language is none the less frequently conceptualised as a semiotic system which is stable, fixed and still, an ideal reference point. Without such a system, the argument goes, communication would be impossible. But this system can only be activated to

serve as a fixed, reference point by putting it in motion, at which point the system of fixed, shared meanings becomes 'present to us through its absence'. (p. 183)

If social practices are "constituted by fictions ... questions of agency, insight and control over meaning" cannot be avoided: they "haunt the law and legal theory" (p. 183). Here we find the meeting place of law, language, and information science. If lawyers believe that the language of contracts "actually involve 'a meeting of minds' (*consensus ad idem*) as a psychological or social fact, then there are legal theorists who wish to remind them that he world does not come already labelled in 'legal categories' and that legal categories do not descend to earth from a Platonic heaven of pure ideas, but are imposed on it by legal analysis" (p. 183-184, references omitted). The reader for whom this does not immediately bring to mind the semantic web and related issues of metadata, tagging, cataloging and relevance ranking should probably waste no time on Hutton's book or the rest of this review. For those who do see the connection, I would like to take a short detour through Hutton's earlier work to make a point.

Hutton's first book, *Abstraction & Instance*, was not a book on legal language, but on semiotic theory, in particular Charles Sanders Pierce's distinction between 'type' and 'token'. That book was essentially, though not intentionally written as, a profound critique of the foundations of Domanovszky's model of 'work', 'expression', 'manifestation' and 'item' in his theory of bibliographic description. The issues treated in the first part of the book "involve an exposition and critical analysis of the different illustrations of the type-token relation made by philosophers and linguists" (p. 3), but neither Domanovszky nor his model are mentioned, and no questions of information science or bibliographical description are ever brought up. In the early chapters Hutton intends to demonstrate "that the intuitive acceptability of the type-token distinction, and the ease with which it can be illustrated, have led linguists and philosophers to underestimate drastically the complexity of the definitional issues involved" (p. 3). Pierce is himself the best example of the problem Hutton investigates, for in Pierce "the strength of the intuition about the type-token relation leads Peirce to assert that two tokens of the same type are identical, whereas it is of the nature of the philosophy, and in particular of his theory of signs, to deny the possibility of such an identity" (p. 3). The third chapter illustrates the problem from examples in art theory:

> The notion of type is illustrated or suggested by those works of art that can be copied, duplicated, reproduced or forged, such as literary works of art, music, paintings, etc. Again we have an intuitive point of departure, the notion that, for example, two different performances of the same piece of music must in some significant sense be performances of the same work. This intuition serves as the basis for a philosophical discussion of the ultimate nature of works of art. Everyday usage and ways of talking about art are invoked to illustrate the distinction under consideration. Thus we talk of *Beethoven's Fifth Sympohony* as being a great work, but also of a particular performance being great. (p. 4)

Hutton argues that the distinction between type and token is "a useful, but not very profound, distinction between different ways of counting" (p. 5). Types are understood to be "atemporal, non-material" entities that endow "the physical object, the token, with meaning", and this involves "an opposition between pure abstraction and pure physical object" (p. 162). The 'intuitive' validity of this model lies in the fact that

> It is part of the explicit practice associated with these areas that creative and interpretative work mediates between, for example, score and performance, or script and the stage. ... Further distinctions can be made with

respect to the distinction between a book and its copies. (p. 163).

Yet Pierce's seemingly 'intuitive' notions of type and token (and clearly Domanovszky's work-expression-manifestation-item as well), when erected into a model of the ontology of the existing linguistic, cultural and communicational material, the concrete facts whose meaning and interrelationships we seek to understand, produces insoluble definitional and ontological problems. *Abstraction & Instance* elucidates those problems but there is barely a hint of political and legal issues, at least not overtly.

Hutton turned to the law at least as early as 1995 with the publication of the paper "Law lessons for linguists? Accountability and acts of professional communication", and then turned his attention to studying linguistic theory under the Third Reich (Hutton, 1999 and 2005). With Harris and Hutton (2007), he returned to language and the law, and in this latest book of his we see the issues of 1990 combined with those of the later 1990's. What unites all these works are "questions of agency, insight and control over meaning" (p. 183) and "accountability and acts of professional communication" (Hutton, 1995). In other words, does language involve anything other than a mechanical matching of tokens with types, or is interpretation involved in *all* questions of meaning and communication? These questions often seem marginal or irrelevant to the professional linguist and the information scientist, but to one who has spent time studying questions of language and law during the Third Reich, questions of control over meaning and accountability cannot be marginalized for they constitute the central decisions concerning life and death.

The operation of law always involves the interpretation of a preexisting text (law) in order to determine its applicability to a particular case that has arisen after the enactment of the law and therefore not present to the authors of the text of the law. The existence of the law, its interpretation and its application to particular cases all involve some form of coercion or the operation of law would be insignificant. What is of particular interest to Hutton is how that coercion is persistently denied and presented as simply the 'facts of language', whether natural language or the technical language of law, rather than acknowledged as a contingent matter of social relations.

We find an exact parallel in information science. Many recent discussions of the semantic web have offered us a vision of a world in which 'meaning' is established unambiguously by urls, statements in the form of triplets, i.e. syllogisms in the language of IT. The claim that all questions of meaning can be solved (or at least solved 'good enough' for machine interpretation) requires that all issues of interpretation, and that means all political, social and legal issues, be banished from consideration and regarded as irrelevant or nonexistant. It is a denial that human communication—via information systems or any other—has any dimension other than a technical operation of matching up signs with meanings (types with their tokens, or works with their expressions, manifestations and items). Such a system of securing meaning through the language of the law has a history much longer than the similar history in information science, and that earlier history is particularly instructive precisely because it was rooted in cultural practices established explicitly for the purpose of and widely believed to be functioning in the interests of the exercise of justice.

The issues in law are identical to the issues in LIS: issues of interpretation (of legal language, laws, cataloging codes and controlled vocabularies), of classifying particular instances (legal cases, documents in a library) in relation to existing precedents (case law, Library of Congress Rule Interpretations), of determining the applicability or non-applicability of a given law (judicial review, cataloger's judgement), and whether or not an infallible, mechanically applicable rule, hermeneutic, heuristic, tool or algorithm can be developed to eliminate the human variability at the heart of the system (judges, catalogers).

If it is assumed that existing law defines justice (as opposed to the notion that the law must seek to determine what is just in each and every case), a means of interpreting existing law that would be not based on the messy psychology and intellectual limitation of humans but on an infallible interpretative rule would provide us with the perfect system for the administration of justice. Hutton's book reveals, page after page, that no legal hermeneutics of such perfection has ever existed, nor can such infallible interpretive rules or tools ever be developed. Why? Precisely because the exercise of law is the exercise of the power of control over interpretation. Exactly the same applies to information science and the design, construction and use of any and all information systems. To misquote Hutton, "Coercion is the element that ties the names to things, and that coercion is enacted through language as a system of rdf descriptions and urls" (p. 3). To deny the existence of this political matter, masking the operation of power and coercion in matters of interpretation by claiming that some techical system such as the semantic web somehow puts interpretation out of business, is simply a mystification that serves only to prevent us from deepening our understanding of information systems and their operation.

So as we design or dream of future information systems for use in any of our social practices, let us imagine ourselves as the users of the system. Imagine that we are before a judge in a court of law. Is an algorithmic justice good enough? Or would we be demanding an accurate presentation of the facts of the particular case and the circumstances surrounding it, a judge who was neither blindly literal nor accepting whatever interpretation the expert system provided him, and a judicial philosophy that sought to determine how the law should be interpreted and applied in a particular instance to establish justice here and now?

The issues Hutton discusses in *Language, Meaning and the Law* do not touch upon the trivial and superficial issues related to the design and use of information technologies and may be of little use in dealing with the many of the everyday problems information professionals will encounter. But to understand information systems on the whole as tools used in social practices involving the making and interpretation of linguistic signs, I recommend *Language, Meaning and the Law* over many other volumes that specifically—and narrowly—address the philosophy and techniques of information science. Anyone who wants to think about the foundations of information science and its relation to social practices will welcome this book. On the other hand, those who imagine that the semantic web will solve all problems of meaning in technical communication will not find it pleasant reading. Unless, of course, they fail to follow the links from law to information science.

References
Harris, Roy and Christopher Hutton (2007). *Definition in Theory and Practice: Language, Lexicography and the Law.* London: Routledge.
Hobbs, Jerry R. (1995). "Sketch of an ontology underlying the way we talk about the world" *International Journal of Human-Computer Studies* v.43 p.819-830
Hutton, Christopher (1990). *Abstraction & Instance: the Type-Token Relation in Linguistic Theory.* Oxford: Pergamon. (Language & communication library, v. 11)
Hutton, Christopher (1992). "Law lessons for linguists? Accountability and acts of professional communication" *Language and Communication* v.16 nr.3 p.205-214.
Hutton, Christopher (1999). *Linguistics and the Third Reich: Mother-tongue Fascism, Race and the Science of Language.* London: Routledge.
Hutton, Christopher (2005). *Race and the Third Reich: Linguistics, Racial Anthropology and Genetics in the Dialectic of Volk.* Cambridge: Polity.
Simmel, Georg (1990). *The Philosophy of Money.* London: Routledge.
Ludwig Wittgenstein (1978). *Philosophical Investigations.* Oxford: Blackwell.

VII

Principia Rhetorica[1]

One of the most discussed topics of the past decade has been the Semantic Web and the various techniques that have been proposed and developed to make it a reality. Given the ubiquitous presence of rhetorical perspectives in virtually every field of academic research during the past half century the complete absence of a rhetorical perspective in the discussions of the Semantic Web is surprising. While a search of the full text EBSCO Library, Information Science & Technology Abstracts with Full Text database using the words *semantic*, *web* and *rhetoric* produced zero citations when I began writing this review, the literature of information science and librarianship is teeming with discussions of issues that are clearly rhetorical. Examples are everywhere: discussions of the order of elements in a bibliographic display, relevance ranking, the language of indexing and description (natural language and controlled vocabulary), Dervin's "communication not information", orientation towards the user, and the reference interview all involve issues of rhetorical practice. Most of these topics have never been discussed from a rhetorical perspective, but several

---

[1] Review of: Michel Meyer. *Principia Rhetorica: une théorie générale de l'argumentation*. Paris: Fayard, 2008.

publications of the last decade have used rhetorical theories in various areas of IT research. Sapienza's (2007) paper on single-sourcing, Potter (2008) on asynchronous learning networks, Argamon et al. (2007) on text classification, and Spinuzzi's (2005) paper on research techniques are excellent examples of how rhetorical theory can illuminate the design, implementation, use and evaluation of information technologies.

Believing that "current rhetorical theories are insufficient" for analyzing the technique called single-sourcing, Sapienza (2007) drew on early 20th century poetics (imagism and acmeism) for his analysis. Like Argamon et al., Spinuzzi and Potter, he made no references to Michel Meyer, nor have I encountered any references to any of Meyer's works in the LIS literature. The present review is not a review of *Principia Rhetorica* as a book on rhetoric, but an introduction to the particular approach to rhetoric Meyer takes—one based on what he calls problematology and which as a search term also does not match anything in the EBSCO database—and its relevance to LIS.

Principia Rhetorica begins with a chapter on the definitions of rhetoric followed by a brief history of rhetoric leading to Meyer's "new vision of rhetoric" based on problematology. Meyer notes that the periods of greatest attention to rhetoric were periods of epistemological uncertainty: classical antiquity, the Renaisance and the 20th century. In earlier works as in the work under review here, Meyer compared the triplets of rhetoric (*ethos, logos, pathos*) with the triplets of Saussure's speech circuit (speaker, language, hearer), of information theory (sender, message, receiver) and philosophy (self, world, other). Here he notes that ancient rhetoric emphasized *ethos* (the speaker), renaissance rhetorics emphasized *pathos* (the hearer/receiver/Other), and 20th century rhetorics emphasized *logos* (the world). A product of the renaissance, science emphasizes *logos*: language as hardware in the brain, messages in a technical system, the world as object of knowledge without reference to a knower. In contrast, Meyer's approach treats *ethos*, *logos*, and *pathos* as equal in importance, related through their participation in the problematic that gives rise to the communicative act.

Two remarks by Meyer serve nicely as demonstrations of his approach and its significance for current research in information systems. Contrasting rhe rhetoric of Aristotle with that of our time, Meyer remarks "What one discusses are theses, (Aristotle), propositions, in the literal sense of the word *to propose*. However, that conception is out of date. What one debates, those matters upon which we reflect, are *questions*, and if there is no problem, there is no discussion." (p. 9; the full significance of this remark for philosophy may be found in his 1994 monograph *Of Problematology*). His remarks on Descartes' four rules in the *Discours de la méthode* could easily have been written about the Semantic Web:

> If one examines the source of these four rules, one immediately sees that they are concerned with transforming each stage of rhetoric into a precise rule of method. Descartes thus transposes *inventio, dispositio, elocutio* and *memoria* into strictly analytical steps, leading to the result that the result is a necessary result rather than simply a reasonable response. ... The dissolution of the dialectic is total. The first rule is very clear in this regard: one must not permit anything that is problematic, since, according to Descartes, the problematic is the doubtful. The alternative is identified with the undecidable. The problematic must therefore be totally eliminated. One must find (*inventio*) the right response, that is to say the response that makes the problem dissappear. From there on it is the task of method rather than rhetoric to produce results that are no longer uncertain. Thus one has judgements that no longer have any thing to do with interrogativity, these being filed away among all things dubious, because we find ourselves in an intellectual universe ruled by a founding self-affirmation of

> the necessary and exclusive affirmation: A without the possibility of having non-A. (p. 45)

This transformation of the problematic, of possibilities, alternatives, disagreement, meaning, metaphor, polysemy, ambiguity, ignorance, the unknown, uncertainty, vagueness, deception and propaganda, into the "machine-interpretable" triplets of RDF is simply the latest version of the cartesian project to eliminate uncertainty. This transformation requires, as Meyer has argued at length in earlier works (e.g. Meyer, 1988 and 1994), obscuring or denying the problem which gives rise to the question that provokes the statement, proposition, response in the first place. The Semantic Web is predicated upon the notion that meaning can be made explicit, i.e. meaning is not problematic, all questions of interpretation will be eliminated. In the Semantic Web there will be definitions and rules. The Resource Description Framework (RDF) and the Functional Requirements for Bibliographic Records (FRBR) alike assume a world that can be described entirely in propositions. The Semantic Web is the "philosophical grammar" of Descartes' contemporary John Wilkins in a new guise. And indeed Meyer's comment

> If one demands "What is X?" this evidently presupposes that X *is* some thing, *a* rather than *b* for example, since one must know what it is we are asking about and not confuse it with some other thing. So to say that X is *a*, or that X is *b*, is already to specify what it is that one is asking for. (p. 26)

echoes Harris's criticism of Wilkins' universal language:

> a classification system that purports to reflect the 'real' organization of the world of Nature cannot be proposed *in advance of* the experimental investigations necessary to determine that organization. (Harris, 2005, p. 61-62)

Moving from the Renaissance into the 20th century, Meyer's comments on Gadamer's hermeneutical approach also seem pertinent to the basic problems for understanding information seeking behaviour. When Meyer quotes Gadamer's remark "one cannot understand a text unless one has understood the question for which the text is a response" (p. 63) I am reminded of Collingwood's critique of propositional logic (specifically mentioned by Meyer several times in publications of the past 30 years) and his famous thesis about understanding historical events: in order to understand human action it is necessary to understand what the actor intended to do, what problem the actor was trying to solve. Gadamer himself argued that even though Collingwood was oriented in this direction, we still have no logic of question and answer. If the meaning of a statement relates to the question it answers, so must its truth. And as many of Collingwood's critics noted, discovering that question is a problem, a problem that will not be resolved in a triplet. It is also *the* problem in the design of any information system, i.e. matching a database to a query that is known to the search system only through the text entered into the system. It is the problem for which techniques as disparate as relevance ranking, keyword searching and controlled vocabulary have been proposed as solutions, but it is a problem, like historical understanding, which remains in the realm of the problematic.

Meyer then devotes two chapters to the distinguishing features of rhetoric and argumentation, followed by the chapters that make the book more than just another book on rhetoric. In the first of those chapters—*Ethos, logos, pathos dans l'interaction rhétorique*—Meyer offers up a discussion of the classical rhetorical concepts of *ethos, logos* and *pathos* that raises a multitude of questions for the parallel sender-message-receiver paradigm of information theory.

> Is there anything more convincing for anyone than one's sense of humanity and capacity to respond to questions that others pose and to which they seek answers? ... The

ethos is presented as the most profound expression of a common humanity, thanks to which we all alike respond to the great questions. ... The *ethos* becomes more distant and "authoritative" as it places itself within the *ad rem*, and more malleable and adaptable to others, more compatible and sympathetic when it is rhetorical, distance there being by definition less conflictual. To create distance one must transform the *ethos* into a principle of authority that excludes all putting in question. (p. 152)

The *ethos*, in becoming a principal of authority, goes from universal wisdom to particular knowledge, from humanism to technical competence. (p. 153)

Reading this I wondered how Meyer's "new" rhetoric would be pertinent to understanding human-machine or machine-machine communication. Was Meyer's "new" rhetoric out of date before it was published? I think not, but questioning information science and the discourse of the Semantic Web in terms of *ethos* (and *logos* and *pathos*) will certainly raise some of those "great questions" that humans ask and to which they respond. What is ethos/authority in machine generated discourse? How is the query entered into an information system related to the inquirer's question? How is the response of the information system to that query related to the inquirer's question? To a human response?

Rhetoric, for Meyer, is the art of speaking and writing about the problematic. In an information system, there are no questions, only answers, for nothing is problematic: every response is an answer that can be accepted or rejected but never argued or debated (the problematic as the debatable being for Meyer the primary characteristic of human knowledge). This would seem to suggest that rhetoric plays no part in an information system, that *logos* (message) alone—to the exclusion of both *ethos* and *pathos*—matters in an information system. Yet if we recognize that the computer is a primary *auctoritas* for our society, *ethos* comes back into the center of the discussion. Furthermore, the source of the data within the system and the designers of the software at work are both largely hidden elements that ought to be examined from the perspective of *ethos* as well. Do ontologies operating "under the hood" act as hidden *ethos*, making them unquestionable authorities? Will the interoperation of ontologies in the proposed Semantic Web distort the *logos*/message of the original author? Will this entail the elimination of *pathos*/hearer/receiver?

The next three chapters are devoted to discussions of *ethos* (Logique des valeurs, logique de la culture [Logic of values, logic of cuture]), *pathos* ("Comment négocie-t-on la distance entre individus?" [How is the distance between individuals negotiated?]), and *logos* (La théorie des variations problématiques [Theory of problematic variation]), a chapter on social aspects of argumentation and concludes with the chapter "Métarhétorique". The chapter on *ethos* concludes with the statement that "social life is founded upon the distance that must be continually negotiated at each encounter", that distance being one of cultural and personal values which lead to different questions. The following chapter on *pathos* discusses the problem of interlocutors reaching understanding of each other's positions, if not agreement on them. Meyer's criticism of his teacher Chaïm Perelman's *universal auditor* appeared earlier in the book and in this chapter he contrasts the auditor/reader as imagined by the speaker/writer—*pathos projectif*, the projective auditor—with the actual or effective auditor/reader (*pathos effectif*). The assumed auditor/reader (in LIS terms, the user) of techniques such as natural language description, keyword searching and relevance ranking is none other than Perelman's universal auditor, a fiction, or, as Meyer puts it, the projective auditor, the reader as we (authors, programmers) imagine her to be, who may or may not have much to do with the actual auditor/ reader/user.

In the *ethos-pathos-logos* relation the *pathos projectif* leads to a triple response: the understanding of what the speaker wants to say ("what is the question?" is the question to him), the adequacy of the response and the persuasive interest of the proposition. If I address myself to someone, I make that triple hypothesis: the difference will be eradicated by persuasion, my response will be judged adequate and the other will necessarily understand my point of view as well as my intentions. But the auditor is not forced to react as I imagine or hope he will. The *pathos effectif*, that is to say the real auditor, is moved by other parameters. (p. 230)

Meyer's discussion of negotiating distance is largely concerned with a direct communication situation, whether in a court of law, mass advertising, reading or face-to-face speaking. Librarianship and information science are largely concerned with mediated communication, whether that mediation takes the form of document-librarian-user, document-cataloger-IT-reference librarian-user or simply document-IT-user. I was led to see that the success of user supplied descriptions (tags, reviews, etc.) attests to the value of addressing a varied readership, an interesting technical response to a problem ignored by standardized thesauri as well as keyword searching. Most importantly, Meyer's problematological rhetoric provides a rigorous theoretical understanding of both the failures and the successes of a number of technical means for dealing with the problems of matching database and reader through a textual query, i.e. negotiating distance using a technical system, for the conflicts between the cataloger's assumption about the user and the actual user and the conflicts between system (designer's) assumptions about the user and the actual user can both be understood in terms of projective versus effective users.

Meyer's theory also provides insight into propaganda and spam:

A successful agent must offer responses that meet the values of the auditor, putting at a distance those that she rejects, exalting her emotions, even passions, and sincerely at that. (p. 234)

However, he continues, the rhetoric most successful in that effort is that of the seducer, the manipulator. In the technical context of IT we call that spam—when we recognize it. While programmers working on anti-spam software will certainly agree with Meyer's remark that "in everyday life those failures and the subsequent adjustments are natural and inevitable" (p. 235), his statement is equally true for all communication.

The chapter on *logos* discusses the problematic of world as word: literature, law and political discourse, with a closing section on the language of advertising. As a key to literary style, he offers a "law of inverse problematicity" in which he states that "the more a problem is literally expressed in the text, the more the text will explicity provide the resolution" (p. 246). The corollary according to this law is that the more the problem is obscured, figuratively expressed, the less the text will attempt to resolve that problem. Applied to political and legal discourse, the law of inverse problematicity is restated. In legal discourse

> The more there is conflict, the more the discourse is affected by *pathos*. The more the discourse diminishes the problematicity of the questions, the more it expresses the resolution of the norm in terms of positive law. (p. 262-263).

while in political discourse

> The more the question is expressly specified, the more the political discourse is literally conditional. The less overt the problem, the more it is taken over by ideological discourse that pretends to resolve everything. (p. 263)

One of my few complaints about this book arises from having read his earlier books: Meyer's examples in *Principia Rhetorica* are the same examples he has proferred in publications of 1988, 1992, 1994 and elsewhere. By now I am a bit weary of discussing the possible questions that could give rise to variations on the statement "Napoleon was the victor at Austerlitz." A more diverse set of examples could have made his points not only clearer, but far more provocative. For instance, whether discussing *ethos* (sender), *logos* (message) or *pathos* (receiver) in information retrieval, the problem is generally approached as a problem of information and users. Yet when confronted with the following responses to a query using the term "peace" we can see how important it is to take account of ethos/authority in the evaluation of those results:

> The State must see that public peace and order are preserved and, in their turn, order and peace must make the existence of the State possible. (Hitler)
> the first premise for every truly human culture ... the individual's capacity to make sacrifices for the community (Hitler)
> socialism is sacrificing the individual to the whole (Goebbels)
> But there is a direction to events, and the sacrifices of the present have not been in vain. ... We are called still to spread liberty, to assure justice, to be the makers of peace. (McCain)
> Americans laid down their lives for this country and for the peace they were there to protect. We revere their service. We honor their sacrifice. (Obama)
> True partnership and true progress requires constant work and sustained sacrifice (Obama)
> Socialism and work are inseparable from each other (Stalin)
> Only under the reign of socialism can peace be fully established (Stalin)

Don't imagine that I came to bring peace on earth. I did not come to bring peace, but a sword! (Jesus)

My point here is NOT to smear Jesus, Obama and McCain by comparing their words to those of Goebbels, Hitler and Stalin, but to demonstrate that how we understand the meaning of *peace* (socialism, sacrifice, work...) is dependent upon who we know as the speaker/writer, i.e. it is a rhetorical matter of *ethos*. Information technologies do take *ethos* into account whenever they rank a page by how "popular" it is, but in spite of a few such techniques, consideration of *ethos* is largely absent from IT system design. And how to incorporate matters of ethos/authority into IT is as much a political matter as it is technical, which is the topic of Meyer's penultimate chapter.

I began my own reading of Meyer's works in my efforts to understand what kind of a rhetorical strategies would be appropriate or necessary for creating machine operable metadata, and conversely, what strategies would be appropriate for library users facing a computer screen. Meyer addresses neither of these questions directly, but in his works and in particular this latest monograph Meyer has raised a host of questions that need to be addressed before tackling the particular questions of human-machine and machine-machine interaction. Although there is a growing body of literature advancing a rhetorical approach to hypertext, internet writing and reading, human-computer communication and related matters, the literature that I have examined is all based on older rhetorics emphasizing only one of the elements of the *ethos-logos-pathos* trilogy, and furthermore generally suffer from being focused on technology rather than the communication situation as a whole. Meyer's problematological rhetoric permits an understanding that is rooted deeply in human experience—difference, disagreement, ignorance, alternative possibilities—focusing on the problematic and the ways in which we respond to questions, aspects of human communication that will not dissappear or become outdated with the next technical development. It is not misleading to characterize problematology as an anti-ontology. Ontology attempts to state what is, while problematology enquires. The question is always prior and persistent; the answers we give (natural language, science, ontologies) are debatable and ephemeral: like hardware and software, they are here today and gone tomorrow.

Philip Agre has described how practitioners of AI "believed that by defining their vocabulary in rigorous mathematical terms, they could leave behind the network of assumptions and associations that might have attached to their words through the sedimentation of intellectual history" (Agre, 2002, p. 131). AI "inherited certain discourses from that history [of Western thought] about matters such as mind and world, and it has inscribed those discourses in computing machinery. The whole point of this kind of technical model-building is conceptual clarification and empirical evaluation, and yet AI has failed either to clarify or to evaluate the concepts it has inherited" (ibid., p. 141). What happened instead, he argues, is that "AI has been left with no effective way of recognizing the systemic difficulties that have arisen as the unfinished business of history has irrupted in the middle of an intendedly ahistorical technical practice" (ibid., p. 131). Agre argued for "a critical technical practice: a technical practice within which such reflection on language and history, ideas and institutions, is part and parcel of technical work itself" (ibid.). It is in that spirit and towards that end that we should read *Principia Rhetorica*. It is not just the meaning of words in a text that matters in information retrieval; authors and readers, information suppliers and information users are equally important agents. *Principia Rhetorica* does an excellent job of describing and theorizing these issues in terms of a problematological rhetoric.

References

Agre, Philip E. (2002). "The practical logic of computer work" In Matthias Scheutz, ed., *Computationalism: new directions*. Cambridge: MIT. p. 129-142.

Argamon et al. (2007) Argamon, Shlomo; Whitelaw, Casey; Chase, Paul; Hota, Sobhan Raj; Garg, Navendu; Levitan, Shlomo. "Stylistic text classification using functional lexical features" *Journal of the American Society for Information Science & Technology* Vol. 58 Issue 6 (April), p. 802-822.

Harris, Roy (2005). *The Semantics of Science*. London: Continuum.

Meyer, Michel (1988). "The interrogative theory of meaning and reference" In Michel Meyer, ed. *Questions and Questioning*. Berlin: Walter de Gruyter, p. 121-143.

Meyer, Michel (1994). *Of Problematology: Philosophy, Science, and Language*. Chicago: University of Chicago.

Potter, Andrew (2008). "Interactional coherence in asynchronous learning networks: A rhetorical approach." *The Internet and Higher Education*, Vol. 11, Issue 2, 2008, Pages 87-97.

Sapienza, Filipp (2007). "A rhetorical approach to single-sourcing via intertextuality" *Technical Communication Quarterly*, Vol. 16 Issue 1 (Winter), p. 83-101.

Spinuzzi, Clay (2005). "Lost in the translation: shifting claims in the migration of a research technique" *Technical Communication Quarterly* Vol. 14 Issue 4 (Autumn), p. 411-446.

VIII

Media and New Capitalism in the Digital Age[1]

In *Media and New Capitalism in the Digital Age: The Spirit of Networks* Eran Fisher attempts to analyze the ideology of the networked world as Weber did the origins of capitalism. The central argument of the book is that the discourse related to network technology, "the digital discourse", is a legitimation discourse, "the 'religion' of an instrumental society" (p. 226). It is a largely successful demonstration that "the spirit of networks is not a critical discourse, but precisely the opposite: it is the discourse of the new capitalism *par excellence*" (p. 227).

The book is divided into three parts. In the first part the author articulates the theoretical and empirical foundations of his argument, as well as the sociological context. In the study of relations between technology and society he distinguishes three positions: technology shapes society ("the most prevalent approach"), society shapes technology ("critical approaches") and the approach that informs his book: "technology as

---

[1] Review of: Eran Fischer. *Media and new capitalism in the digital age: The spirit of networks.* New York, NY: Palgrave Macmillan, 2010.

discourse—cultural, social, political, and ideological" (p. 17). In the strong version of the "technology as discourse" approach, "Technology discourse is 'ideological' to the extent that political issues are treated as technical ones" (p. 19). His focus is not on technology in general, but current popular discussions of the network—primarily articles published in *Wired* magazine, "an epitome of the digital discourse"—and how this particular form of technical realization is believed or assumed to establish new rules and a new rationality for "four key transformative sites" (p. 5): new markets, new forms of work, new modes of production, and new humans (and posthumans).

The second part deals with each of these four areas in turn. He discusses in detail Kevin Kelly's articles in *Wired*, especially "New rules for the new economy" (Kelly, 1997). In that article "dumb chips" in a network produce smartness and rationality. Fisher comments:

> It is important to infer what Kelly is suggesting, especially as it pertains to the status of nodes *vis-à-vis* a technological network or that of individuals *vis-à-vis* markets and society. If consciousness (as well as smartness and rationality) is the result of the cooperation of dumb neurons (as well as dumb chips, nodes, or individuals), the corollary is that *reflexivity* (i.e., the ability to evaluate rationality, or the ability to apply rationality to asses rationality...) resides not in any single node but only in the network. None of these small nodes can comprehend the complexity of the network's rationality. Kelly ... therefore redefines smartness as an inherently network quality. (p. 50)

In Kelly's articles we find an early expression of an idea that many later authors would embrace as "the wisdom of crowds", "swarm intelligence", "spontaneous order" and other such oxymorons which "tie together the irrational (the fuzzy and undirected) with the rational (the instrumental, purposive, and focused)" (p. 51). According to this view

> superior rationality can solely be the product of networks. Intelligence and rationality are achieved not by improving on the performance of individual nodes but by connecting them to each other. Sophistication and progress is created by very limited, short-sighted, and unreflexive agents. (p. 51)

What are the implications of this for social and economic theory? Because the network is imagined as a biological development ("biology has taken root in technology" Fisher (p. 56) quotes Kelly as writing), the chief features of biological systems become the chief features of the network, economy and all of society: evolution, perpetual disruption, unpredictability, incalculability, turbulence, uncertainty, disorder, chaos.

> The digital discourse does not simply describe the chaotic nature of the digital economy but also insists on the inevitability and benevolence of chaos. It suggests that since chaos is part and parcel of the network economy, it would be worthless and even dangerous to react to it defensively and try to counter this economic reality with a political and social action. In this context, Kelly invokes the anti-Luddite maxim that perceives any opposition to technologically induced change as a reactionary and futile struggle waged by shortsighted people. (p. 59)

And of course the shortsightedness of the Luddites would be the basis of intelligence if the Luddites were to connect to the network.

Fisher notes that Kelly contrasts the industrial economy with the network economy by describing both as natural objects, the character of both understood as independent of political and social action. He notes that the industrial economy as understood in the digital discourse of *Wired* magazine ignores "the fact that the stability and predictability of industrial economy was ... precisely a product of the political and social barriers put forth by governments on markets" (p. 62), something which John Gray (1998) has argued at length from his very different perspective. Responding to Kelly's remark "the prime goal of the new economy is to undo—company by company, industry by industry—the industrial economy" (quoted by Fisher on p. 62) Fisher remarks

> It is precisely the undoing of the political constraints put on markets and the layer of social arrangements that were constructed throughout the twentieth century in order to insulate individuals from an unforgiving, unpredictable, and irrational market (in the broader sense of substantive rationality) that the digital discourse is calling for and legitimates through a naturalization and technologization of flux and chaos. What the digital discourse constructs is a structure of the network market as a chaotic but self-regulating mechanism, the operation of which is best achieved by leaving it to its own devices and in no way regulating it politically. (p. 62-63)

Fisher follows this with a discussion of these issues in liberal and neoliberal theory, particularly in the work of Hayek. In contrast to both classical liberalism, in which "individual liberty in the marketplace is seen as a natural, unconditional right ... a *normative legitimation* for the free market" (p. 66), and neoliberal theory, where individual liberty is seen "as a prerequisite for the successful operation of the market ... a *scientific legitimation* for the free market" (p. 66), the digital discourse "transforms the argument for individual liberty into a technologistic legitimation" (p. 67):

> To the extent that individuals are reconceived as nodes within a technological network, and to the extent that

these nodes must be atomized, flexible, and adaptable to network fluctuations, individuals must be free in order for spontaneous order to occur. Hence, the argument for the liberty of individuals in the context of free markets is asserted thrice: first, on normative grounds, second, as a scientific discovery, and, finally, as a technological necessity (p. 67)

In this view of economy and society, "economic rationality is redefined as emanating solely from the operation of networks" (p. 75), and "political issues are treated as technical issues" (p. 77). The analysis here follows and updates that of Habermas from the late 1960's.

After the discussion of the nature of markets as described by advocates of the network economy, Fisher devotes a chapter to the nature of work as these same advocates understand it. He analyzes the "worker" as that character appears in Douglas Coupland's story "Microserfs", pointing out one of the more important issues that narrative touches upon but avoids reflecting upon: "the unproblematic blurring of the dichotomy between workers and employers" (p. 95). This blurring of the boundaries at Microsoft Corporation Fisher compares to slavery and serfdom—a comparison forced upon readers by the very title of Coupland's story—and "its blurring—indeed, annihilation—of the distinction between work and leisure, between private and public life" (p. 95). This is then contrasted with the self-image of the members of the digerati and "technology as an axis of professional identity" (p. 97).

Chapter five discusses the forces of production as imagined by the digerati. In the network economy, the technologies used themselves provide "a more democratic, participatory, and inclusive mode of production ... making it more human and engaging for individuals by welcoming and harnessing human facets" (p. 107). Network technologies offer "power to the people" and individual empowerment:

> Thanks to the Web, creativity, enthusiasm, cooperation, and personal expression are reintroduced into the spheres of production and consumption from which they have been traditionally excluded and revitalize them. (p. 110)

Consumers and audiences—passive categories—disappear in the network mode of production, and in their places we find participation and collaboration. The result of that participation and collaboration "turns out to be superior to anything we have experienced in the past ... a depository of knowledge, furnishing humans with a newfound and a quasi-transcendental view of the world" (p. 111) which is, in Kelly's words, "spookily godlike" (p. 111).

There is a good discussion of crowdsourcing in this chapter, especially good because it focusses on issues that are never discussed in either the popular articles in praise of the practice, nor in the scientific literature that evaluates its potential. Stating the issue bluntly, Fisher writes

> The network is seen in the digital discourse as a new repository for cheap labor, a mechanism for extracting hitherto unexploited resources. ... [C]rowdsourcing is ultimately interpreted in the digital discourse as a new source of profitability. In that sense, crowdsourcing offers not a break but a continuation of the long history of capitalist exploitation, based on increasing levels of surplus value (rather than simply increased levels of productivity). ... In the uncritical, even triumphant language of the digital discourse, this is not seen as exploitation at all because labor is done by "amateurs," it is "latent," and it is done outside of productive time. (p. 118-119)

Fisher follows this observation by questioning the reference to the "latent" power of the crowd. If, as the network discourse claims, "only network technology is able to uncover and mobilize this talent and work power into productive results ... why is it latent, and why can it only be uncovered and mobilized with network technology?" (p. 119). Fisher develops the argument that because "workers are redefined as independent freelancers who are compensated solely for their successful accomplishment" all the costs of their labor are externalized by the companies who utilize them in crowdsourcing. Everyone—professional and amateur alike—becomes, in other words, a piece worker perpetually competing in a global market. Using examples from iStockPhoto and InnoCentive to Lego, he argues that "a networked mode of production such as InnoCentive is economically more rational only from the point of view of companies rather than the system, or society, as a whole" (p. 128).

In these first chapters on markets, labor and production, Fisher contrasts the humanist critique of industrialism with a social critique. The humanist critique is based on values linked with the arts—"authenticity, self-expression, noninstrumentality, and critical distance from the prevailing social order, particularly from its most systemic structures; the market and the state" (p. 105)—leading to its "demand for a less alienating, more satisfying and creative work process" (p. 143). The social critique, on the other hand, is concerned with mitigating exploitation, "the need for social security, stability, and equality" (p. 217). This is an interesting and revealing mode of analysis which becomes more and more pronounced as the book unfolds. The digital discourse and the networked world that it imagines and preaches is, according to Fisher, a continuation of "the traditional critique of capitalism" (p. 143) in its humanist forms. In that universe of discourse, "network production is constructed as a transcendence of the pitfalls of industrial and Fordist production" (p. 142), but that is not the end of the story.

> The digital discourse offers at one and the same time an affirmation and inclusion of the humanist critique of capitalism into the spirit of contemporary techno-capitalism, and a rejection and exclusion of its social

> critique. At the same time that the new spirit of networks promises more engaging roles for individuals in the process of production, it also accepts and naturalizes the individualization, atomization, and privatization of work life, and the liquidation ... of protective structures and mechanisms. As it promises more flexibility and creativity, the spirit of neworks also accepts and legitimates greater precariousness, instability, and vulnerability. (p. 142)

In chapters six ("Network human") and seven ("Network cosmology and the exhaustion of critique"), Fisher discusses some of the further reaches of theory, speculation and religious nonsense that not only surrounds but informs much of the discussion of the network world. The anthropomorphization of computers and the simultaneous reduction of the human to information technology that one can find in *Wired* and related literature is a matter that I have long been familiar with, but some of the essays that Fisher discusses were so ludicrous that they shocked even me.

> According to the digital discourse, ... human beings in the most technologically advanced regions of the world have been inextricably fused with network technology. Under these new circumstances, humans can no longer be thought of within the framework of humanism as distinct from technology but instead as network humans. Network humans are commensurable with network technology. (p. 173-174)

This view of humans—Surprise, Surprise!—fits a post-Fordist society's reproductive needs. "Humans are reconceptualized to fit their place in the new mode of production and a new society" (p.174). Thus, "a network market, network work, and network production require the reconceptualization of humans as commensurable with network technology as informational, flexible, and distributed and as nodes in a techno-human network" (p. 178). With the boundaries between human and information technology blurred or rejected, there is now the possibility "for a more meaningful, emancipatory, and natural interaction of humans with technology" (p. 175). Instead of "the disciplining of humans to industrialism" (p. 175) as Gramsci described things, the network human "can now be unleashed and flourish with network technology" (p. 180).

The cosmological speculations which Fisher finds in *Wired* are truly remarkable as much for their grandeur as for their lack of sophistication. Technology gets theologized and religion becomes a mystical doctrine of... computation.

> The notion of universal computing—this most basic rule of the universe, or the "operating system" of the cosmos —is, according to Kelly, what binds us all together. In the "mystical doctrine of universal computing ... we are linked to one another, all beings alive and inert, because we share, ... an immaterial source. This commonality, spoken of by mystics of many beliefs in different terms, also has a scientific name: computation." (Fisher, quoting Kelly (2002), p. 200)

The upshot of making a religion of computation, is that the entire world is explained in terms of a particular technique. Fisher notes that this cosmological view makes "technology the axis of social explanation" and rests on three assumptions: the neutrality, inevitability and benevolence of technology. With biology, society and the universe assimilated to information technology, Kelly and others construct "a framework where the political dimensions of social structures... are uprooted altogether and excluded and where the social is reduced to the technological" p. 190-191). The circularity of reasoning in the arguments and positions discussed by Fisher is obvious, and the complete disolution of any meaningful categories follows; there is no longer any distinction between technology and biology, technology and anthropology, technology and religion, technology and society. In the discourse of the digerati, everything has the same explanation and it is not god but it just as well may be. To explain everything by one term is to explain nothing, least of all that term.

> It is obvious that the use of the language of nature and biology to explain technology and society is not simply metaphorical but points to a conflation of these worlds *in reality*. In this case, the social (economy) and the technological (which underlies the networking of the economy) are understood to be overtaken by nature. The crux of this depoliticizing narrative comes from anchoring of the social in the technological, which in turn is anchored in the natural. (p. 191)

I liked this book a lot and was particularly interested in the author's analysis of how the network ideology addresses the humanist critique of industrialism and capitalism. It is this power of critique, Fisher argues, that has led to its wide influence. As one example he notes that the anti-globalization movement is founded on this critique:

> It entails the decentralized assemblages of disparate groups, which convene ad hoc around a specific political project. The movement is also dehierarchized: there is no overdetermination for any essentialist political analysis, project or identity. ... It is worth noting that to a large extent the target of this movement has been post-Fordist capitalism itself, and perhaps for that reason the spirit of networks is commonly assumed to harbor a critical potential. (p. 225)

In this book Fisher wants to point out the insufficiencies of limiting our critique to the humanist critique (as he has described it), arguing that we must base our critique on a social critique (again, as he has described it). My only substantive complaint with the book is that Fisher appears to argue that one must found a political culture on one or the other critique. That, it seems to me, to be unnecessary, as both can—and should—inform political culture. The distinction that he has made between the two forms of critique can indeed be distinguished in analysis as he has done, and can be justified by historical references to various past criticues. But at bottom, this is an analytical distinction that need not lead to statements such as "A political culture founded on the social critique is inherently more political" (p. 223). What of a culture founded on both and then some? Perhaps I have misunderstood his intention here, as he does in fact insist that we must incorporate in our critique what we can learn from the network discourse as critique.

In spite of that reservation, I agree with his analysis as with the conclusions mentioned in my opening paragraph.

> The spirit of networks, with its explicit critique of the pitfalls of Fordism, legitimates the shift to post-Fordism first and foremost by depicting this shift as *progress*. Since the contemporary post-Fordist condition is intertwined with network technology ... the social formations that stem from it are also conceptualized as being of a higher stage, a social development. The shift to post-Fordism, in other words, is understood as technologically induced and, therefore, as apolitical, asocial, and inherently progressive. (p. 224)

In opposition to the views of the editors and contributors of *Wired*, Fisher insists that political and social questions have not and will not dissappear with network technology. His book is also an important reminder that the relationship of information science to the economy, society and politics is not an extramural and peripheral issue for information science, but constitutive of the discipline itself. And his book is well worth reading not just by information scientists, but by anyone who works for a living as well as many of those who wish they could.

References
Coupland, Douglas (1994). "Microserfs", *Wired*, January 1994.
Gray, John (1998). *False Dawn: The Delusions of Global Capitalism*. New York, New Press.
Kelly, Kevin (1997). "New rules for the new economy", *Wired*, September 1997.
Kelly, Kevin (2002). "God is the machine", *Wired*, December 2002.

Part Two

Integrational Linguistics and Information Technology

IX

Ethos, Logos, Pathos
or
Sender, Message, Receiver?

A problematological Rhetoric For Information Technologies

Abstract
In this paper I examine information science through the problematological rhetoric of Michel Meyer. Meyer's critique of philosophy (and ontology in particular) he calls problematology, and it is founded upon the recognition that every statement is an answer to a question arising from a particular problem. In problematology it is assumed that even the most self-evident or trivial statement (fact, proposition) can be disputed or there would be no point in making the statement. If something can be questioned, it can be debated, and how we debate any issue is a matter of rhetorical practices, all of which involve ethos, logos and pathos. These concepts, familiar from Aristotelian rhetoric, have their counterparts in information science: sender, message, receiver. Unlike ethos, logos and pathos, the concepts of information science are rooted in a technical understanding of

sender (author, self, human or machine) markedly different from the ethical ethos of classical antiquity, an ontologically based propositional understanding of message (language, information, world), and an abstract understanding of receiver (auditor/ reader, user) as human or machine with a straightforward, statable, interpretable and answerable question. If we begin with the assumptions that the world is not known but is "what is in question", that "what is in question" may be answerable by multiple alternative answers or be unanswerable, and that questions are inseparable from the time, place and person of the questioner, then our understanding of the relationship between information technologies and their users must move from metaphors of mining, fishing, hunting and finding to a rhetoric of ethos (source, authority), logos (description, argument) and pathos (questions, desires, satisficing). A rhetorical approach illuminates many aspects of information production and use, from spamming and computer viruses to user supplied metadata and reuse of metadata in different contexts. Of particular interest are the implications of a rhetorical approach for the creation of metadata for 1) human users of IT, and 2) machine interoperability (e.g. the Semantic Web).

1. The Mathematical Theory of Communication

Claude Shannon began the second paragraph of his 1948 paper *The Mathematical Theory of Communication* with the following remarks:

> The fundamental problem of communication is that of reproducing at one point either exactly or approximately a message selected at another point. Frequently the messages have *meaning*; that is they refer to or are correlated according to some system with certain physical or conceptual entities. These semantic aspects of communication are irrelevant to the engineering problem. The significant aspect is that the actual message is one *selected from a set* of possible messages. The system must be designed to operate for each possible selection, not just the one which will actually be chosen since this is unknown at the time of design. (Shannon and Weaver, 1949: 3)

This remarkable passage acknowledges four of Shannon's assumptions about communication, each of which are significant from a rhetorical and linguistic perspective.

First, the "fundamental problem of communication" is assumed to be one of reproducing a given message, that is to say, neither the message itself nor its production and comprehension are a part of the problem of communication, only its reproduction. Crucially, what a message is in this theory remains unstated. Rather than providing a definition or even a discussion of what a message is, Shannon gives an *ad hoc* list of types of messages: "a sequence of letters ... a single function of time .. a function of time and other variables as in black and white television ... two or more functions of time ... several functions of several variables..." (ibid.: 4-5). We learn that a message can be "transmitted" and that it has an intended destination (person or thing). Weaver in his comments on Shannon's paper informs us that an "*information source* selects a desired *message*" which "may consist of written or spoken words, or of pictures, music, etc." (ibid.: 98). But what a message is, and how it is to be understood theoretically, we are not told.

The second assumption is that a message may or may not mean anything. Weaver in his comments states that among the possible messages from which an information source chooses "two messages, one of which is heavily loaded with meaning and the other of which is pure nonsense, can be exactly equivalent, from the present viewpoint" (ibid.: 99).

Shannon's third assumption is that the meaning of a message is "irrelevant to the engineering problem." Note that the meaning of the message *is* considered to be one of the "semantic aspects of communication" but not of the engineering problem. What has happened in this sentence is not at all clear: has Shannon simply abandoned a theory of communication in favor of the engineering problem of the transmission of signals? This seems both unlikely in view of the title of the paper and irreconcilable with the immediately preceding remarks on the fundamental problem—reproduction of a message—and the possibility of meaningless messages. It appears that Shannon is simply and straightforwardly assuming that communication is indeed an engineering feat and that communicative activity that is *also* meaningful activity is simply one type of communicative activity, a corollary of assumption two, i.e. a message may or may not mean anything. Given that assumption, the "semantic aspects" of any particular communicative act are simply empirical facts of particular messages and therefore of no theoretical import. As Janich described it, "meaningful or meaningless, true or false, useful or useless, understandable or incomprehensible play no role" in the functioning of communication technologies (Janich, 2006: 113).

The fourth assumption is that for Shannon a message (whatever that is) is not something created to fit a communication situation but one among a number of possible messages available for selection and transmission. The question here is: What exactly is a possible message or a "set of possible messages"? Clearly this is not a question that can be answered if the notion of message itself remains unstated and undefined. What is clear is that this stock of possible messages preexists the communication situation since "the actual message is one *selected from a set* of possible messages" (Shannon and Weaver, 1949: 3). Janich criticised this position, remarking "The concept of a 'stock of possible messages' has nothing to do with the openness of human communication, but with the functional limitations of a technical system and the use of tools" (Janich, 2006: 72), later adding "The traditional theories of information and communication never ask why. Information and communication are always already there, and as natural facts at that" (ibid. 147).

Finally, given these assumptions, Shannon recognizes that the engineering problem is to design for probabilities rather than realities. As Weaver puts it, information in Shannon's theory "has nothing to do with meaning", treats "the statistical character of a whole ensemble of messages" rather than with particular messages, and "in these statistical terms the two words information and uncertainty find themselves to be partners" (Shannon and Weaver, 1949: 116).

In his remarks on the paper Weaver asks whether or not Shannon's theory is merely a theory of the technical problem and answers this question with the statement that the theory "is, at least to a significant degree, also a theory" of the semantic problem and the effectiveness problem. Weaver associates these three problems of a theory of communication with three questions: 1) the technical problem: How accurately can the symbols of communication be transmitted?; 2) the semantic problem: How precisely do the transmitted symbols convey the desired meaning?; and 3) the effectiveness problem: How effectively does the received meaning affect conduct in the desired way? (ibid.: 96). These three problems and questions reflect three of the basic elements of Shannon's diagram of a communication system: the transmitter, the message and the receiver. A look at Shannon's diagram, however, reveals five parts through which a message moves first as message, then transformed as signal, and finally as reproduction of original message. Those parts are: an information source, a transmitter, a channel, a receiver and a destination. The diagram itself suggests the tripartite division of Weaver's three problems, and indeed the subsequent discourse on the Shannon model has largely tended to discuss it as a model of sender, message and receiver. Just what are the terminal points in the Shannon model, and what is their significance?

Both Shannon's conception of the activity of the information source as being selection of a possible message and Weaver's identification of the technical problem as being the transmission of symbols betray the theoretical nullity of both the "information source" and the destination. The information source is simply the terminus of the system at one end, with the destination being the terminus at the other end. Neither play any role in the operation or theoretical understanding of Shannon's communication system. "The receiver's answer plays no role" in this view Janich observed (Janich, 2006: 82), and indeed what we find in Shannon and Weaver is simply a message presented to the transmitter within a technical system which converts it to a set of signals or symbols—a significant equivocation—to be reconverted by the receiver (also still within the technical system) and deposited at the opposite terminus, the intended destination. Why, whence, from and to whom the message was "selected" and transmitted are all irrelevant questions for the operation of such a system of "communication" as well as for its understanding.

Particularly revealing on this point is Weaver's discussion of Shannon's diagram in which he states that "When I talk to you, my brain is the information source, my vocal system is the transmitter, and your ear and the associated eighth nerve is the receiver" (Shannon and Weaver, 1949: 98-99). Weaver actually serves to muddle the picture with his remarks, since the "information source" is identified not with the speaking "I" but with the brain of the speaking "I", and the destination of the message is not you with whom I am talking but rather your brain. As Roy Harris has pointed out this is a mereological fallacy, "one which involves attributing to parts of a human being (or animal) features and functions that logically belong only to the whole creature" (Harris, 2008: 141).

Dupuy criticized the concept of information as found in Shannon and Weaver's work on the grounds that it is only when you ignore all matters related to the creation of information and its meaning that you can treat it as a thing in a technical system (Dupuy, 1980), but this—transmitting a signal through a technical system for no other reason than to adequately reproduce it at the other end—was precisely Shannon's task as an engineer. There could be no information technologies as we know them if the designers of the system had to deal with actual messages, their creation and their meanings at both ends of the system.

2. The Rhetorical Theory of Communication.

Ancient rhetoric was based on three primary assumptions: 1) there is a speaker who 2) has something to say 3) to someone. Thus rhetorical theory from Aristotle to the 20th century has distinguished three concepts of argumentation, the first concerning the facts (*logos*), the second the interpretation of the facts (*pathos*), and the third the legitimacy of the speaker (*ethos*). Meyer suggested that these three concepts can all be unified by recognizing the interrogativity that underlies them. He noted that by viewing argumentation—and all rhetoric—from the perspective of interrogativity, a clear distinction between two uses of rhetoric becomes clear: a rhetoric focused on the question or "white rhetoric" and a rhetoric focused on an answer or what Barthes called "black rhetoric". The former is a rhetoric that brings to light and clarifies facts, interpretations and the manner and motives (logic, passion) for the arguments given, while the latter manipulates, striving to present as "conclusive, true and just what in reality is the very matter in question." In fact, Meyer argues, "To consider a matter interrogatively, or on the other hand not to care about the question, is all that separates white from black rhetoric, critical usage from manipulation or closure" (Meyer, 1993: 42-43).

In rhetorical terms, communication theories based on the Shannon and Weaver model deal with *logos*—messages—exclusively, regarding all matters pertaining to *ethos*—the authors or creators and the creation of information—as well as *pathos*—the receiver, auditor, reader, interpreter, interlocutor—as stochastic processes rather than ethical agents. Understanding communication as *logos* alone provides no grounds from which to make any ethical enquiry since ethical issues require ethical subjects, responsible agents as participants in communicative action.

Rhetorical theory in ancient Greece and Rome was concerned with public speaking and more broadly with the art of effective communication, emphasizing the speaker's qualifications, knowledge and skill, which can be concisely stated as matters of *authority*, or in Greek, *ethos*. Aristotle defined rhetoric as "the faculty of observing in any given case the available means of persuasion" and followed this definition with a discussion of how rhetoric differs from other arts:

> Every other art can instruct or persuade about its own particular subject-matter; for instance, medicine about what is healthy and unhealthy, geometry about the properties of magnitudes, arithmetic about numbers, and the same is true of the other arts and sciences. But rhetoric we look upon as the power of observing the means of persuasion on almost any subject presented to us; and that is why we say that, in its technical character, it is not concerned with any special or definite case or subject. (Aristotle, 1954: Book 1, Chapter 2, Part 1)

This is a particularly interesting passage in light of the previous discussion of Shannon and Weaver. Like the mathematical theory of communication, Aristotle understood rhetoric "in its technical character" as having no concern with the particulars of any communicative activity. Yet unlike Shannon and Weaver, Aristotle does not ignore the "information source" nor does he give short shrift to the audience or "destination", for he follows the definition quoted above with remarks on the three "modes of persuasion" or proofs (*pistis*) which convince the hearer (or reader):

> Of the modes of persuasion furnished by the spoken word there are three kinds. The first kind depends on the personal character (*ethos*) of the speaker; the second on putting the audience into a certain frame of mind (*pathos*); the third on the proof, or apparent proof, provided by the words of the speech itself (*logos*) (ibid.)

Ancient rhetorics emphasized *ethos* and that emphasis is fairly clear in the passage just quoted: both *pathos* and *logos* are conceived as elements of communication strictly from the point of view of the speaker. In Meyer's rhetoric *ethos*, *logos* and *pathos* are all of equal importance, and in this respect—as in many others—his rhetoric provides a basis for a far-reaching critique not only of earlier rhetorics but of philosophy, communication theory, linguistics and information science.

Meyer offers a new definition of rhetoric: *rhetoric is the negotiation of the distances between human beings in regard to a question, a problem* (Meyer, 1993: 22). He derives his definition from a statement by Aristotle:

> [T]he use of persuasive speech is directed to a judgment (there is no further need of speech on subjects that we know and have already judged). (Aristotle, 2007: Book 2, Chapter 18:1)

We can not, Meyer insists, "allow rhetoric to be limited to the art of persuasion" without losing sight of communication's other dimensions (Meyer, 1993: 23). Of particular importance is Meyer's insistence that rhetoric is not a technique for manipulating others (as the Sophists and public relations departments would have it) but a negotiation, a general social practice arising from the perception of a problem. The problems and questions that arise in life's situations lead us to engage others; although persuasion is one type of communicative activity, human communication is not limited to that kind of interaction alone. "In fact" Meyer writes,

> rhetoric is the encounter of men and of language through exposing their differences and their identities. They affirm each other in order to recover, to reclaim, to find a moment of communion, or on the contrary, to evoque the impossibility of communion and to acknowledge the wall that separates them. (ibid.: 22)

Meyer's rhetoric is rooted far deeper in human experience than Aristotle's or indeed any previous rhetorical theory. It is not our knowledge but our problems and the questions to which they give rise that constitute the starting point of all communication. The consequence of putting questioning first is that all answers are responses to an originary question which remains. Knowledge becomes a contextual matter: the answer given need only solve the problem faced; it can never eliminate the question of what *really is* but only how to proceed in our business. With epistemology unseated, ontology with its being and essences vanishes and the syllogism stops dead in its presuppositions, for *what is* is always *what is in question*.

> The syllogism is a synthesis, which means that it requires that we start from the known to determine the unknown ... Just because a conclusion follows naturally from certain premises does not mean that it is known as such. Likewise, knowing the premises which lead to a conclusion does not mean that one necessarily knows the particular conclusion which may result from them. (Meyer, 1995: 108)

The syllogism requires "that we start from the known", that we agree on the premises from which we are to draw the conclusions: Socrates is a man, All men are mortal. But "what one individual knows is only relative and is different from what others know" (ibid.: 109) so every premiss is a presupposition that itself can be debated. Socrates is, after all, Stanford's library catalog, just as Melvyl is Berkeley's, and whether they are mortal or not depends entirely on what you mean by "mortal." And for that matter, many have declared that other Socrates "immortal." It is this kind of problem, whether we describe it as a problem of homonymy, polysemy, ignorance or alternatives, that prompts Meyer to go back to the Socratic question "What is X?":

> If one demands "What is X?" this evidently presupposes that X *is* some thing, *a* rather than *b* for example, since one must know what it is we are asking about and not confuse it with some other thing. So to say that X is *a*, or that X is *b*, is already to specify what it is that one is asking for. (Meyer, 2008: 26)

And here Meyer joins Roy Harris who provides a complementary analysis of Aristotle's understanding of language and communication:

> Aristotle's account already implies or presupposes a theory of linguistic communication; namely, that the hearer understands what the speaker says in virtue of knowing the set of conventions to which the speaker's utterances conform. Only thus can the hearer grasp *what* it is that the speaker is saying. ...
> However, there is an elementary difficulty. How is it that the hearer can relate the sounds the speaker articulates to the same things as the speaker—in his own mind— relates them to? For while the sounds the speaker utters can be heard, what he means by them is not audible.

> Aristotle ... preempts the difficulty by declaring that the world is the same for everybody. ... So what *Grass is green* means for the speaker must mean exactly what *Grass is green* means for the hearer *if the same linguistic conventions apply in both cases.* In other words, these conventions themselves are anchored by everyone sharing a common pre-linguistic experience of the world and what it looks like, feels like, sounds like, smells like, etc., *irrespective* of whatever language they happen to speak. (Harris, 2009: 81)

Aristotle wanted—indeed, needed—to guarantee understanding among interlocutors and chose language as that guarantee. If language, *logos* alone, rather than the speaker, is the source of meaning and the guarantee of understanding, then it is not you and I who speak and who must be trusted or not trusted, but, as Heidegger famously declared, it is the Sprache that sprichts (although of course it is not sprichting so well in this sentence.) Of this move away from human responsibility Harris and Hutton remarked:

> Thus the postulate of semantic determinacy makes it possible to transfer the responsibility for making meaning from the individual to the collectivity, and from the circumstantial to the macrosocial level. ... Words come to be construed as autonomous signs that can and do function semantically without support from any other semiological source, providing the essential self-sustaining mechanisms for the facilitation and regulation not only of human interactions but of human thought itself. (Harris and Hutton, 2007: 203-204)

And just as in the mathematical theory of communication, we are left with no grounds for ethical investigation of any speech act for it is not we but the language, our "stock of possible messages," that determines what is meant.

There is one further element in Meyer's theory of rhetoric that I wish to discuss before directing my attention to the design and use of information technologies, and that is his notion of the *projective ethos* and the *projective pathos*. Since "social life is founded upon the distance that must be continually negotiated at each encounter" the speaker must "integrate that distance a priori in the form of a relation, even though that may fail. He must construct an image of the other just as the other must construct an image of him." The distance is one of cultural and personal values which lead to different questions, and since we "never truly know people ... we are obliged to supplement ... the fragmented reality with which we are confronted." Thus it is inevitable that there be "a mismatch between the projective *ethos* [how the speaker is imagined by the interlocutor] and the effective *ethos* [the speaker as he or she really is] and between the projective *pathos* and the effective *pathos*." The projective auditor, the reader as we imagine her to be, may or may not have much to do with the actual auditor/reader/interlocutor/library user, and all that we intend to accomplish by communicating may come to nought (Meyer, 2008: 228).

In the *ethos-pathos-logos* relation the *pathos projectif* leads to a triple response: the understanding of what the speaker wants to say ("what is the question?" is the question to him), the adequacy of the response and the persuasive interest of the proposition. If I address myself to someone, I make that triple hypothesis: the difference will be eradicated by persuasion, my response will be judged adequate and the other will necessarily understand my point of view as well as my intentions. But the auditor is not forced to react as I imagine or hope he will. The *pathos effectif*, that is to say the real auditor, is moved by other parameters (ibid.: 230).

3. Ethics, Rhetoric and Information Technologies
The preceding discussion of rhetorical and linguistic matters has been too brief to do justice to the depth and rigour of both Meyer's problematology and Harris' integrationist philosophy

of language. I trust that certain elements of their critiques will be clear enough to allow a preliminary interrogation of information science and certain presuppositions underpinning much research and development of information technologies. Time does not permit more than a cursory discussion of three items, namely the problem of *ethos* in dealing with information sources, the creation and use of metadata, and the idea of a Semantic Web.

The differences between the "information source" as conceived in the mathematical theory of communication and the *ethos* of rhetorical theory, whether Aristotelian, problematological or any other, are multiple. One of the chief differences concerns issues of authority: Does the source of information have any bearing on the particular contexts of information seeking? The mathematical theory hides this issue under the concept of noise—disturbances arising from a channel other than the one being utilized—while treating all messages from whatever information source as equivalent. The *logos* or message matters, the *ethos* or source does not. In contrast, from a rhetorical perspective *ethos* or information source is a crucial factor.

Meyer argued that the deemphasis or even denial of the significance of both *ethos* and *pathos* is characteristic of twentieth century rhetorics, and both Derrida and the history of information science present clear examples. Commenting on Derrida's statement "All writing, then, in order to be what it is, must be able to function in the radical absence of any empirically determined addressee in general" (Derrida 1972: 375, quoted in Harris, 2009: 156) Roy Harris remarks that this means that a text "is intrinsically complete. ... An interpreter is surplus to requirements. The text needs neither the presence of the author nor the presence of a reader" (Harris, 2009: 157). Harris associates this with the developement of literacy:

> In preliterate societies, words are part of the vocal activities of speakers, and what words mean is part of what the speaker means on some particular occasion. ... In

literate societies, by contrast, words are abstractions that take priority over both their vocal and their scriptorial manifestations, and over both speakers and hearers simultaneously. The speaker loses his privileged role of being in absolute control of what his utterances mean, for the words used can now be referred for arbitration to a source independent of both speaker and hearer." (ibid.: 140)

The modern disregard of *ethos* and *pathos* is thus a result of the decontextualization of the products of communicative activity (texts or utterances) and has characterized information science from its origins. In a fascinating book on the Internet—sadly ignored in the United States—Philippe Breton compared the ideas about cummunication and society held by pioneers of informatics like Turing and Wiener with similar ideas current in the culture of the Internet. From the perspective of an understanding of humans as information processing systems, Breton writes, a human being is simply "a program among programs". I quote at length:

> A program among programs, the human being is sometimes hardly able to determine whether the one to whom he writes on the networks is human or the software of a computer. There we are in the heart of that famous proof which the English mathematician believed would prove that machines could "think"...
> This test that Turing called the "imitation game" consisted in a device where a questioner addresses two separate partners in two distinct rooms and asks them all sorts of questions without any direct physical contact with them. If the questioner is not able to tell the difference between the two, then they are fundamentally similar. The first version of the test was applied to the distinction between a man and a woman, the second between a human and a machine, in this case, a com-

puter. Turing was convinced that soon a computer would be indistinguishable from a human being in the game.

Behind that test was a more fundamental point of view which was described by Turing's biographer Andrew Hodges: "The discrete state machine, communicating by teleprinter alone, was like an ideal for his own life, in which he would be left alone in a room of his own, to deal with the outside world solely by rational argument." That "ideal of life" shows us that the idea of the network, of the human being made by the network preceded by far its concrete realization. Let us imagine for just an instant that Turing's ideal of life were fully realized: this means that just as humans talking among themselves would not know whether they were conversing with another human or with a machine, so machines could not know whether they were addressing a human being or one of their own...

For Turing, who very well expressed the thinking of the first informaticians as well as that of the current Internet fundamentalists, man and woman, human and computer, all belong, in essence, to the same category, which we have called the "informational androgyne". (Breton, 2000: 69-70)

The reference to gender in the above passage should not be missed. In an earlier work appropriately titled *À l'image de l'homme*, Breton traced the history of humanity's imagination of artificial life in both artistic and literary forms as well as attempts to physically create an imitation human (e.g. robots) (Breton, 1995). His study revealed that with the sole exception of the medieval Golem, all these creations served to replace the human female with an obedient slave, fashioned to *answer* our desires, not to *question* them like a real woman would. And according to Breton, the most spectacularly successful of all these attempts was the virtual sex slaves created for the world of the internauts. A creature that says only what we permit it to say, means only what we want it to mean, does what we tell it to, when we tell it to, and always infallibly. Sound familiar? Is the Spider Woman of our dreams weaving the Semantic Web?

Matters of ethos surround much more mundane issues as well. Suppose someone interested in libraries and library catalog developments is looking for information on libraries and metadata issues. Among the items available on the web is a blog post by a man (or woman?) named Jon. Jon wrote "I haven't felt the need to set foot in a library, except for a meeting, in the last 10 years. I haven't used a library OPAC or ILS, except for the purpose of researching the system itself in at least a year." (http://managemetadata.org/blog/2009/02/25/embrace-the-chaos viewed 2009, no longer available in June 2020). For a mathematical theory of communication this is just another message from just another information source and like all the rest it is offered as "relevant" to all those interested in metadata and library information systems. In contrast, from a rhetorical perspective the value of the message is inextricably related to the character, knowledge, experience, beliefs and values of its source or author. The question thus becomes one of why someone interested in library catalogs should listen to someone who neither uses the library catalog nor even sets foot in the library? And to make myself as clear as possible, let me emphasize that the QUESTION becomes one of why listen to this voice; the ANSWER to that question will differ from one reader to another, and the question Why attend to that particular voice? will remain so long as the voice remains (and POOF! it dissappeared sometime between 2009 and 2020).

The questions, problems and possibilities associated with the term metadata itself as well as the practices and policies associated with the term are of considerable interest to me as I am both a creator and user of metadata any way you define it (and I will not). One of the most important metadata related questions is 'How should metadata be produced?' Some suggest that the human production of metadata item by item is too costly, that given the explosion of information resources, production of metadata by humans is out of the question, that automatic means of generating metadata are good enough for most purposes and therefore we should concentrate if not wholly rely on computational analysis and other automated methods. Others, noting the evident inadequacy of such methods for many purposes argue for the retention or even increased use of human production of metadata. Still others, probably the majority of those seriously involved in metadata matters, admit the value of utilizing both human created and automatically or computationaly derived metadata, each for what they alone can provide. The question for those among the latter tribe is then when to provide the one or the other or both, for what materials, for which purposes and for whom. The debate continues because *there is no right answer*: the right answer depends on what you want to do for what purposes, for whom and so on.

A fascinating precursor to this debate over human versus algorithmic decision making involves no less a figure than Norbert Wiener. Breton mentioned Wiener's views on law and justice in the context of the Internet, writing

> The rejection of the Law goes hand in hand with a taste—often immoderate—for the rule, the procedure, the algorithm, that adequately describes a problem and permits the "self-regulation" (another key notion) of its resolution. Norbert Wiener ... translates into his own terms the sentiment held by many in informatics circles that the law and justice are arbitrary, given over to questionable judicial procedures and the rhetoric of speech, whereas a good description of the problem in terms of information allows for "non-arbitrary" and incontestable solutions. In the new cult of the Internet, rule replaces the Law and self-regulation replaces the norm. The ideal resolution of a problem rests in the algorithm. (Breton, 2000: 57)

The production of metadata by algorithms or any other means has even more troubling complications relating to *ethos*. Communication presupposes that we are doing something for a reason for this is the sole hope the auditor or information seeker has that the communication has any value at all. We must assume that the one speaking-writing-signing means something by that activity. If we cannot trust the source of the information, we cannot rely on the information provided. This problem exists not only for human users but is probably much more severe for programmers and the systems they are designing, as Brooks pointed out:

> The Web is not a benign, socially cooperative environment, but an aggressive competitive arena where authors seek to promote their Web content, even by abusing topical metadata. As a result, Web crawlers must act in self defense and regard all keywords and topical metadata as spam. (Brooks, 2003)

Since Web crawlers cannot distinguish between meaningful and meaningless subject metadata all communication via subject metadata must be treated as meaningless. The counterpart of this is the creation of useless, misleading and incorrect metadata by librarians in their cataloging operations, whether this is performed by human action or by automated means: faced with an information environment in which the meaning of the results cannot be interpreted the user must act just like the web crawlers and ignore it all.

The third matter that I wish to discuss is the nature and role of ontologies and the Semantic Web as ideas, ideologies and ongoing projects. An ontology, we read,

> provides the semantic bases for metadata schemes and facilitates communication among systems and agents by enforcing a standardized conceptual model for a community of users. (Jacob, 2003)

and ontologies

> furnish the vocabulary necessary for communication between social agents and Web pages, defining relations between concepts ... in practice, an ontology defines terms associated with the texts it describes, what they mean themselves, and the formal axioms that restrict the interpretation and use of those terms. (Pickler, 2007: 72)

Here we see spelled out with as much clarity as naivité the belief that our concepts and language can be furnished, even forced upon us, by the builders of ontologies. One of the great ironies of these ontological efforts is that they are being developed in large part as attempts to overcome the limitations, biases and ambiguities of the linguistic behaviour of the community of users whom they are designed to serve (hence, the language of enforcing and restricting). Ontology designers/theorists suppose that they are dealing with language alone, what terms *really* mean in themselves. The term ontology itself is taken from philosophy where the discussion relates to the real world, Platonic essences or names of concepts that are more real and unchanging than our messy human language. A term in such a philosopher's ontology should thus represent not a possibility much less a bias but the correct name for this or that fact of the real world. Yet in information science the definitions in an ontology are a guide to proper usage rather than the real world of the philosophers; the natural world is not in question, only "natural" language. Dahlgren for one blandly stated that

> A linguistically-based ontology corresponds to the way people think about objects. It is a useful way to predict their thinking about the knowledge in structured databases. (Dahlgren, 1995: 810)

while Hobbs went even further, mixing up both what words mean and the theory or "understanding of the world" that we can find in language:

> If we are going to have programs that understand language, we will have to encode what words mean. Since words refer to the world, their definitions will have to be in terms of some underlying theory of the world. We will therefore have to construct that theory, and do so in a way that reflects the ontology that is implicit in natural language. (Hobbs, 1995: 819)

Presumably, when writing in English, the "ontology that is implicit" in English does not vary among the speakers of English, the underlying theory of the world revealed in the discourse of English speaking junkies, computer scientists, televangelists, poets, philosophers, truck drivers and pop stars all being identical.

Is "enforcing a standardized conceptual model for a community of users" as Jacob puts it, something other than enforcing one's own biases and opinions? How reconcile the "wisdom of the crowds" so popular these days with the practice of definitions and standards forced upon all of us by some unknown programmer or group of programmers? Have these writers ignored the lexicographical problem noted by Harris and Hutton (2007: 49) that a "definition can only be as effective as the context allows it to be, and the context includes the situation of the person seeking to understand the meaning"?

We read that "Ontologies codify the knowledge of a domain and are made to be reusable" (Romaní, 2006) as though knowledge is static and theoretically defined terms (like ontology) are never misused to mean their opposites. Do Dahlgren, Hobbs and Romaní believe that "the way people think about objects" is uniform across time and culture? Do they believe that theory is not hotly debated and changing all the time? Or is an ontology an attempt to prevent scientists from changing the terms of the discourse or even squelch dissent among scientists? And the misunderstandings propagated through popular science and among philosophers of science—has no one read Lévy-Leblond's *Aux contraires*?[1]

The real reason why the spiders spinning the Semantic Web assume knowledge and language to be more serviceable when rendered immobile and lifeless is evident in almost every paper on the subject: the world they are designing is a world of machine-machine communication, and the more that people can be made to act logically like a machine, the better we can interact with that system. The seminal paper by Sir Berners-Lee offers plenty of grounds for questioning the Semantic Web:

> A program that wants to compare or combine information across the two databases has to know that these two terms are being used to mean the same thing. Ideally, the program must have a way to discover such common meanings for whatever databases it encounters. (Berners-Lee, Hendler and Lassila, 2001)

The program "wants," "compares," "knows," and "discovers." Are we dealing here with metaphors, 21st century anthropomorphization, or a belief that programs actually engage in these activities in no significantly different sense than humans are said to do? Have Berners-Lee and his colleagues misread Vico and decided that if programs can immitate these human activities, however poorly, then the programmers have actually understood not only what they are doing and what their programs are, but what humans do when doing these things and that programs are doing the same things that we are? Philippe Breton again offers

---

[1] See Jean-Marc Lévy-Leblond, *Aux contraires: l'exercice de la pensée et la pratique de la science* (Paris: Gallimard, 1996), one of the most fascinating books on language and science ever written, worthy companion to Roy Harris, *The Semantics of Science* (London: Continuum, 2005).

some provocative reflections, especially for those putting all their eggs in the Web2.0 and open source baskets:

> How should one consider viruses? There also, it is indeed the world of beliefs developed around the Internet that permits one to see something other than simply an aberration, or gratuitous acts of pure delinquency. The reality is more complex. If one analyses viruses by taking into account the paradigm which we describe here, we discover that viruses are not special or marginal products: they are programs like the others, even closer to normalcy than other programs. In effect, the virus—technically small pieces of software—is the prototype of a program which circulates most easily and is constructed so as to get around whatever obstacles may get in its way. From the point of view of the belief in the freest possible circulation, this is the best software there is. (Breton, 2000: 62)

In the Semantic Web as imagined, there are no obstacles, no problems, and no questions. There are only answers, for nothing is problematic: everything is defined and programmed prior to any use. The Semantic Web can only deal with axioms, definitions and probabilities, it knows no questions and offers only programmed responses, meaningful or not. It is imagined that the Semantic Web will interact with human users in exactly the same manner in which web applications interoperate, for all language will be controlled and human users can only operate with the language and the rules of interpretation provided them by the folks who create the Semantic Web. Ethics here gets personal: the Semantic Web in the form of LibraryThing has the author of *Responsible Librarianship* and *Khubilai Khan and the Beautiful Princess of Tumapel* identified as the same David Bade as the Dutch painter whose works appear in the exhibition catalogue *1001 Nacht.* Because that catalogue was given an overall rating of 2 by some LibraryThing user, the author page for David Bade, also known as David W. Bade, lists several of my books—as well as *1001 Nacht*—and provides an overall rating of two for the author—not bad considering I was expecting a big zero.

It is certainly possible for someone—anyone—to go into LibraryThing and change the author information, combining or disambiguating David Bades according to what they know or think they know or what they want others to think, but apart from the ethical issues involved in any such possible action, we must acknowledge that neither LibraryThing nor any Semantic Web technology can do anything other than exactly what it has done in the case of the multiple David Bades. There are no ethical issues, no true or false for the Semantic Web as these issues exist only for the programmers and users of these technologies. The Semantic Web, all computer programs and web applications are not like people at all. People believe and disbelieve, agree to disagree, debate, misunderstand, do not worry about ambiguity unless it is a problem for them and their interlocutors, and continuously break the rules. We do these things not because our programmers want us to simulate human beings but because we ARE human beings. We need the flexibility of a language that is not pre-made in order to deal with a world that is ever in the making. We do not wish to be slaves, nor to have our words defined, redefined, ambiguated or disambiguated, nor to have our questions "reformatted" by anyone other than ourselves. Some of us are even appalled by such attempts:

> Frankly, I'm appalled! I don't want to have a machine guessing what I mean and then address me, as a person, with that kind of unsolicited questions!
>
> What I mean is my business and mine alone. When I make mistakes entering search terms, that's my problem and mine to solve, using my own intelligence and judgement when looking at inadequate results or "zero

hits". This kind of features only raises unrealistic expectations and creates a trust where mistrust in technology is vital and trust in one's own capacities must not be eroded but supported.

This bending over backwards to spare the user the "zero hits" experience is, I think, counterproductive in an insidious way. All to easily, timid souls are apt to turn over their judgement to the machine instead of working on it.

IOW, use neutral, unobtrusive, unpatronizing formulations for functions that a reader might or might not want to use, esp. when what the algorithm blurts out can easily be patent malarkey. Don't create the impression that there's more intelligence inside the machinery than there can possibly be. (Bernhard Eversberg, posting to NGC4LIB list, Feb. 20, 2009)

"Mistrust in technology is vital and trust in one's own capacities must not be eroded" Eversberg wrote, and I would like to end on that note.

References
Aristotle (1954). *Rhetoric*, translated by W. Rhys Roberts. New York: Modern Library.
Aristotle (2007). *On Rhetoric: a theory of civic discourse*. Translated by G.A. Kennedy. Oxford: Oxford University Press.
Berners-Lee, Tim; James Hendler and Ora Lassila (2001). "The Semantic Web" *Scientific American* 284:5 (May 2001): 34-43.
Breton, Philippe (1995). *À l'image de l'homme. Du Golem aux créatures virtuelles*. Paris: Seuil.
Breton, Philippe (2000). *Le culte de l'Internet. Une menace pour le lien social?* Paris: La Découverte.

Brooks, Terrence A. (2003). "Web search: how the Web has changed information retrieval," *Information Research* 8:3 (April 2003)
Dahlgren, Kathleen (1995). "A linguistic ontology," *International Journal of Human-Computer Studies* 43.
Derrida, Jacques (1972). *Marges: de la philosophie.* Paris: Minui.
Dupuy, Jean-Pierre (1980). "Analyse de systèmes et critique de la société informationnelle," in F. Gallouedec-Genuys, ed., *Les enjeux culturels de l'informatisation.* Fontefraud: Centre Culturel de l'Ouest.
Harris, Roy (2005). *The Semantics of Science.* London: Continuum.
Harris, Roy (2008). *Mindboggling: Preliminaries to a Science of the Mind.* Luton: The Pantaneto Press.
Harris, Roy (2009). *Rationality and the Literate Mind.* New York: Routledge.
Harris, Roy and Christopher Hutton (2007). *Definition in Theory and Practice: Language, Lexicography and the Law* London and New York: Continuum.
Hobbs, Jerry R. (1995). "Sketch of an ontology underlying the way we talk about the world," *International Journal of Human-Computer Studies* 43.
Jacob, Elin K. (2003). "Ontologies and the Semantic Web," *Bulletin of the American Society for Information Science and Technology* 29:4 (April/May 2003).
Janich, Peter (2006). *Was ist Information? Kritik einer Legende.* Frankfurt am Main: Suhrkamp.
Lévy-Leblond, Jean-Marc (1996). *Aux contraires: l'exercice de la pensée et la pratique de la science.* Paris: Gallimard.
Meyer, Michel (1993). *Questions de rhétorique: langage, raison et séduction.* Paris: Le livre de poche.
Meyer, Michel (1995). *Of Problematology: Philosophy, Science, and Language.* Chicago: University of Chicago Press.
Meyer, Michel (2008). *Principia Rhetorica: une théorie générale de l'argumentation.* Paris: Fayard.

Pickler, Maria Elisa Velentim (2007). "Web Semântica: ontologias como ferramentas de representação do conhecimento," *Perspectivas em Ciência da Informação* 12:1 (jan/abr)

Romaní, Mar (2006). "Webs semàntiques, les webs de segona generació" *Item: Revista de Biblioteconomia i Documentació*, v.42 (Jan-Apr):7-19.

Shannon, Claude E. and Warren Weaver (1949). *The Mathematical Theory of Communication.* Urbana: The University of Illinois Press.

X

The Zheng He dilemma
Language identification and automatic indexing

Abstract
Proper names present special problems not only for theories of language but also for indexing and language identification, whether performed by human or mechanical agents, especially so when the names may also be understood otherwise than as names. The problem is compounded in the case of transliterated text and multilingual publications. If the indexer cannot understand the meaning of the text – whether name, phrase or sentence – a heuristic decision process cannot decide amongst various possibilities.

Databases in the late 20th and early 21st centuries are compiled sometimes through individual input of information and sometimes by optical scanning techniques or by software collecting information from the many sources available via the Internet. Databases of information about books are no exception, and such databases as Amazon.com are compiled by downloading or searching other databases, while the OCLC corporation maintains a large database built and maintained by an army of librarians and library clerks inputting information about books one book at a time, transcribing the information directly from the book which sits in front of the inputter/cataloger/indexer.

The rules for bibliographical description have been designed on a heuristic model: if X then Y; if not X, then Z. The heuristics developed for the human work of bibliographic description and the heuristics for automatic interpretation of title pages are similar: find the title page; title starts at the top; next line is author, etc. The basic intention of these rules is to eliminate interpretation since interpretation presumes sufficient knowledge, takes time, costs money, and inevitably leads to different interpretations. What is wanted is a high degree of uniformity of results and consistency of interpretation, both of which are more easily achieved if decisions are stringently rule-bound and interpretation severely restricted. As an engineer would say, a machine in need of interpretation is a machine in need of repair.

So far, automated bibliographic description does not work well at all, in spite of the development of detailed heuristics. Human description also only works well when the one doing the work (hereafter referred to as the indexer) can interpret the meaning of the black marks on the title page (assuming of course that the indexer can identify that page); in the absence of that linguistic ability, the indexer is liable to make exactly the kinds of mistakes as are produced by an automated process. The following account of the production of a description of a book is deliberately written as if the operation were carried out pedantically, following the rules which follow the spatial layout of the book and its various sources of information (title page, top to bottom, etc.) exactly as an automated process would have to do but as no intelligent human being would ever do. Or at least I hope not. In practice, human indexers in libraries and elsewhere, can see an entire cover and title page at a glance, identify a multitude of clues and resolve many ambiguities instantly. The point of this exercise is to illustrate how the effort to develop a set of heuristics for the interpretation of such a simple and extremely brief text as a title page containing only 22 discrete alphabetic and numerical sequences can reveal remarkable interpretive complexity.

We begin with the book before it is opened. The spine of the book has the following written on it (see Fig. 1).

| SCMA 15 | Salmon/Ptak · Zheng He | Harrassowitz |

Fig. 1. Spine

Given only this what can an indexer infer as to the language of the work in question? What does *SCMA* mean? That one cannot know. And *15*? *Salmon/Ptak* · *Zheng He*? *Harrassowitz*? Authors? Title? Is this a book in English about the fish *salmon*?

If the indexer knows written Chinese in its pinyin form, *Zheng He* may be recognized as the pinyin form of a combination of one of the 25 (or more) Chinese characters corresponding to *zheng* and one of the 31 (or more) characters corresponding to *he*. Which characters in combination will depend on what sense can be made of the combination, either as compound noun, proper name, phrase or sentence. If the indexer is familiar with Chinese naval history and its treatment in historiographical and fictional works, a definite possibility arises: there was a famous Chinese naval officer of the 14th/15th centuries named Zheng He. *Zheng He* is perhaps the name of that officer written in the pinyin variety of written Chinese. But the question remains: Author or Title? And what of *SCMA 15*? *Salmon/Ptak*? *Harrassowitz*?

If the indexer knows neither the Chinese language (at least not the pinyin form) nor Chinese naval history, then this information is uninterpretable no matter what language it is written in and therefore neither the author(s) nor the title can be identified, much less the language.

If the indexer knows neither the Chinese language nor who Zheng He was but does know German, then the author and title remain uninterpretable, while *Harrassowitz* may be tentatively identified as the publisher's name, which may further suggest that the book is in German. The indexer will still need to investigate further to ascertain the significance of *SCMA, Salmon/Ptak* and *Zheng He*.

If the indexer knows only that Harrassowitz is the name of a German publisher, the assumption might be made that the book and its title are in German and the indexer would perhaps reach for a German–English dictionary to look for the entries for *Salmon, Ptak, Zheng* and *He*.

In libraries, the first rule of bibliographical description is that the primary source for obtaining the information about a book should always be its title page. This book, like most European and American publications, has a title page. So the book is opened and we find two pages facing each other. On the left-hand page the following appears (see Fig. 2).

South China and Maritime Asia

Edited by

Roderich Ptak and Thomas O. Höllmann

Volume 15

2005
Harrassowitz Verlag · Wiesbaden

Fig. 2. Series title page.

The indexer who knows English at this point understands the *SCMA 15* of the spine and interprets this page as being the series title page, not the title page of the individual volume. The indexer who does not know English will have to make a decision whether this is the title page or not, a decision which will not be easy if the text cannot be understood.

151

Determining the title page, distinguishing it from series title pages, half-titles, titles in other languages, advertisements and tables of contents is so rarely a problem in an Anglo-American world of standardized publishing practices and English title pages that the extent of interpretive activity which takes place before settling upon the title page is simply overlooked. That work of interpretation occasionally surfaces in spectacular fashion when monolingual American (English, French, German, etc.) librarians attempt to describe books published in African and Asian languages.

A glance across the page yields a totally different layout and textual contents. In order to determine that this is indeed the title page, the interpretive work mentioned in the previous paragraph would have to be performed, but for the purposes of exposition, the identification of this second (right-hand side) page as the title page will be assumed to have been made and the work of description begun in earnest (see Fig. 3).

Zheng He

Images & Perceptions
Bilder & Wahrnehmungen

édité par/editedby/herausgegeben von
Claudine Salmon/Roderich Ptak

2005
Harrassowitz Verlag · Wiesbaden

Fig. 3. Title page

The first line of the page is as follows:

Zheng He

which tells the indexer no more than what was on the spine. Fortunately, there is a second line:

Zheng He
Images & Perceptions

This was not on the spine, and the choices are now completely different: German has dropped out of the picture as far as language of the title is concerned, while *Zheng He* may appear to be some kind of oriental name and therefore perhaps the author. A now superseded rule in libraries used to assume that the title page began with the title; if the indexer determined that in fact the author was at the head of the title page, a note such as the following was required: "At head of title: Zheng He."

If the indexer knows Chinese or who Zheng He is as well as English and French, then this title, due to the ampersand, may be interpreted either as English or as French. Whether *Zheng He* is the name of the author or title remains undecidable; either *Zheng He* is the name of the author, or the main title must be *Zheng He* in pinyin spelling appearing in a book the text of which is perhaps English (*Images and Perceptions*) or perhaps French (*Images et Perceptions*).

If the indexer either knows Chinese or who Zheng He was and also knows either English or French (but not both), then the probable interpretation will be that the title is in English or French, depending on which language the indexer knows. But whether *Zheng He* is the name of the author or the main title remains undecidable.

If the indexer does not know Chinese nor who Zheng He was, but does know both English and French, then the title/subtitle will be interpreted as being in either English or French. Unless the indexer looks for more clues to identify the language, identification of *Zheng He* as the name of the author or main title will remain an enigma, or else *Zheng He* will be presumed to be an isolated instance of a foreign word, phrase or name appearing as the title, and probably the subject of the book. The indexer must then find out (by perusing the book further or using a French or an English language encyclopedia) what or who Zheng He is/was.

The situation will be similar if the indexer does not know Chinese nor who Zheng He was and knows only English or French but not both: the language will be understood to be English for the indexer who knows English and French for the indexer who knows French, and the author/main title interpreted as in the paragraph above. Neither the monolingual English indexer nor the monolingual French indexer will be aware of the fact that the second line is both English and French.

The indexer scans the next line below and now all of the previous interpretations are further complicated:

Zheng He
Images & Perceptions
Bilder & Wahrnehmungen

The indexer who knows Chinese, English and French, or any one of these, is now confronted with text which is problematic. Therefore, whatever the language of the text inside the book, the title, at least, must be bilingual, and perhaps multilingual.

If the indexer knows Chinese, then *Zheng He* may be assumed to be the author of the book the title of which is *Images & Perceptions* and which has either a subtitle or a parallel title *Bilder & Wahrnehmungen*. How these titles/subtitles are interpreted will depend upon this indexer's knowledge of English, French and German.

If the indexer knows German but not Chinese, English and French, then this third line of the title page will be understood, but its relationship to the previous two cannot be determined because they remain uninterpretable. The ampersand and parallel structure of lines two and three may suggest to the indexer parallel titles in two languages. (To many experienced indexers who could not read any of these languages, such an interpretation would not be resisted even if it were incorrect; just such problems may be found in many library catalogs. The assumption of a common format and typography trumps understanding.)

If the indexer does not know German but knows both English and French, the title, whether it begins with *Zheng He* or with *Images*. . . will be taken to be in English and/or French, while the third line in an unidentified language may be preliminarily assumed to be either a subtitle (if the title begins with *Zheng He*) or a parallel title in another language (if the title begins with *Images*). Remembering that the publisher was Harrassowitz, the indexer, if aware that Harrassowitz is a German publisher, may guess that line three is in German.

In every case, further investigation is required. One more line down provides the following new information:

Zheng He
Images & Perceptions
Bilder & Wahrnehmungen
édité par/edited by/herausgegeben von
Claudine Salmon/Roderich Ptak

Some clarification at last. The indexer who knows all of the languages involved will read three languages, and even the experienced indexer who does not know all of these languages will reinterpret the preceding lines in light of this line, and whether the indexer knows English or French or German (any one, two or all three), the language of the title (and perhaps the text within) will be assumed to be in all of these languages, some of which may remain to be determined. Whether *Zheng He* is the name of the author or title remains to be decided on the basis of further examination. Perhaps Salmon and Ptak have edited a Chinese text by Zheng He and published it here? Or English, French and German translations of his text?

Turning the page, we find the "Table des matières/Contents/Inhalt" listing four essays in German, three in French and one in English. We will assume at this point that the indexer has been able to identify at least one of these languages and found some means of determining what the other languages are (e.g., by asking someone else). The languages of the texts within the book are now known and identified. Zheng He is also now known to be the title and the subject of the book, since in the titles of each of the essays some aspect of the life of Zheng He or the literature about him is mentioned.

What still remains to be decided is the language of the main title. Here, we are stuck, since in the essays within the volume *Zheng He* appears as German, French and English. But we also know that *Zheng He* is simply and unquestionably originally pinyin Chinese, which is the romanization system used in American bibliographical databases. Yet we do not want to code this book as being in pinyin or romanized Chinese, since nothing other than the title of the volume could be so represented.

Perhaps the editors deliberately planned this multilingual play, for their use of the ampersand leads to the necessity of a multilingual interpretation of the subtitle. In fact, what we get is the following:

Zheng He = Main title in Chinese, English, French and German
Images & Perceptions = Subtitle in English and French
Bilder & Wahrnehmungen = Subtitle in German
édité par/edited by/herausgegeben von = statement of responsibility in French, English and German
Claudine Salmon/Roderich Ptak = authors' names in French, English and German?

When we write *Zheng He* in what language and script are we writing? In what language is the title of the book described above? The answer can only be that it is not in "a language" at all, but is in Chinese, English, French and German to be read and understood in whichever language(s) the reader understands. Yet the question, for most readers, is completely irrelevant. *Zheng He* is *Zheng He* in whatever language. The problem of interpretation arises only because in an electronic database, *Zheng He* must be input as two sequences of letters in some specific writing system, whether directly transcribed or transliterated, of some specific language. Only with this specification can the search engines of the database limit or specify searches by language, a limitation which is often desired by monolingual readers and sometimes necessary for others due to the simply overwhelming number of matches if some limits are not specified. This task is easy enough for a librarian to do, provided one of the languages can be understood: there are three putative languages in the text, so pick any one, for the choice does not matter. An indexer (whether human or machine) who cannot understand the text and follows a heuristically determined decision process cannot make that choice because he/she/it cannot understand that the choice – the language label required by the software – does not matter to anyone who can read.

XI

Relevance Ranking Is Not Relevance Ranking or, When The User Is Not The User, The Search Results Are Not Search Results

Relevance Ranking

As a technical term, "relevance ranking" refers to various statistical methods for ordering documents matching a search term. While common determinants of relevance ranking are known, the exact nature of the formulae used remain largely unknown to the public since these are valuable intellectual property for their owners. How these formulae are understood and advertised differs widely among the companies offering relevance-ranked displays and those evaluating the results, including librarians. Compare the description of relevance ranking provided by PLWeb Turbo with the description given by the makers of C2.

Relevance ranking for PLWeb Turbo:

Simply put, relevance ranking arranges a set of retrieved records so that those most likely to be relevant to your request are shown to you first. That is, after PLWeb Turbo retrieves all documents that satisfy your search query, it uses relevance ranking to arrange them based on a measurement of similarity between your query and the content of each record. [1]

In the first paragraph the writers of this description claim that PLWeb Turbo finds "all documents that satisfy your search query". *Satisfy* is obviously used in a special sense here for what PLWeb Turbo does is simply match the text string entered with documents in which that same (or similar) string is found. None of those items may "satisfy" the user, they may all be irrelevant. A more accurate description would replace "satisfy" with "match". Exactly the same conflation of meanings follows when the user's question (known only to the user) and the search term entered into the system are both refered to as "query". This is clear in the comment that relevance ranking orders the results using "a measurement of similarity between your query and the content of each record." Using the same term for the searcher's question and the search term entered into the system leads to a serious confusion about what is being matched with what. The software matches the search term(s) (called the query) selected to express the searcher's real question (also called the query) with the contents of the documents so what is being measured is not the similarity of the query as searcher's real question but the similarity of the text entered into the system: only the particular text entered is present to the system, not the searcher's question, intention or desire.

The second paragraph begins with the half-admission that it is probability of relevance that is being measured ("the likelihood of relevance") rather than true relevance:

What determines the likelihood of relevance? PLWeb Turbo performs a content analysis of records in your database by using a combination of the following indicators:

- **Breadth of Match.** *The more distinct query terms that appear in a document, the higher the weight of relevance.*
- **Inverse Document Frequency.** *Rare terms (within the entire database) receive a higher weight of relevance.*
- **Frequency.** *The number of times a query term occurs in a document.*
- **Density.** *The comparable length of retrieved documents.*

Consideration of these combined criteria produces intelligent on-the-fly evaluation of a record's likelihood of satisfying the intent behind your query. [1]

In this description we see clearly that the searcher, with all of her/his questions, intentions and desires is absent and relevance is being determined strictly from an analysis of the distribution and frequency of the matches for the search terms as they exist in the database. Yet this is followed by a fairly accurate description of what relevance ranking actually is: *Consideration of these combined criteria produces intelligent on-the-fly evaluation of a record's likelihood of satisfying the intent behind your query.* The only suspect element in this description is the word "intelligent" since it is clear that the intelligence involved in determining the criteria and writing the algorithms is not actually at work in the ordering performed by the software. The intelligent user may indeed find some of the initial results relevant but may just as readily find all of the results irrelevant —relevance ranking being doubly irrelevant—and in some cases "relevance ranking" may even be an obstacle. Whole classes of materials may drop to the bottom of the list of items retrieved regardless of their relevance, e.g. older materials or materials in other languages where the search term appears only in a low-weighted field.

---

[1] http://uscode.house.gov/help/htmlsrc/relrank.html

This allows you to find more relevant information with less effort. Regardless of how many records your search query retrieves, you will have to review relatively few of them, because moving down the ranking means moving toward less relevant records. With relevance ranking, you will spend less time reviewing search results before deciding whether they are satisfactory.

Additionally, you are free from the burden of composing complex logical queries, which are used to reduce the amount of retrieved data to manageable proportions. You don't have to care about how many records are retrieved, as long as you know that the best information floats to the top.[2]

In these paragraphs misleading claims of finding "more relevant information" and "moving toward less relevant records" replace the accurate understanding evident in the final sentence of the preceding paragraph. The concluding statement is doubly misleading: no one *knows* "that the best information floats to the top" for what "floats to the top" is nothing more than a statistically determined guess at what the searcher might mean, so the thorough searcher does indeed "have to care about how many records are retrieved."

Relevance ranking according to the description provided by the designers of C2 repeats many of the false claims found in the PLWeb Turbo description:

Relevance Ranking

... Relevance retrieval provides a mechanism with which the system determines the degree to which the retrieved records are relevant to the user's original query.

---

[2] http://uscode.house.gov/help/htmlsrc/relrank.html

The paragraph *Term Weighting* does describe accurately what C2 does, but the paragraph *Benefits to Users* is as false as the PLWeb Turbo account and for exactly the same reasons: it is not relevance that is being measured but something that the programmers hope will produce an acceptable substitute for relevance.

Term Weighting

Relevance ranking is a process by which C2 assigns significant values to each search term used in the query. Each document retrieved during a search is assigned a weighted value. The retrieved documents are then ranked in descending order according to the weighted value. The ranking algorithm used in C2 is based on the inverse document frequency (IDF) formula, where search terms are assigned a higher weight if they occur less frequently in the database and more frequently in documents. The term weighting is calculated on a logarithmic scale.

Benefits to Users

Retrieved records are ranked according to their relevance to the user's request. Records that are highly relevant are ranked first, followed by records that are less relevant. Since the most relevant records appear at the top of the list, users do not need to look through long lists to find records of interest.[3]

Again the words *relevance* and *query* shift between accurate descriptions of what is actually being done—term matching and weighting in a given corpus—to unjustified claims of indicating and ranking relevance. The descriptions are awash with shifting terminology, reifications and substitutions of surrogates for the intended object. What relevance is made to mean in these definitions and descriptions of relevance ranking

---

[3] http://contecds.com/library/c2/relrank.htm

is simply not the same thing as the meaning of relevance from a user's perspective but it is relevance from that perspective that is being claimed. This points to failure on another front: the role of the user in the identification of relevance. In these descriptions the user exists only as his/her query term(s). Relevance is treated as though it consists solely of statistical relationships among terms rather than in each and every case a unique judgement fitting a given user's situation. This reification of relevance is also found in many discussions of relevance by those evaluating the results of "relevance ranking."

The Fictional User
Those who have sat through product demonstrations by library systems companies will all have observed one after another salesperson perform "searches" in the system being demonstrated. These "searches" always have two things in common. First, no real researcher past the sixth grade would search a library catalog, Google or any database at all for "American history", "Civil war" or "Chemistry" using only those terms. Not even Toynbee would have gone for such searches as "Civilization" or "History." The second common feature of these demonstrations is actually the origin of the first: the searches do not arise from any real research question, need, project or assignment. They are simply mock searches to demonstrate technical features of the system.

This problem, characteristic of product demonstrations, also characterizes most discussions of users and information seeking in general. An especially clear case can be found in Karen Schneider's *How OPACs Suck, Part 1: Relevance Rank (Or the Lack of It)*[4]. In order to demonstrate the value of what is called "relevance ranking" she searched her own library's catalog using Endeca software with its relevance ranking algori-

---

[4] http://www.techsource.ala.org/blog/2006/03/how-opacs-suck-part-1-relevance-rank-or-the-lack-of-it.html

thms and compared the results with what she found in "two dozen online catalogs from around the country." What was her search? Million. Nothing else, just *million*.

Her results were interesting. She reproduced some of the items listed on the first page of results in library catalogs around the country, declaring that "the first page of hits—often the first or second hits—for those catalog searches should not include" the following items:

Hog heaven: the story of the Harley-Davidson empire
The rock from Mars: a detective story on two planets / Kathy Sawyer
The Johnstown Flood
Mosby's 2006 drug consult for nurses
Hotel Rwanda
Teens cook dessert

The obvious questions are of course "Why not? What were you looking for?" Perhaps the answer to those questions can be discerned by looking at what she calls the "satisfying results" from the first page of hits from Google. Following the link to the Google search for "million" given on her website, the following items were retrieved on 11 April 2007:

Million - Wikipedia, the free encyclopedia
The Million Dollar Homepage –
Million, Billion, Trillion...
Cynthia Lanius' Lesson: A Mathematics Fantasy I'll take that million.
Books-A-Million Online Bookstore : Buy Discount Books
Who Wants to Win a Million Dollars? –
Million Dollar Baby (2004)Million Dollar Baby on IMDb:
Million Dollar Baby DVD -
A Million Thanks To Our U.S. Military Men and Women

Million Dollar Challenge An offer of $1000000 to anyone that can demonstrate paranormal abilities under laboratory conditions.

Why should these results be more satisfying that those found in library catalogs? The presence of the word million is obvious, but the question "What was she looking for?" remains, since these items, like those in the library searches above, appear to have no relationships among them other than an accidental one.

She then gives the first seven results from her own catalog which are ordered according to relevance ranking remarking that "For a search-engine aficionado, those NCSU search results are mmm-mmm good." Those results were:

12 million black voices
Million man march
million dollar directory
Black religion after the Million Man March
Le Million
Million dollar prospecting techniques
Green groatsvvorth of vvit, bought with a million of repentance

In her quest for "relevant" ranking of items retrieved the Google results were "satisfying" and the NCSU results "mmm-mmm good". Yet these two sets and their ordering have only one thing in common—the presence of the word million in each item—while within each set of results there is really nothing in common. The question remains: What was she looking for? The conclusion can only be that she simply wanted to see the word *million* prominently located in each item displayed.

Is it possible to conceive of any library user actually conducting such a search? There may be only two such types of users: the bored child who wonders what will pop up if s/he types in *million*, and a librarian or salesperson who wants to demonstrate a technical feature of a search engine. Other users might want to search for books on the Million Dollar Man television series or the Million Man March, newspaper articles on a million dollar Prada theft, or trailers and reviews of the film Million Dollar Baby. Clearly Ms. Schneider was not looking for any particular one of these or she would have to admit that all of the other items retrieved were irrelevant, that her success in the library catalog was at best two in seven, and in five cases one out of seven, with all other possibly desired results faring even worse. The hits in her catalog had just as much to do with the "satisfying" results in the Google search as they did to the unsatisfying results in other library catalogs.

While none of the responses to Ms Schneider's posting clearly grasped the fundamental problem with her assumptions and example, some of them came close. Mack Lundy (posted March 14, 2006) asked whether

your test is revealing what you think it is.... While you don't specify, it looks like you want the 245 to have more weight that other tags. ... An argument could be made that the search results at NCSU's catalog present an appearance of relevancy, rather than a true representation of a searcher's intent.

When one accurately understands relevance ranking as an ordering with a probability of being relevant (as Schneider does in the second installment of this article[5]), an ordering created with no other information about the searcher's intent than the term(s) entered, then there is no argument necessary: relevance ranking can never present anything other than an appearance of relevancy. If the user's intention, the real query underlying the

---

[5] This is how Ms Schneider describes it in *How OPACs Suck, Part 2: The Checklist of Shame*: "Relevance ranking—As I explained earlier, on TF/IDF (term frequency/inverse document frequency), relevance rank is the essential building block to ensure the most likely search results rise to the top." http://www.techsource.ala.org/blog/2006/04/how-opacs-suck-part-2-the-checklist-of-shame.html

choice of search terms, is unknown—as they must be to the programmer, the software and every one but the user herself—then no assumption about placement or frequency has any relation other than chance to the user's notion of relevance.

In a later posting (March 15, 2006) Lundy pursues the matter again, directly challenging the validity of an abstract user model: "What assumptions can you make about a user of an academic library?" Assumptions about users are key. Relevance ranking algorithms are produced according to certain assumptions about users: figuring linking patterns, document currency and cooccurence of terms into the algorithms assumes certain attitudes for all users. What would it take to adjust relevance ranking for a target audience? Relevance ranking that was of the same nature as the relevance determinations of the searcher.

In a library catalog every element in a MARC record represents the interpretation and judgement of a human being, the subject headings being in fact the cataloger's assertions of relevance according to a defined taxonomy. The format itself has been designed to maximally support specific searching according to the kind of information desired: author, title, publisher, subject. Using a general keyword search ignores the information supplied by acts of intelligence isomorphic with the searchers intelligence (i.e. not by statistical weighing of data but by judgements based on human knowledge and experience in information seeking); using algorithms to weigh the results is simply an attempt to produce a substitute for that judgement using methods different in kind.

Emily Lynema noted the impossibility of knowing what users want ("There is no way for a catalog to auto-magically know what users are looking for when they type 'million' into a general keyword search" posted March 16, 2006) and again the next day "I just don't think it's always possible to know exactly what they need by the term they enter" (posted March 17, 2006). The truth is that it is never possible to "know exactly what they need." But Ms Lynema concludes her March 16th post with the disappointing remark "at least they can see a sensible connection between the word they entered and the results they got".

A sensible connection? No, rather a visible connection that makes the librarian happy. Ms Schneider's conclusion is the assumption which informs her evaluation of the results: term in the title proper indicates the most relevant item for any and all searchers and searches. Any ranking which ranks term in title proper over all other occurrences of the term is therefore relevance ranking; any other ranking cannot be relevance ranking because she has defined highest relevance as the presence of the search term in the title proper.

Another respondent (Will Stuivenga, 15 March 2006) complained about the lack of research on the effectiveness of relevance ranking. Even if Mr Stuivenga did not find it there has been research, and the best of it suggests that relevance ranking by algorithms is sometimes useful and sometimes not (more on that research in the next section). Ms Schneider's "research" itself demonstrates clearly the chief problems of relevance ranking algorithms. The results of the relevance ranking algorithms which Ms Schneider praises are (apart from the two items for the Million Man March) a set of totally unrelated items—exactly like both the library results which she criticizes *and* the results from Google—no one of them of any relevance to anyone looking for any of the other items. The only thing the items in her retrieval set have in common is the purely accidental characteristic of having the word *million* in the title proper. Nothing is relevant to the search because the search itself was a fiction, like the user who *might* search just the term *million*. When relevance is replaced by surrogates and the searcher an unreal abstraction, then the search is not a search, the search results are not search results and the whole exercise is an exercise in irrelevance, the discussion total nonsense.

Relevance Ranking and the Real User
Objective relevance is context free Borlund (2003) maintained, but information seeking is never context free. In every infor-

mation seeking task, relevance is always determined by the particular user within given circumstances and a specific goal, all of which are known to the particular user but unknowable for software (i.e. for the designer(s) of the software). A recent two-part article by White describes the dilemma in terms of Sperber and Wilson's relevance theory.

Sperber and Wilson write almost exclusively about how relevance is created in dialogues between persons. Information scientists focus on a different sort of dialogues - those between a person seeking information and a system designed to provide it, the system being a literature-based artifact whose human designers are absent. In the latter dialogue, both questioner and answerer are governed by views of what constitutes relevant information, but a distinction has long been made between what the nonhuman system deems relevant output and what the human user does, because they are by no means necessarily the same. Here, the assumptions relevant in a context are not the user's. A measure of relevance based on term counts is a system measure, and the assumptions are the system's, as instructed by its human designers. (White, 2007a, p.536-537)

In order for the technical system to actually determine (weigh, measure) relevance, it would have to be designed anew by the user for every search. While some systems *are* designed from scratch to deal with a specific research question, what we usually find instead are systems designed to be as useful as possible over as many different situations and users as possible. This means abstraction, generalizations, heuristic, statistical and probabilistic treatment of data and presentation of results. It means a high degree of indeterminacy, choice and failure in the task. Even limited success can often be achieved only through the persistent intelligent actions, reactions and adjustments of the user, frequently with the aid of another person or persons familiar with the research area of interest, the technical system, the database or collection being searched, the likes and dislikes

169
of the person (professor, department head, client) for whom the research is being done, or other resources whether printed, mechanical or human.

Given the abstract nature and limited potential of the technical system when dealing with particular searches, it is the decisions made by the user her/himself that renders the technical system usable as a tool, i.e. what to enter into the search box, how to enter it, and which box to use. One can not adequately explain this within an engineering theory of communication. David Weeks' recognition of the user's role in determining the results of a search was due to his accurate perceptions and understanding of the process. In his words "the decisions that determine the response to an enquiry are made primarily by the user himself" (Weeks, 1963, p. 9). Like the best system designers, he understood that what makes the system work is not the hardware or software but a purposeful agent beyond the parameters of the theory.

An algorithm must be based on criteria determined by a programmer and it must operate over an historical corpus, i.e. a corpus of data gathered and analyzed prior to the particular search; even when the search itself initiates a real time analysis the analysis is done over a historical corpus and is not an analysis of the user's assumptions, usage, questions, meanings or intentions. The questions which certain search terms prompt in many systems (Do you mean...?) are not the result of taking into account the specific users, their questions and their intentions, but a programmed event following from particular stemming or spell-checking algorithms.

Statistically analyzing a preexisting corpus and ordering results according to variously weighted factors such as place of occurrence, co-occurrence, proximity, frequency of use by other searches within the same corpus, degree of similarity between searched terms and other terms *may* all be combined to provide both a useful set of results and a useful ordering of those results, but just as often they provide perfectly useless nonsense. What must be understood is that these techniques do *not* select anything nor order anything according to the user's judgements but they select and order results strictly according to the surrogates for relevance determined by a programmer. The programmer finds or decides that certain factors often are associated with real users' judgements of relevance and then writes a program that assumes that those factors are straightforward or at least fairly reliable indicators of relevance in the abstract, apart from all users and uses—and in certain situations that assumption may prove useful. Yet since judgements of relevance are always unique judgements in unique situations the results of any search and their ordering according to algorithms is never anything more than a probabilistic inference based upon the past history of searches over a preexisting corpus.

The usefulness of the result set and its ordering must also be understood as being the result of users and their social practices rather than a technical production. This can most clearly be seen in the case of subject data supplied by authors, indexers and catalogers, but is in fact characteristic of all language use. It is the social demands for proper spelling, proper usage and plain speaking/writing which alone creates a corpus which when statistically analyzed will yield useful correlations and orderings. Were there no standardized orthographies authorized in dictionaries, then spell-checking, stemming, and useful statistical analysis would all be impossible. In specific discourse communities words and phrases often acquire very precise meanings and these social practices are what establish the correlations and probabilities that statistical analysis discovers.

For those assuming a particular universe of discourse, the correlations and rankings which the algorithms produce may be judged to be relevant when they match the linguistic practice of the searcher ***but not in any other case***. At this point ontologies can be brought into the searching technologies. Like other relevance ranking algorithms, ontologies can provide useful inclusions/exclusions from the data set as well as a useful ordering for specific searches, but exactly the same kinds of problems as noted above remain. Judgements of relevance can only be made by the individual searcher with each search performed.

The real problems with relevance ranking algorithms such as those weighting term frequency (tf) and inverse document frequency (idf) White locates in how they direct the searcher's attention.

The real significance of tf*idf weighting thus lies in how it directs attention. It is designed to put the items whose relevance is easiest to see where people are most likely to see them and to put titles whose relevance is harder to see down where people are less likely to look. It fills up the plausible browsing space with items that anyone can match on noun phrases - items that are topically relevant - and not with items that are relevant only to a special claim. It thus seems fair to say that lists ranked by tf*idf weighting are designed to appeal to people without special claims, people who can make only the easier relevance judgments - students, librarians, readers unfamiliar with a literature, hired judges in information retrieval experiments. Presumably, the designers of document retrieval systems want this outcome because it makes their systems look good to anyone, expert or not. (White, 2007a, p. 547)

Mr White understands all too well the librarian's delight at the ordering of her retrieval set. Arranging items in this manner "to indicate how easy it is to perceive their relevance" leads frequently to the user finding "more than enough to read." The searcher can therefore quit without ever looking at most of the items, an outcome that White feels is likely "for all but the ambitious scholar" (White, 2007a, p. 549) since the results are "structured so that the items beyond any desired limit can be ignored" (White, 2007a. p. 550).

White's research in the ISI citation record revealed "that scholars and scientists repeatedly make relevance judgments of less obvious kinds" (White, 2007a, p. 548). While relevance ranking algorithms promote "easy-to-see relevance... relatively hidden connections could be the very ones that most interest domain experts" (White, 2007a, p. 552). The most important connections or relevancies in real human interactions are "deducible from the input and context together, but from neither input nor context alone" (White, 2007a, p.552, quoting Wilson and Sperber). The ISI citation record revealed that the kinds of connections made by researchers is not readily available to mechanical operations such as matching and weighting.

In the second part of his essay White declares that "Information science... is the science of *artificial* relevance" (White, 2007b, p. 585; italics in original). When people engage a computer in the task of information seeking, there is a mismatch:

At the problematic interface, a user blindly implies interests to a system that cannot infer. The system instead shows the consequences of matching the verbal form of the user's message against a stock of written language - a very different thing from understanding what the user really wanted. (White, 2007b, p. 585)

Systems, White insists, are idiot savants, offering the searcher only an artificial relevance.

What is being ranked? Relevance as property and relevance as judgement
The larger part of LIS research is rooted in an engineering understanding of communication as transportation, positing an abstract sender and receiver of things called messages. The concrete user embedded in a personal biography, social environment and pursuing idiosyncratic ends is reduced to two technical roles—sender and receiver—filling now one role and now the other in relation to a certain class of objects known as information. The problem of "relevance ranking" and our understanding of it lies in this theoretical basis, which itself arises from a problematic semantics of science. Borlund (2003) was of

the opinion that research and debate on relevance had "resulted in an improved understanding of the concept" (p. 913) claiming that "a consistent and compatible understanding of the relevance concept" (p. 923) had been achieved. Jacsó (2006) has recently suggested otherwise: "It is an understatement to say that there is no consensus even in the meaning and definition of relevance, let alone in measuring the effectiveness of ranking results by their objective relevance" (p. 71).

Cooper (1971) contrasted *logical relevance* with *utility*. He defined logical relevance in the following manner: "A stored sentence is *logically relevant* to (a representation of) an information need if and only if it is a member of some minimal premiss set of stored sentences for some component statement of that need" (p. 24). Logical relevance for Cooper was an either-or matter, while utility was a matter of degree. Slightly altered and refined, the distinction has been retained in recent literature under other terms. Jacsó (2006) contrasts *pertinence* (subjective relevance, or "direct utility, usefulness and applicability") with objective relevance, or *topicality*.

There are two main objections to this way of understanding objective and subjective relevance. The first is that any relevance judgement by any human being will always be subjective to some degree, no matter how objective that person may strive to be. The second is that nothing is relevant to anything for any machine. What a machine retrieves is what it has been programmed to identify, match and retrieve: nothing more. A machine orders the items matched not according to relevance, but acording to a programmer's rules for ordering those results, a program written without any knowledge of or reference to the topic, the search terms, the user or the user's questions.

From Cooper to Jacsó objective/logical relevance has been assumed to be something that is an inherent property of a particular information object, strictly determined by an analysis of that object without any reference to users, their questions and all other factors which may influence the actual user behaviour during the search process. Objective relevance is understood to be something (topicality) which an objective observer could identify and describe, and therefore something which should in theory be identifiable and describable by that most objective observer, the machine. Borlund (2003) discusses what Saracevic (1996) refered to as manifestations of relevance, one type of which "describes the relation between the query (terms) and the collection of information objects expressed by the retrieved information object(s)" (Borlund, 2003, p.914). Another type of manifestation of topical relevance is "an intellectual assessment of how an information object corresponds to the topical area required and described by the request(s) for information. ... An observer makes the judgement" (Borlund, 2003, p. 915), i.e. one instance of Cooper's utility and Jacsó's pertinence.

Is not objective relevance also a judgement, albeit a judgement without a context, determined in advance of all contexts by the programmer? A theory of relevance as a judgement rather than a property (or manifestation thereof) of an information object will lead to a very different understanding of relevance, an understanding which will both clarify and explain the differences between objective (context-free) and subjective (context-dependent) relevance. It will also sharply distinguish between the context-free, mechanically determined algorithmic estimates of relevance and objective human judgements of topical relevance in such practices as indexing and subject analysis. Finally, a theory of relevance as judgement would illuminate the known problems with both human supplied subject data as well as mechanical forms of indexing, abstracting and relevance ranking.

One problem remains: the terminology. According to the Oxford English Dictionary the term *relevant* first appeared in the 16th century but was a rarity prior to 1800. Its meaning is given as "Bearing upon, connected with, pertinent *to*, the matter in hand." *Relevancy* also appears in the 16th century, but the use of this word has largely been replaced by *relevance*, the first occurrence of which the OED dates to 1733. Theoretical confusion entered the history of discussions of relevance the first time someone used the word relevance to describe the process of the probabilistic determination of relevance using algorithms, a history that the OED does not provide any evidence for, although it does include an interesting reference from a 1955 article: "**1955** *Bull. Atomic Sci.* Apr. 126/1 Relevance is another one of these non-assessable quantities which circumstances require to be assessed."

How to dissipate the confusion? Human relevance judgements are what programmers attempt to estimate and predict by means of algorithms. The results of the use of the algorithms are estimates and predictions of relevance judgements that some user might make, measurements of surrogates and orderings of items of information which are completely different in kind from all human judgements of relevance. The confusion will vanish as soon as relevance once again means only human judgements of relevance in a given context, and the programmers' context-free estimates based on surrogates and expressed in algorithms are called something else.

Another Means for Making Relevance Judgements
Algorithms based on surrogates for relevance are not the only methods for determining relevance, nor are they the earliest means. A much more effective method for determing relevance has long been practiced in libraries and by indexing and abstracting services, a method rooted not in surrogates, heuristics and statistical analysis but in a knowledge of linguistic and scholarly practices not available to any statistical analysis or indeed to any purely technical approach. That practice is the provision of subject information by persons who analyze the contents of each item with a view to providing a description appropriate to users working within the framework of a socially or institutionally defined universe of languages and practices. In academic libraries for instance, the language, scholarly methods and research practices such as citation, literature review, and theoretical framework inform the work of subject description.

Subject analysis by human beings is never context-free, distinguishing it in every case from system determined algorithmic relevance. Subject analysis done by human beings always takes place within a human world of social practices such as reading, writing, research, academic life and discourse, surfing the Internet, book buying, product innovation, marketing, trouble-shooting and a vast array of social practices that differ from one political community to another, one linguistic community to another, one interest group to another, one time to another, one age-group to another and so on. Subject analysis is a communicative act directed towards a particular group of users, even though much of the time the nature of that user group is only vaguely present to the one doing the subject analysis. The assumptions are usually general, encompassing language (e.g. English), purpose of information seeking (e.g. thesis research) and the social practices of that particular time and place and the activities for which the information is assumed to support. It is always within a particular context that the subject analyst determines—judges—topicality.

While it is true that within restricted domains of highly regulated practices subject thesauri and ontologies can provide some context, both the unique context and the wider context of socially embedded and embodied life in a time and a place is in every case unavailable to mechanical means of relevance ranking. That larger context permits the subject analyst to attempt to communicate information about topicality and relevance to unknown future users. Yet because the analyst cannot directly interview the unknown user, considerations of what Jacsó calls pertinence can never enter into the act of subject analysis and in this respect human supplied subject data are in a sense context-free or objective, exactly like algorithmic relevance, with all of the failures and short-comings of the latter.

One crucial difference between subject analysis and relevance ranking is collocation. Relevance ranking collates nothing. Subject analysis as an intellectual judgement about topicality is an attempt to bring like materials together, not to rank them. Like Cooper's logical relevance, subject analysis is an either-or proposition, not a matter of degree.

Weinheimer (2007) described his experiences teaching library users how to use the library catalog, emphasizing the difference between subject headings and relevance ranking:

Headings are the entire power of the catalog and this was pretty much lost through the keyword search. I truly believe that people want the (what I call) "clusters" of materials that are found in the card catalog (and now the online catalogs), and when I have shown people the power of this and say: "Would you rather find everything on World War I in one place or do you want to sit and think of all the different words that could be used and still miss a few?" then absolutely *everybody* likes the "clusters."

I then explain that these "clusters" are only as good as the people who make them, and that just because you might be an expert on the subject of World War I, you may not be able to make the clusters correctly....

I discuss "relevance" ranking by doing a Google search and asking why these materials are more "relevant" than something else. How does this machine know what is relevant to me by two or three words that I have typed into a little box? Does it read my mind or what? Then I discuss citation indexing and that Google works through a secret algorithm based on citation indexing and that "Mr. and Mrs. Google" decided to call "relevant." Then I ask them what kind of a word "relevance" is in this case: it is propaganda. They could just as well have called it "irrelevance ranking" or "citation ranking" but they decided to use an inappropriate word that makes people feel more secure. I can go on about finding materials (some truly excellent ones!) in Google Books, or rather *not* finding them because the relevance searching just completely breaks down.

As Weinheimer pointed out, the value and relevance of subject headings will vary depending upon who creates the headings and the conditions of their creation. Subject description can provide the terms for great precision in searching but it is equally possible that the results will be nearly identical to title or general keyword searching, particularly if the descriptors are entered as isolated terms (single words). If the creation of subject headings is restricted (whether by choice, the rules for subject description, or a heuristic) to words found in the title, table of contents, index or abstract then the results will be superior to mechanical indexing only in respect to gathering materials in all languages under a single language of description (not a small advantage). The primary difference between the results of machine indexing displayed according to relevance ranking algorithms and keyword subject description of whatever sort is that the latter provides only those terms considered useful to a potential reader who is searching by subject. In the purely mechanical approach, there is no judgement of the value of the words for subject access: all words are indexed; term weighting is simply an attempt to correct that indexing *faux pas*.

The difference is evident in the results described by Ms. Schneider. Any human being who indexes a book like "The Million Man March" would be expected to provide a subject phrase "Million Man March" (perhaps adding the place and date, Washington, D.C., October 16, 1995) and not simply offer three disconnected words to be searched out of context. Indeed, one would expect any searcher to search for the phrase rather than simply "million", and the smart searcher might well add place and or date as search terms. On the other hand Ms. Schneider's final example in the list of results from her own library catalog is a book that only Ms. Schneider would both search for using only the term "million" and be pleased with its appearance high on the list of relevant items.

2013. Coming soon...

I suggested above that in order for any system to determine real relevance it would be necessary for the system to be designed anew by the user for every unique search. That was not a *reductio ad absurdum*. Jatalla.com "relies exclusively on relevancy evaluations performed by live human beings, not computers." (http://jatalla.wordpress.com/about/) While many librarians remain enthralled with the mechanical dreams of the 1950-1990s, others who recognize the necessity of the searcher/user determining relevance are working toward a more user-friendly future. From their website "a little vision of what Jatalla will (hopefully!) look like in, say, 2013 or so":

In that future world, Jatalla will allow users not only to submit their own search relevance rankings but also to write, store and share their own user-generated search algorithms. Specifically, you will be able to create an algorithm that includes several "components", ... Such an approach will allow you to combine link-to (i.e., "citation-ranking" a la PageRank) results with lexivote results and pay-for-placement results to produce a single final list of results that are ranked according to the remainder of the formula that you create. You will then be able to store your search engine and deploy a search box on your website that uses your search algorithm to search and rank documents from the specified database.
(http://jatalla.wordpress.com/about/)[6]

If indeed systems can be designed to incorporate real relevance judgements, perhaps we will all be catalogers in 2014.

---

[6] Alas, we did not all become catalogers in 2014. Instead on 24 September 2007 Jatalla announced "We have wrapped up the Jatalla prototype search engine. The results were excellent, and we'll hope to bring you a more complete version of the collective-intelligence-powered search engine in the future. Thanks to all who participated!" (https://jatalla.wordpress.com/2007/09/24/wrapping-up/) and nothing more has been heard from them since.

References.

Borlund, P. (2003). "The concept of relevance in IR" *Journal of the American Society for Information Science and Technology*, Vol.54, No.10, pp.913-925.

Cooper, W.S. (1971). "A definition of relevance for information retrieval" *Information storage and retrieval* Vol. 7, pp. 19-37.

Jacsó, P. (2005). "Savvy searching: relevance in the eye of the search software" *Online information review* Vol. 29 No. 6 pp. 676-682.

Jacsó, P. (2006). "Savvy searching: pertinence in the eye of the user" *Online information review* Vol. 30 No. 1 pp. 70-76.

"Relevance" *Oxford English Dictionary (OED online)*

Saracevic, T. (1996). "Relevance reconsidered '96" in P. Ingwersen, & N.W. Pors (eds.), *Proceedings of CoLIS2, second international conference on conceptions of library and information science: Integration in perspective, Copenhagen,* Royal School of Librarianship, Copenhagen, pp. 201-218.

Schneider, K. (2006a). How OPACs Suck, Part 1: Relevance Rank (Or the Lack of It), available at: http://www.techsource.ala.org/blog/2006/03/how-opacs-suck-part-1-relevance-rank-or-the-lack-of-it.html (accessed 11 April 2007)

Schneider, Karen (2006b). How OPACs Suck, Part 2: The Checklist of Shame, available at: http://www.techsource.ala.org/blog/2006/04/how-opacs-suck-part-2-the-checklist-of-shame.html (accessed 11 April 2007)

Weeks, David (1963). "Information system theory as the foundation of practical design." in Howerton, P.W. (Ed.), *Information Handling: First Principles*. Spartan Books, Washington, DC. pp. 1–17

Weinheimer, James (2007). RE: Weinheimer's glorified card catalog. Posted to Autocat, 22 March 2007.

White, Howard D. (2007a). "Combining bibliometrics, information retrieval, and relevance theory, Part 1: First examples of a synthesis." *Journal of the American Society for Information Science & Technology*, 2007, Vol. 58 No. 4, pp. 536-559

White, Howard D. (2007b). "Combining bibliometrics, information retrieval, and relevance theory, Part 2: Some implications for information science." *Journal of the American Society for Information Science & Technology*, 2007, Vol. 58 No. 4, pp. 583-605

XII

It's About Time!
Temporal Aspects of Metadata Management in the Work of Isabelle Boydens

One of the principle emphases in Roy Harris's writings on language and communication is the element of time in communicative action. According to Erik Hollnagel, one of the critical features of all work is the temporal dimension. Both the cognitive psychologist Dietrich Dörner and the professor of management Guy Callender found that a failure to consider temporal developments was characteristic of managers whose decision making produced catastrophic failures in similated (Dörner) and real (Callender) situations. The temporal dimensions of database construction, management and use have been a matter of frequent reflection on my part, but I have never pursued the issue in any depth (not enough time, perhaps). Nor do I recall running accross any sustained discussion of the issue in the literature of library and information science during my searching over the past decade. Clearly my failure, as Isabelle Boydens' 1999 book *Informatique, normes et temps* proves. My only excuse is that searching EBSCO's *Library, Information Science & Technology Abstracts with Full Text*, Wilson's *Library Literature and Infor-*

mation Science Retrospective and LISA (CSA Illumina)—all of them—today (26 January 2011) turns up not a single reference to Boydens.[1] That is shocking, so shocking in fact that someone ought to find out what it is these databases are doing and why a prolific author like Boydens is not in any of them. Her book is in the OCLC database, but when I tried to find a copy, only two US libraries were listed as having copies. That is all the justification I need for this issue's column, and indeed, for *The International Observer* column itself.

Like Carlo Revelli's work discussed in the last *International Observer* column, the number of Boydens' publications and the length of *Informatique, normes et temps* presents just too much to go through in detail, even though I really would like to. At times the level of technical detail goes over my head, and at other times I had difficulty imagining how this would translate into cataloging practice (i.e. my world) as opposed to database management efforts by programmers (definitely not my world). Yet even in what were for me the heaviest sections of her monograph, the synthesis at the end of each chapter (a very nice feature of her book) invariably increased my level of understanding and led me to some heavy underlining. Rather than a detailed review of twenty years of publications, I shall comment on a few themes in her major work *Informatique, normes et temps* that particularly interested me, and follow that with comments on some of her other publications as well as those of her former student Seth van Hooland.

Before discussing some of the particulars of her published work (chiefly in French, but a few papers in English), I would like to mention two notable characteristics of her writing. First of all, in spite of the technical topic, her writing is easy to read and understand. In many academic papers every statement is justified by one, two or ten references which are then either never discussed, or when discussed at all, the discussion only proves that the authors did not really read the works cited. Other

---

[1] For a complete list of Prof. Boydens' publications see her web page: http://www.ulb.ac.be/cours/iboydens/

authors insist on filling half the book with quotations and the other half with footnotes (the pot is calling the kettle black here and he is well aware of it). Readers of Isabelle Boydens' book will suffer none of these horrors. References, quotations and footnotes are neither obtrusive nor excessive, and are always pertinent, with their importance for the argument made clear in the discussion that follows. One might think this is just a matter of style, but good writing like hers is generally the product of clear thinking, and that is the second characteristic to note.

When Boydens mentions or quotes Raymond Aron, Fernand Braudel, Norbert Elias, Gilbert Hottois, Friedrich Nietzsche, Max Weber or Ludwig Wittgenstein (which she does), the reference is presented as the basis for a discussion that takes those remarks and elaborates what they mean for database management. Not only information scientists but philosophers, sociologists and historians inform her discussion—they do not merely embellish it. Theories developed outside of information science and long before its origins inform her work, principally hermeneutics and historical criticism. Her discussion of metadata (she uses the term 'méta-information' and has been publishing on the topic since 1993) in the third chapter of *Informatique, normes et temps* ("Bases de données et incertitude") is a good example of how the depth of her analysis is rooted in theories and concepts that have been developed outside LIS. If one compares her discussion of metatada with the widely acclaimed works of philosopher and metadata advocate David Weinberger, the latter comes off as Timothy Leary to Boydens' Edmund Husserl. Her 'méta-information' is neither everything (and therefore nothing) nor miscellaneous (and therefore meaningless) but theoretically introduced in the chapter on the problem of uncertainty in databases. With a notion of metadata rigorously and theoretically defined in its philosophical, social and technical significance, she clarifies many issues that plague metadata managers and is able on that theoretical basis to proceed towards the development of automated methods for managing particularly difficult problems.

The chief issue she addresses in her book appears to be simple enough. Time, she insists, is an aspect of the real world that must be taken into consideration by database managers from the very beginning. The problem? The world changes, whether the data which we utilize in our decisionmaking regarding that real world does or not. Her metadata is, therefore, not just meta- as in higher generalization (metaphysics), but meta- as in change (metamorphosis). Her book is, however, more than just a treatise on information science the author of which had more time on her hands than most. The preface is a very good indication of the diversity of approaches she takes to database management as well as the multiple means for addressing the problems of temporal databases. In that preface four authors (all of whom I am going to have to read after reading professor Boydens' use of their work) address the four principle dialogues that inform her monograph. In her book information science confronts public administration and management (Alain Pirotte), hermeneutics (Françoise D'Hautcourt), history (Jean-Philippe Genet) and epistemology (Jean-Louis Besson). That was more than enough to propel me through the next 550 pages.

After a general introduction to the problem that her book addresses and the structure of her argument, the first three chapters present the state of the art in research on how to evaluate and improve the quality of databases. Included is a discussion and marvelous critique of the MIT "data quality management" research program of the early 1990s, a discussion of current methods of managing data quality, and the problem of uncertainty which was at the heart of her critique of that research: "the question of the accuracy of a database can find no satisfactory response because of the absence of referentiality that would allow the validation of the adequacy of the information [in the database] to the real world it represents". Uncertainty, she notes, "designates that which is neither fixed nor determined *a priori*."

> For operational reasons, most current database models rest on the hypothesis of a closed world: all the facts not

included in the database are interperted as false. Theoretically, a database is thus considered as complete (all the values logically deriving from a given state of the database are present) and coherent (all the present values are correct), inside the area specified by the schema of the database. Nevertheless, in practice databases come to have incomplete or incoherent values.[2]

And how do databases come to have incomplete or incoherent values? Time changes the world that the data must accurately reflect if the database is to be usefull at all. Time also changes the database structures, schema and sources of data, as well as the social forces that determine what information needs to be in the database, e.g. database users' desiderata, legislation, as well as discoveries and inventions, all of which may make all-important what was previously insignificant (and vice versa).

One of Boydens' chief arguments concerns the limitations of the TDQM (Total Data Quality Management) approach associated with Redman, Wang and MIT in the 1990s. She begins her critique by noting that the solutions proposed by these researchers "has as its object the improvement of procedures for treating the inadequacy of formally identifiable and measurable errors (incoherencies, incompleteness, programming errors)".[3] Boydens reminds the reader that beyond such formal errors there is a particularly important matter that TDQM approaches to data quality do not address at all, and that is the human interpretation of information.

> the measure of the accuracy of a fact rests upon an hypothetical bijective relation between a value v contained in the database and the corresponding true value v'. Yet because of the absence of referentiality in any empirical domain of application, what these authors call the

---

[2] Isabelle Boydens, *Informatique, normes et temps* (Bruxelles: Bruylant, 1999), p. 100.
[3] Ibid., p. 57.

"*correct value v*" is in absolute terms "unknowable". For example, to verify the validity of the name of a salaried worker presupposes that one has available a precise and determinate definition of the concept of "salaried worker". Yet, the juridical and informatic norms that permit the representation of the concept, exactly like the real world alongside it, never cease to evolve. ... *A fortiori*, to verify the validity of the names of several hundreds of thousands of individuals supposes that one can identify the whole of the population at every moment."[4]

She proceeds to outline the "ontological foundations" set forth in a famous paper by Wand and Wang[5] and three postulates upon which those foundations rest:

- The world is composed of discrete, unequivocal elements that are clearly identifiable and perceptible;
- Combinations and knowledge of these elements are governed by laws;
- It is possible to establish a bijective relation between the observable reality and its informational representation by virtue of the isomorphism that links the one to the other.[6]

Her critique begins simply enough: "Wand and Wang's approach is tautological".[7] Ockham gets the credit for refuting Wand and Wang's logic seven centuries ago, and Gilbert Hottois leads her to the observation that "the absence of a

---

[4] Ibid., p. 58.
[5] Y. Wand and R.Y. Wang, "Anchoring data quality dimensions in ontological foundations," *Communications of the ACM*, 39:11(November 1996): 86-95.
[6] Boydens, op. cit., p. 62.
[7] Ibid., p. 63.

'contradictory' observation is not sufficient to prove the validity of a proposition but only a temporary indication".[8]

She then develops an argument on the basis of census databases, the semantics of which are, she insists, "precisely characterised by the absence of any isomorphism with the corresponding reality and that for three reasons".[9] First, a census can never be complete. Second, the evaluation of census data can never rest on the available sources. And finally all economic and statistical observations are artificially attributed to a given period of time when in fact there is always of necessity a discrepancy between the state of the real world and its measurement.[10] A few pages later she quotes Stuart Madnick:

> There are often real reasons why different people, different societies, different countries, different functions, different organizations may look at the same picture and see something different. To assume that this can be prevented is a mistake. We must accept the fact that there is diversity in the world".[11]

Boydens herself goes further, arguing that "even in the case of a single fact and of a single observer, an unequivocal informational representation of 'observable reality' is illusory".[12] This leads her to suggest in the final sentence of the first chapter that the question TDQM researchers asked—Is the information contained in the database correct?—should be replaced by the question "How is information constructed over time?" This change in the question we ask of databases is itself a splendid example of her thesis and the reason for the new question: the world changes *for us* because we ask and expect different things of it at different times; that being so, both our data and our metadata need to

---

[8] Ibid., p. 64.
[9] Ibid., p. 65.
[10] Ibid., p. 65-66.
[11] Madnick, quoted in Boydens, ibid., p. 68.
[12] Ibid., p. 68.

change to reflect that new state of the world. This is quite a strong claim, namely that neither data nor metadata have some ontological status that remains unchanged regardless of the user, the uses and the questions that ground each use of the database.

As mentioned above, chapter three theoretically puts metadata in its place: the management of uncertainty and change. Boydens argues that systems of metadata should be constructed on the basis of four tasks: the identification of a minimal group of metadata based on usage, a compromise between economy and completeness of information, assessment of the organization within which the metadata will function, an effort at minimizing manual labor.[13] It is preferable, she insists, "to forego schema enrichment rather than adding elements" if the organization lacks the human resources that updating such metadata would require, since the provision of partial or dubious metadata would be "a remedy worse than the problem being addressed".[14] The validity of probabilistic or "fuzzy" indexing in a real—and therefore uncertain—environment is liable to be even more uncertain than the original uncertainty of the real it is intended to represent.[15]

The third part of the book describes the database that the author studied (the Belgian social security database, LATG) and the principle methodologies informing her approach: heuristics, historical criticism, and hermeneutics. Historians, like database users, "confront the absence of referentiality".

> In order to verify the correctness of some value, one must have available a normative reference. Yet, in an empirical domain of application, that reference does not exist. ... In order to verify the correctness of the information contained in a database, one must ideally know *a*

---

[13] Ibid. p. 117.
[14] Ibid.
[15] Ibid., p. 118.

priori a reality that only that database allows one to know.[16]

For the historian, the past is past and inaccessible directly, while in a database, each item of information it contains reflects a different past state of affairs that has changed since the effort of data collection. This remains true even in a "live" system; the only difference being the shorter time interval between data capture and data use. The opacity of a networked system decreases as the capacity of access increases, yet

> from node to node, from context to context, information is transformed in the act of circulating. And the user, further and further from the source producing the information, does not necessarily have the resources that would allow him to decode the meaning of the data obtained.[17]

Any information scientist who cites the Belgian philosopher Gilbert Hottois—and Boydens does, as I mentionied earlier—gets my attention, but anyone who quotes the British philosopher Robin George Collingwood not only gets my attention but gives me great pleasure. In her chapter on hermeneutics for databases, we get to read Collingwood's own words in French translation:

> Data, on the one hand, and principles of interpretation on the other, are the two elements of all historical thought. But they do not exist separately and then undergo a combination. They exist together or not at all.[18]

---

[16] Ibid. p. 144.
[17] Ibid. p. 152.
[18] Collingwood, from *The Philosophy of History* (London: Published for the Historical Association by G. Bell and Sons, 1930), quoted by Boydens, ibid. p.161.

She follows this with the remark "the interpretation of the same concept varies according to the place, the period, the context and even the author. Scientific questions themselves have their own histories".[19] This issue is further elucidated in the sections entitled "The interpretation of the norm interacts with interpretations of the facts"[20] and "The interpretation of the facts interacts with that of the norm".[21] And with her introduction of Braudel's notion of time levels and Elias's evolutive continuums, we have entered into the heart of the problem that she addresses and her approach to dealing with that problem.

That is a very brief summary of the first two parts/six chapters of Boydens' book. The remaining sections deal with the management of the flow and change of data, proposed methods for automating as much of that effort as possible, and general conclusions. In this book and in subsequent publications Boydens illustrates "how hermeneutics, embodied through the use of a temporal framework, can help to interpret changes in the quality of empirical databases and lead the way to operational recommendations".[22] The management strategies described in her publications apply "to all information systems whose structure evolves according to the interpretation of the realities that they aim to grasp. This is particularly true of empirical databases, in which the homogeneity of the formal codifications clashes with the heterogeneity of the empirical categories".[23]

One of the most interesting aspects of studying the LATG database was that the data really mattered, mattered to the people affected (pensioners, the unemployed), and to the responsible administrative agencies. National and international legal regimes enforced both the collection of the data and its

---

[19] Boydens, ibid., p. 161.
[20] Ibid. p. 163.
[21] Ibid. p. 164.
[22] Isabelle Boydens and Seth van Hooland, "Hermeneutics applied to the quality of empirical databases," *Journal of documentation*, v.67(2011), nr.2: 287.
[23] Ibid.

interpretation in a never-ending and frequently retrospective sequence of changing and sometimes conflicting laws. To construct and manage a database that really matters requires a very different mindset than that frequently encountered in the library literature. Related to that is another matter that I should have noted myself, and long ago, but never have: database quality isn't only a matter of human knowledge, ignorance and error, nor of human error directed and exacerbated by bad policies, rather it is above all a matter of the very structure of existence in time. It is that insight that has informed professor Boydens' work since the early 1990's, and the implications of which are now being pursued not only by Boydens herself, but also by some of her present and former students. A few remarks on that growing body of research follow.

Many of the themes treated in depth in *Informatique, normes et temps* were discussed in a few earlier papers that may be easier to find and to read than the monograph. Using historical criticism to think about database management was the topic of two early papers "Informatique et qualité de l'information. Application de la critique historique à l'étude des informations issues de bases de données" (1993) and "La critique historique face aux sources informatiques" (1996)[24] and metadata was the topic of a few papers of the late 1990's and the past decade.[25]

---

[24] Isabelle Boydens, "Informatique et qualité de l'information. Application de la critique historique à l'étude des informations issues de bases de données," *Belgisch Tijdschrift voor Nieuwste Geschiedenis. Revue belge d'histoire contemporaine*, vol. 3-4 (1993): 399-439; Isabelle Boydens, "La critique historique face aux sources informatiques," in *Actes de la Journée de l'histoire contemporaine 1996 - session "Internet pour les historiens" - Vereniging voor Geschiedenis en Informatica (VGI). Université Catholique de Louvain-La-Neuve, 27 April 1996*: 15-17.

[25] Isabelle Boydens, "Les systèmes de méta-information, instruments d'interprétation critique des sources informatiques," *History and Computing*, v. 1, nr. 8 (January 1996): 11-23;

Managing data transformation and data quality over time were the particular concerns of three papers in 1998,[26] though this is really the basic concern in all of her published work. Since the publication of her monograph in 1999, Boydens has touched on topics such as controlled vocabulary,[27] the conflict between the disorder in the real world and the order constructed within a database,[28] Web2.0[29] and the semantic web.[30]

Isabelle Boydens, "Les systèmes de méta-information," *Techno, publication technique de la SmalS-MvM*, nr.1 (April 1997); ISabelle Boydens, "E-gouvernement en Belgique: un retour riche d'expériences," *L'informatique professionnelle*, nr.217 (octobre 2003): 29-35.

[26] Isabelle Boydens, "Analyser le processus de transformation de l'information : du "stemma codicum" au "data tracking"," in Roelants-Abraham J., éd., *Information et documentation : du réel au virtuel* (Bruxelles : Infodoc-ULB, 1998): 57-70; Isabelle Boydens, "Evaluer et améliorer la qualité des bases de données," *Techno, publication technique de la SmalS-MvM*, n° 7 (January 1998); Isabelle Boydens, "Managing time in historical and contemporaneous databases," in *International Congress on Historical Information Systems, November 6th-8th 1997* (Vitoria-Gasteiz : Juntas Generales de Alava, 1998): 159-172.

[27] Isabelle Boydens, "Déploiement coopératif d'un dictionnaire électronique de données administratives," *Document numérique*, v. 5 nr.3/4 (2001): 27-43.

[28] Isabelle Boydens, "Les bases de données sont-elles solubles dans le temps?" *La Recherche hors série ("Ordre et désordre"). Hors série* n° 9 (November-December 2002): 32-34.

[29] Isabelle Boydens, E. Bruillard, P.-A. Caron, G. Gallezot and D.K. Schneider, "Entretien," *Revue distance et savoirs*, v.7 nr.3 (Numéro spécial: *Informations scientifiques et pratiques numériques acadéques*, ed. by Timini I., DelaMotte E. and Peraya D. Paris: Editions Hermès Sciences-Lavoisier): 479-500.

A number of recent papers in English present in concise and updated form both the theoretical approach and the operational strategies that she has developed during the past decade. Her latest paper describes the use of her approach to data quality in electronic government in Belgium. In E-government databases "the pooling of data and dematerialization of procedures demands interoperability between sectors and departments, and this potentially multiplies the interpretation difficulties to be overcome."[31] She describes the three methods developed for dealing with these problems in Belgian government databases:

1. *Master Data Management* is a general methodology to analyze and improve the quality of the concepts and flows judged to be the most fundamental within the information system.
2. *Anomalies and Management Strategies* are an original operational approach that we applied in the scope of our research about interpretation of the Belgian social security database.
3. *Documentation of Application and Services* aims to present an electronic data dictionary (glossaires de la sécurité sociale) that was implemented in Belgium to improve interpretation of e-government databases by the Belgian Data Quality Competency Center presented in the introduction.[32]

---

[30] Isabelle Boydens, "Du "Web sémantique" au "Web pragmatique"," *Research Note* - SmalS-MvM, n°5 (April 2004), 19 p. (slides)
[31] Isabelle Boydens, "Strategic issues relating to data quality for E-government: learning from an approach adopted in Belgium," in S. Assar, I. Boughzala and I. Boydens, eds., *Practical Studies in E-Government : Best Practices from Around the World* (New York: Springer, 2011): 113-130; quotation from p. 128.
[32] Ibid., p. 121.

"Hermeneutics applied to the quality of empirical databases" (with Seth Van Hooland) is a short but comprehensive introduction in English to Boyden's approach to database management,[33] and a forthcoming paper coauthored with Van Hooland and Eva Méndez Rodriguez, also in English, is a very interesting and iconoclastic empirical study of user-generated metadata in cultural heritage institutions.[34] In this latter paper the authors note that studies of user-generated metadata in Web2.0 environments have focused on the usefullness and efficacy of such metadata for current users, but the authors are particularly interested in other questions, namely the responsibility of cultural heritage institutions towards the past we are preserving and future uses of those materials. (It is amazing how differently we can evaluate a practice depending on the questions we ask of it!) In a 2010 paper she describes centralized/hierarchical and distributed/anarchic systems of knowledge organization in the Western world from the medieval era to our own.[35]

Two of the papers mentioned above were written in collaboration with Seth van Hooland, current holder of the chair in Digital Information at the Information and Communication

---

[33] Isabelle Boydens and Seth van Hooland, "Hermeneutics applied to the quality of empirical databases," *Journal of documentation*, 67:2 (2011): 279-289.

[34] Seth van Hooland, Eva Méndez Rodriguez and Isabelle Boydens, "Between commodification and sense-making. On the double-sided effect of user-generated metadata within the cultural heritage sector," in Marty P. F. and Kazmer M. M., eds, "Involving Users in the Co-Construction of Digital Knowledge in Libraries, Archives, and Museums", special issue of *Library Trends,* (forthcoming).

[35] Isabelle Boydens, "Hiérarchie et anarchie : dépasser l'opposition entre organisation centralisée et distribuée?" *Les cahiers du numérique* (Numéro thématique « Organisation des connaissances et Web 2.0 », M. Hudon and W.M. El Hadi, eds) 6:3 (2010): 77-101.

Science department of the Université Libre de Bruxelles and a former student of professor Boydens. One of the major topics that van Hooland has researched is the changing nature of description and the role of changing technologies and government policies in that development. That is one of the central issues discussed in his thesis[36] and in personal communication he has indicated that he is working on a paper looking at the successive records created for a single object over the past 150 years, in collaboration with museums and libraries in Brussels and Berlin. His paper (in Dutch) on the history of metadata looks at how successive technologies bring us different kinds of metadata and consequently different possibilities, from the card catalogue to Web2.0.[37] Other papers in English (van Hooland 2006; van Hooland, Kaufman and Bontemps, 2008) and French (van Hooland 2007) deal with metadata, folksonomies and ontologies in museum collection databases.[38]

---

[36] Seth van Hooland, S. (2009), *Metadata quality in the cultural heritage sector: stakes, problems and solutions*. PhD thesis, Université Libre de Bruxelles. Available at: http://homepages.ulb.ac.be/~svhoolan/these.pdf

[37] Seth van Hooland and H. Vanhee, "Van steekkaart tot webinterface. De evolutie van metadatabeheer in de culturele erfgoedsector," in B. de Nil and J. Walterus, *Erfgoed 2.0.* (Brussel: FARO, 2009): 87-106. Available at: http://ia700200.us.archive.org/20/items/VanSteekkaartTotWebinterface.DeEvolutieVanMetadatabeheerBinnenDe/Erfgoed2.0_vanhooland_vanhee_87_106.pdf

[38] Seth van Hooland, "Spectator becomes annotator: possibilities offered by user-generated metadata for image databases." Paper presented at Immaculate Catalogues: Taxonomy, Metadata and Resource Discovery in the 21st Century, 13-15 September 2006, University of East Anglia, UK, available at: http://homepages.ulb.ac.be/~svhoolan/Usergeneratedmetadata.pdf ; Seth van Hooland, "Entre formalisation et déconstruction: état de l'art critique de l'application documentaire des ontolo-

I am myself just beginning to think about the philosophical and practical implications of taking time seriously when thinking about databases and in using them. Boydens and Van Hooland have given me much to think about along those lines. But they are not armchair philosophers: they both really understand the nuts and bolts of information technologies and their intention is not only to understand how metadata works, the limitations and possibilities that metadata (however produced) offers to users of databases, but also how to ameliorate the limitations and enhance the possibilities through operationalizing metadata management. That is where they go way beyond anything I have done or ever will do.

It is not often that anyone manages to open up a whole new dimension to any field, but by bringing research into the problems and questions associated with heuristics, hermeneutics and the study of history, professor Boydens has not only broken new ground in approaches to database management, but opens up an entirely new dimension of reflection on cataloging and classification. Those whose interest veers toward the philosophical questions associated with cataloging and classification will find Boydens' publications, from the first paper to the forthcoming, among the most interesting research produced during the last few decades.

---

gies et folksonomies dans le domaine de l'indexation du patrimoine culturel numérique," in *Organisation des connaissances et société des savoirs : concepts, usages, acteurs. Actes du colloque ISKO 2007, Université Paul Sabatier IUT, Toulouse, 7 and 8 June 2007* (Toulouse, 2007): 33-47; Seth van Hooland, S. Kaufman and Y. Bontemps, "Answering the call for more accountability: applying data-profiling to museum metadata," in *Proceedings of the International conference on Dublin Core and metadata applications, 22- 26 September 2008, Berlin* (Berlin: Dublin Core Metadata Initiative, 2008): 93-103.

XIII

IT,
That Obscure Object of Desire:
On French Anthropology, Museum Visitors, Airplane Cockpits, RDA Online and the Next Generation Catalog

And the first error was, and remains, the belief that the solutions to problems of description and communication were purely technical.—Martine Poulain[1]

Don't let the title fool you like it did the search algorithms that led you to this article. This column is neither about RDA online nor about next generation catalogs. It is about research projects at the *Centre national de la recherche scientifique* (CNRS) and elsewhere in France that have been studying the adoption and appropriation of new information technologies from anthropological, sociological and semiological perspectives for the past two decades. The relevance of that research to the current situation of cataloging in libraries is the topic of this column.

---

[1] Preface to Joëlle Le Marec, *Dialogue ou labyrinthe? La consultation des catalogues informatisés par les usagers.* (Paris: Bibliothèque publique d'information, Centre Georges Pompidou, 1990. Études et recherche): 9.

In 2005 I stumbled upon Victor Scardigli's book *Les sens de la technique* as part of my continuing research on understanding success and failure in the use of technical systems.[2] I liked the book, enough so that I looked around and found a later book of his: *Une anthropologue chez les automates*. That book was the result of a succession of research projects at CNRS: "Socioanthropologie des technologies nouvelles", "Pilote, contrôleur et automate", and "Intégration de la dimension socioculturelle dans la conception et la conduite des avions fortement automatisés".[3] As I read his ethnographic description of cockpit designers, the cockpits they designed and their intentions in designing them as they did, and how those designs were understood, used and sometimes misunderstood, misused and even refused by the intended users of those cockpits, I thought how relevant his research was to studies of library users. Pursueing

---

[2] Victor Scardigli, *Les sens de la technique*. (Paris: Presses universitaires de France, 1992). For an interesting review of Scardigli's book, see Nicholas Nova, "Victor Scardigli, the meaning/direction of technique" on his blog Pasta & Vinegar (viewed 14 October 2011) http://liftlab.com/think/nova/2008/03/27/victor-scardigli-the-meaningdirection-of-technique/ Nova is the author of *Les flops technologique: Comprendre les échecs pour innover* (2011) and *Les médias géolocalisés: Comprendre les nouveaux espaces numériques* (2009), both published by Éditions FYP, Limoges. He writes of himself "I study people's practices as well as usage of technologies and turn them into insights, ideas, prototypes or recommendations to inform design and technology foresight." Another and very different review by Yann Leroux is "L'imaginaire de la technique: Victor Scardigli" on Socialmediatoday. com http://socialmediatoday.com/index.php?q=SMC/113999 (viewed 14 October 2011)

[3] "Automates et anthropologie: Le monde de l'aviation comme société digitale", *CNRS Info* no.392 (Avril 2001), Accessed 14. 10.2011:http://www.cnrs.fr/Cnrspresse/n392/html/n392a07.htm

his work I found a volume coedited by Alain Gras, Bernward Joerges and Scardigli: *Sociologie des techniques de la vie quotidienne*. Inside, not only Gras (whom I already knew and appreciated), but Philippe Breton and David Le Breton as well, two of my favorites. And then I noticed an article on libraries by someone named Joëlle Le Marec.

Looking for more by Le Marec I discovered that she had founded the research group "Communication, Culture et Société" in 2002. The work of her group introduced me to a number of other authors and publications that proved to be equally relevant and interesting: Igor Babou, Cécile Dérioz, Yves Jeanneret, Emmanuel Souchier and others. Some of the names I found associated with this research already carried a lot of weight with me: Isabelle Stengers is listed as a member of the jury of Le Marec's *habilitation*, and Jean-Marc Lévy-Leblond was on the jury of Igor Babou's. There was a special issue of *Hermès* (the journal of the Institut des sciences de la communication du CNRS) devoted to information technology with an article by André Vitalis on Ellul. There were others, like Le Marec herself, Yves Jeanneret and Emmanuel Souchier, whom I soon came to respect just as much. One big surprise was the presence of Oxford linguist Roy Harris; he had been invited to CNRS right at the beginning, and his book *Sémiologie de l'écriture* appears to have had a major impact on thinking about reading and writing, texts and technologies among researchers at CNRS.

The year 1990 is the best place to begin for in that year Le Marec published *Dialogue ou labyrinthe?*, her study of how visitors to the Bibliothèque publique d'information in the Centre Georges Pompidou used its new catalogues Geac and Lise which went public in 1988.[4] Although this may seem to be too outdated to have any bearing on the problems of our plans for 'next-generation catalogs', that is not at all the case. In its time

---

[4] Le Marec, *Dialogue ou labyrinthe?*

her study was a brilliant critique of previous user studies, as Martine Poulain notes in the preface to her book.

In our time Le Marec's study is still a brilliant critique of user studies, but it appears to have been little studied accross the Franco-American divide: for the United States, OCLC listed only the New York Public Library as having a copy when I sought to obtain her book last year (many copies are available in Canadian libraries), and there are now only two copies listed, the other having been purchased by the University of Chicago Library at my request. Many library user surveys and studies of research practices have been published in the United States and Great Britain during the past decade and subsequently studied, promoted and used as the basis for planning and forecasting the future of libraries and library catalogs, yet to my knowledge none of them have cited Le Marec's 1990 study nor any of her subsequent publications on the use of information technologies in scholarly communication. The British Library/JISC report "Researchers of Tomorrow" [5] in fact cites not a single work in any language other than English, and in this it is exactly like the OCLC sponsored study by Palmer, Teffeau and Pirmann.[6] Twenty years of fascinating, brilliant, ground breaking, interdisciplinary and multidisciplinary research on the uses of new in-

---

[5] British Library. *Researchers of Tomorrow: a three year (BL/JISC) study tracking the research behaviour of 'Generation Y' doctoral students. Annual report, 2009-2010.* June 2010. Accessed 20 October at:
http://www.efc.co.uk/projects/rot/RoT%20Year%201%20report%20final%20100622.pdf

[6] Palmer, Carole L.; Teffeau, Lauren C., and Pirmann, Carrie M. *Scholarly Information Practices in the Online Environment: Themes from the Literature and Implications for Library Service Development.* Report commissioned by OCLC Research. Published online and accessed 20 October at:
http://www.oclc.org/research/publications/library/2009/2009-02.pdf

formation technologies in research and scholarly communication, including studies of library catalogues, was simply ignored on this side of the Atlantic.

There have been some interesting survey results and observations published in the United States, but all of them have left me with a feeling that something was wrong. As I read the reports from the Library of Congress Working Group on the Future of Bibliographic Control and the reports from Indiana University and the University of California, the pictures of the library users that these studies presented seemed to me to be too much an artifact of the survey instrument, test design or the researchers' assumptions. When I first read the British Library/JISC report mentioned above it was immediately after reading Le Marec's monographs; I wrote on it throughout "cf. Le Marec." After reading Le Marec, the problems with those two studies were obvious.

If we wish to study the users of libraries and library catalogs what sort of questions ought we to be asking? Of whom? To what degree does the study of library users itself—the questions asked, the subjects interrogated and the manner of that interrogation—determine the object of study? In their study of Geac and Lise, Le Marec's research team decided at the start to "take the point of view of the users and study the system's characteristics through observing the visitors' practices"[7] rather than adopting the methodology of earlier studies. This approach differed from a simple evaluation of the effectiveness of technical systems because it allowed them to avoid making their study a comparison between the new and the old systems. A comparison between the old and the new systems, the team believed, "would easily and almost irresistably be influenced by ideas about the new system that were all the more powerful for not being fully formulated." Chief among those ideas was that "the visitor, thanks to these systems, would be capable of doing everything the old system could do, and better, as well as many more

---

[7] Joëlle Le Marec, *Dialogue ou labyrinthe?*, p.21.

things." Those new capabilities would be "intrinsic to the machine, determined by its design" and could be observed directly in the practices of users.[8] They decided instead to adopt an entirely qualitative methodology and to study not what they thought the new catalog could do, but to observe the actual usage of the library's visitors.

The first point Le Marec makes in her discussion of the results of the study is that the technological object attracted those who came to the library, "very probably increasing the number of users of the library catalog."[9] Some users of the new systems had never used a library catalogue before, and the extreme case of one person interviewed who had no interest in the library but came on the advice of a friend solely in order to try the new technology. The keyboard with a screen, "that obscure object of desire... is not neutral, nor is its placement. ... Before the visitor decides what he is interested in, the new tools are arranged in front of his eyes. The simple fact of having seen them can influence the decision of whether or not to use them."[10]

One of the most interesting discussions in the book concerns the effects of the test on user behaviour. During the first stage of their study the researchers had simply observed and recorded usage, while during the next stage they asked test subjects about the searches they performed and their search strategies.

> During test conditions, the variety of individual approaches that were observed in the first part of the study disappeared. ... In the presence of the researcher, notably, the users often preferred to formulate their query using keywords rather than sequences of words in ordinary syntax [the opposite of what happened during the purely

---

[8] Ibid., p.22.
[9] Ibid., p.27.
[10] Ibid.

observational stage—DB]. ... The test conditions "conditioned" a certain type of procedure: an analytic procedure by stages, explicit and in anticipation of the succesive situations. ... The experiment destroyed what we wanted to observe.[11]

The title of Le Marec's book draws attention to the discrepancy between the user's expecation of a dialogue with the system and the reality of search strategies in a labyrinthine catalog. Thinking of the online catalog in terms of queries and responses prevented the users from realizing the dynamics of the system as one of programmed discontinuities. Interestingly, the help screens of those systems were least likely to be imagined as places of dialogue by the users (p. 50). She suggested that improvements to the system should involve both efforts to prevent the user from misunderstanding their search as a dialogue and efforts to present more clearly to the user information about what is actually happening during the search in order to permit the users to understand better what they have done, what were the results of their actions, and what are the options for proceeding. Not more under-the-hood programming, but more tools, information and guidance out in the open for the users.

In his book *Un anthropologue chez les automates*[12] Victor Scardigli interviewed and studied a very different set of users of information technology—and a very different technology—but what he found nicely complements Le Marec's studies in libraries and museums. The Centre national de la recherche scientifique announced the publication of his book in April 2001 with a short notice in which we read:

---

[11] Ibid., p. 42.
[12] Victor Scardigli. *Un anthropologue chez les automates: de l'avion informatisé à la société numérisée.* (Paris: Presses universitaires de France, 2001)

With the development of cockpit engineering, one aim has been to replace those involved in flight by machines. Automation is spreading : the highly computerized Airbus 320 has already challenged the pilot's superiority inside in the cockpit. Data-link networks could soon connect a large number of planes and decision centers, bringing about a kind of technological sociability between navigation and surveillance computers that would supplant traditional interaction between humans. However, on several occasions, this trend has been thwarted by pilots and controllers. Does the reluctance of the users reveal an irrational, anti-scientific attitude or self-interest ? ...

Two human communities with diverging cultures came to light. When engineers build the technological framework for tomorrow's civilization, they implicitly refer to their own vision of the world, based on an abstract understanding of time and space, accidents and human factors. Distrusting the user's human motivations and weaknesses, they deny his/her expertise and autonomy. ... But the users—and the citizens—of this information society will keep to their own, more composite vision of the world: one where science and intuition, empirically-based expertise and tradition are combined. Flight systems follow the designers' Cartesian logic, which is sometimes quite different from pilots' experience.[13]

In a column such as this I cannot go into the kind of detailed discussion that this book deserves, much less deal with all the related material published by CNRS researchers. What I will do is to offer a fast run through the book by means of my notes

---

[13] "Robots and anthropology," *CNRS Info*, no.392 (English edition, April 2001) Accessed 20 October 2011 at:
http://www.cnrs.fr/Cnrspresse/n392/html/en392a07.htm

on it, most of which were fast and rough translations or abstracts of passages. While reading my notes on Scardigli's book the reader should keep in mind statements emanating from the library world such as the following:

> Nextgen catalogs do not currently have a search algorithm that is robust enough to pull up perfect results every time. This shows that commercial search engines are more advanced than library search engines. It also probably means there are problems with the back-end data.[14]

> Much as I am also irritated by users who don't know a keyword from a hole in the ground, the tendency to blame the user for not knowing how to use a catalog is exactly the kind of thinking that got us into this mess to start with. Yes, users are idiots. But good systems are designed for idiots and help idiots be successful despite their idiocy. That's why Google is so popular, and why catalogs are not. Any tool that requires "instruction" to use is doomed.[15]

> Generation Y doctoral students, in common with others, are quite risk averse and 'behind the curve' in using digital technology, not at the forefront; and this despite the fact that the majority of Generation Y students

---

[14] Jenny Emanuel, "Next Generation Catalogs: what do they do and why should we care?" *Reference & User Services Quarterly* v.49 nr.2 (2010): 117-120 (Accidental technologist column)
[15] Online comment by commentarius - September 29, 2009 at 03:50 pm to the article by Marc Parry, September 28, 2009 "After Losing Users in Catalogs, Libraries Find Better Search Software" *The Chronicle of Higher Education* 56 no. 6 (Oct. 2, 2009) p. A13 Accessed 20 October 2011 at: http://chronicle.com/article/After-Losing-Users-in/48588/

answering the survey and in the cohort appear to be keen users of the latest technology applications in their personal lives.[16]

Perfect results every time, users are idiots, and not adopting the latest technology makes you 'behind the times' rather than an intelligent consumer who does not run after every new commodity available solely because it is available: here we see in splendid honesty the ideological world of technology imagined as the best of all possible worlds (perfect results every time), as that which makes life possible for idiot humans (rather than learning), and rejection of which damns you as a backward opponent of progress and utopia realized. If we abandon these ideological prejudices, the big question, in both airplane and library catalog design, remains how to design systems for intelligent human beings who live in the real world rather than for the imaginary users and systems of an all too human designer.

Scardigli notes in his introduction that his research grew out of a "feeling that the digital paradigm seems stuck, whether by a dominant school of thought or by engineers who have failed to master the complexity of the world but blame the incompetent users instead" (p. 8). In the first chapter "Who is creating the information society?" he notes that digital technologies presuppose that the whole of reality is transformable into quantifiable information; that transformation is not innocent (p. 11). The engineers whom he studied refused or forgot the corporal dimension of the human being in the cockpit, eliminated social relations, and regarded automation as the ultimate object of the information society. He notes that one significant consequence of automation is that it leads to a great distance between any action and the one who planned that action (p. 12). Automation is often seen as a threat to individuals but he found that a more important effect of automation was upon social relations and culture in the anthropological sense (p. 14). Products of technic-

---

[16] British Library, *Researchers of tomorrow*, p.4.

al production are rarely understood as an act of persons within a culture who are realizing a project—technical objects are understood technically but not socially (p. 23). A single logic of power determines the changing techniques for aviation, with each change the engineer gains power over the actual users of the system who become ever more dependent on the designers (p. 29).

In the second chapter "Almost without a pilot" he discusses how in the face of problems and crashes following the installation of automated cockpits aeronautic engineers blamed the pilots: it was not a problem with the technologies but the pilots who did not understand how to use the software or how to dialogue (remember Le Marec!) with the computer; do the actions of the pilots (upon which blame for accidents was placed) reveal the irrationality of the pilots or the discordance between two rationalities of action during the actual conditions of flight (logical versus empirical representations of the world)? The engineers reacted to criticism as injured lovers yet the role of passion and personal involvement was denied in the engineers' description of their role as the working out of a pure disembodied rationality (p. 40). How do cockpit designers respond to the conflict between design for a predictable model and the realities of the unpredictable real world of flight? They claim that there never was a goal of complete automation (i.e. they denied what they advocated when the project was proposed); they suggested that everyone calm down and they would try again; eventually they abandoned working alone and integrated their design efforts with the point of view of the users of the system treating them as equal partners in a man-machine system (p. 41). Every real flight takes place in a reality completely different from that which the designers foresaw and how they thought of their invention (p. 43); the automated systems and their manner of operation are far removed from the pilot's manner of thinking and acting (p. 44). The actions arising from the logic of the system are not entirely predictable in any real world conditions because no one can know exactly what information the system is getting and therefore what actions it will do without the pilot's knowledge; the result is that the pilots are unsure what the system may do: in the user's view those systems became unpredictable and capricious and hence untrustworthy, and this led to pilot associations refusing to use the new systems (i.e. the pilots were rational in rejecting a system that appeared to act irrationally) (p. 45).

Chapter three describes why the design teams brought in pilots to participate in the design. The old cockpits were made for physical beings, persons with bodies of specific dimensions and needs; the new cockpit was made for an immobile intellect, a thinking observer, not an acting body (p. 58). The pilots in the cockpit cannot know the entirety of the information available to the system, whether programmed into it or acquired during operation, yet they are required to master the laws of the system's functioning (p. 61). The history of cockpit automation reveals that the progressive putting into place of the digital society has not been the ineluctible result of a purely technical evolution but rather the result of a human choice underwritten by a project relentlessy pursued: progress towards a different social organization through the complete transformation of a human activity into information (p. 71).

Chapter four, on how engineers think about their work, is based on interviews with cockpit designers. The designer decides what is good and therefore what is bad; he participates in a choice for society, his decision altering the social relations of aeronautics (p. 80). System failures leading to airplane crashes or other accidents are understood in terms of the statistical probabilities of an accident; accidents are normal and expected (cf. Perrow). But when a human is found to be at fault, the accident is no longer normal, no longer a statistical probability but a moral fault, and the pilot is judged according to moral values, not statistical probabilities (p. 91: let us bring this matter into the discussion of metadata!).

Chapter five discusses the various social classes of actors involved in aeronautics. In practice the automated system requires human decision making and this, the engineers argued (again, in interviews), must be done by the control center not the pilot. This, Scardigli notes, is a social organizational revolution and not a technical revolution (p. 116). He quotes an engineer who insisted that the automatic features are a necessity imposed by the performance demands of the clients; the engineers are completely guided by the passengers who are the real driving forces in these technical evolutions. Scardigli remarks that in reality the passengers were never consulted at any time in the design process. The engineer interviewed believed that only the best technical innovations would catch on, that there would be no other options, and that people would have to adapt to the technologies, for the reverse is impossible. The engineers believed that technical innovation will transform society and human beings will adapt to it, as they always do (p. 117).

I will skip over chapter six on the philosophical attitudes of members of the design teams, and go on to chapter seven regarding the sense of mission and ideas about progress of those designers. Boolean algebra is the language of thought and thus the language of God, who is apparently imagined as a pure intelligence (p. 143); the perfect machine requires the elimination of the fallible human actor (p. 152); from the designers' point of view, human communication poses a major problem; accidents are often due to pronunciation errors, translation errors, misinterpretation, inattention; perfect operability demands the elimination of the human factor (p. 153).[17] Technical relations—links —will replace social relations and human communication (p. 154). How relevant is that to the next generation catalog?

---

[17] I have written of parallel developments in the railroad industry in "Signs, language and miscommunication: an essay on train wrecks" *Language Sciences*, v.33 nr.4 (July 2011) p.713-724.

Chapter eight discusses the crisis brought about in the early 1990s by the acknowledgment of the complexity of the real world after the investigation of accidents. The cultural diversity of pilots throughout the world—such as the fact that they did not all speak or read English well or even at all—was finally admitted to be an unavoidable factor in the operation of a global aeronautics communication system (p. 164). Instead of being the guarantee of system safety, automatization had led to an increase in complexity for the pilots—the reverse of what had been claimed and expected; with the increasing complexity of the system even the designers could no longer predict how the system would represent flight conditions to itself, much less how it would represent its own condition to itself, a problem greatly compounded with more and more planes in the same flight space; the problem of complexification and unpredictability follows all technological development in the global information society (p. 169). What was previously regarded as human fallibility came to be understood as human flexibility in a world that was real rather than a designer's model, a flexibility that automation could not supply (p. 170).

The next chapter brings us to the beginning of the network era. Just when the designers had recognized that their failures were due to their inadequate understanding of the users and uses of technology and had not only brought those users back into the design process but began again to design tools in which the human user would be in control, the internet was invented by Al Gore.[18] The book stops shortly thereafter (cerca 1998), pos-

---

[18] This reference to the remark "I took the initiative in creating the Internet" by then United States vice president Al Gore in a 1999 speech was deleted by the editors of *Cataloging and Classification Quarterly* in which this paper was originally published. For readers too young to have lived through this amusing moment in United States history, see:
https://en.wikipedia.org/wiki/Al_Gore_and_information_technology (viewed 30 June 2020). It is a pity that our august Library Science has no sense of humour.

ing questions about how to keep the system user in the center of the design process under those new and developing social and technical conditions. The following chapter "Correspondences" glances around at other areas of technical innovation and attitudes towards users. In a discussion of user-modeling Scardigli notes that it is often argued that in designing human-machine systems artificial agents and non-artifical agents must be conceived according to the same model for they must function together as a system; since the non-artificial agents can only function as purely cognitive systems of information gathering, representation and decision, the human must also be modeled as a purely cognitive system. With that, we are back to 1977 with only a few minor changes (p. 198).

Scardigli addresses a central concern of mine in his concluding chapter. The increasing complexity of technical systems requires that they be trusted rather than understood, and in this they require a belief in magic as a condition of their efficacy (p. 229). Furthermore we have returned, he writes, to a traditional society that is faith-based rather than a society based on scientific evidence and proof because scientific specialization has led to a situation in which no specialist can understand anyone outside his own speciality and so must take what others say based on trust rather than on knowledge. And without that trust, no one would dare make an airplane, much less get on it. New technologies announce an impossibility, Scardigli argues: a human being that is a purely cognitive system, a human being without humanity, deprived of all the values, culture, conscience and emotions of our species. Such a creature, he writes, could neither trust nor use, much less create the technologies whose designers imagine and assume his existence (p. 230). Scardigli's anthropological concerns appear here clearly: the cockpit designers revealed themselves in their interviews to be involved in a grand project of creating a perfect machine, and that machine was a reflection of how they thought of themselves in comparison to the users: without fault and without a mistake strewn history, to which Scardigli added, without reality (p. 231). His conclusion is that our society places a great value on the expertise of the inventors of complex tools, but denies that expertise and any corresponding value to the users of the technologies. Remember the librarian's comment quoted above: "Yes, users are idiots."

That is a great deal of space to devote to Scardigli, so I will stop here rather than discuss other work by him. Almost everything he has discussed in this book as in others[19] has a direct relevance to our work since we work with tools designed for users of libraries, databases and a wide variety of electronic resources. Many of the issues discussed by Scardigli appear in the other research projects which I want to discuss briefly since all these projects—from Le Marec in 1988 to Tardy, Davallon and Jeanneret in 2007, and presumably beyond in works I have not read[20]—focus on users of information technology.

Some of the main issues that I would like to bring into the discussion of cataloging which are brought together in the writings of Le Marec and Scardigli as well as other members of their research groups include understanding cataloging as one form of technical communication, as a part of scholarly communication, as a linguistic practice, as a practice that is carried out in many linguistic and cultural forms, as being part of and heir to centuries of a number of related practices (research, reading,

---

[19] In addition to *Les sens de la technique* mentioned above, see also Victor Scardigli. "Déterminisme technique et appropriation culturelle: l'évolution du regard porté sur les technologies de l'information" *Technologies de l'information et société* v.6 num. 4 (1994) (Technologies de l'information et modes de vie): 299-314 and Victor Scardigli, Marina Maestrutti and Jean-François Poltorak, *Comment naissent les avions: ethnographie des pilotes d'essai* (Paris: L'Harmattan, 2000).

[20] Francis Jaureguiberry and Serge Proulx have just published *Usages et enjeux des technologies de communication* (Ramonville Saint-Agne: Érès, 2011), a book I have ordered but not yet been able to read, but it promises to be well worth reading.

writing, bibliography, quotation, citation) and technologies, and as a practice that must not be thought of as a merely technical procedure but as a fundamentally social practice that is not bound to any particular technology, whether the card catalog or the latest social media. In these research projects carried out for decades in France I have found all of these matters studied in great depth, current ideas and attitudes questioned and challenged, and most importantly everywhere the engagement has been with the actual use of technologies rather than an emphasis on what users could do or what the systems will someday be able to do for us.

The work of Roy Harris has been immensely influential in my understanding of cataloging, and in some of this research his influence is directly evident (i.e. in citation). *Lire, écrire, récrire : Objets, signes et pratiques dans les médias informatisés* edited by Souchier, Jeanneret and Le Marec is a collection of essays on writing and reading using information technologies.[21] The presence of Harris is most marked in the editors' introduction and in the paper by Davallon, Noel-Cadet and Brochu. The latter studied the use of Gallica (the digital library of the National Library of France) by looking at how other web sites linked to it and how they put those links in context.[22] Users of Gallica who provided links to it on their web pages always did so with accompanying description directed at particular kinds of users for particular kinds of uses. This, the authors noted, contrasted markedly with the manner in which the contents of Gallica were listed on the Gallica site itself, i.e. it was designed for a generic user present only in the minds of the system's designers. Usage

---

[21] Emmanuël Souchier, Yves Jeanneret, Joëlle Le Marec (sous la direction de) *Lire, écrire, récrire: objets, signes et pratiques des médias informatisés*. (Paris: Bibliothèque publique d'information, 2003) (Études et recherche).

[22] Jan Davallon, Nathalie Noel-Cadet, and Danièle Brochu, *"L'usage dans le texte: les "traces d'usage" du site Gallica."* In: Souchier, et al. *Lire, écrire, récrire*, p.47-89

of a digital library reveals that the semiotic, social and technical are present equally in the objects mediated as in the social practices of the users. One of the conclusions in this paper was that when studying the usage of digital libraries if we look at usage from the dynamic point of view of the users rather than the static point of view represented in the system design then our understanding of the functioning of a website must be completely revised (p. 80). They offer a critical perspective on an approach to digital libraries that understands the media object as fashioning the practices in which it is involved.

Also in that collection is a paper by Babou and Le Marec, "De l'étude des usages à une théorie des 'composites': objets, relations et normes en bibliothèque" [From the study of use to a theory of 'composites': objects, relations and norms in the library].[23] The notion of 'composite' was developed at greater length in Le Marec's habilitation.[24] Composites are "situations in which individuals mobilise the significance of material objects and representations, acting upon them and putting into action systems of norms or regulations all at the same time." The situation the authors studied: catalogers at work. This is a unique, iconoclastic and brilliant study of catalogers as professionals from a semiotic and ethnological perspective. Just a glimpse until someone translates it and publishes it in CCQ:

> Ethnology furnishes us with keys for interpretation. The question regarding the relation to change in societies as

---

[23] Joëlle Le Marec and Igor Babou, "De l'étude des usages à une théorie des 'composites' : objets, relations et normes en bibliothèque", in : Emmanuel Souchier, Yves Jeanneret and Joëlle Le Marec (eds.), *Lire, écrire, récrire - objets, signes et pratiques des médias informatisés*, p. 233-299. Available at: http://hal.archives-ouvertes.fr/docs/00/15/91/80/PDF/composites.pdf

[24] Joëlle Le Marec. *Ce que le "terrain" fait aux concepts: vers une thérie des composites.* Habilitation à diriger des recherches, Université Paris 7, Cinéma, communication et information, 9 mars 2002.

posed in certain works could help us escape from the narrow perspectives of the sociology of innovation that are focused on the effects of technological changes in the wake of information technologies. The attitudes of actors in the face of change brought about by the introduction of networks could be seen otherwise than as reactions to that innovation in terms of resistance or acceptance. Ethnology allows us to avoid adhering *a priori* to a conception of change as being either naturally positive or technological in its very nature: it puts the practices and the institutions studied in larger spatial and temporal perspectives.[25]

In their conclusion they ask whether anyone would take seriously an effort to write a sociology of pencils in order to analyze writing practices in libraries. Certainly not, but we are doing the same thing when we focus on information technology as a technical object and with that object as a given we proceed to examine library practices involving those objects. Their point is that a pencil was never a purely technical object but was used in many social practices, and the same is true of our technologies today. We must stop making the technologies the central object of study and the unit of analysis and make the users and their practices the focus of our attention. And we will find, as they did, that penciled messages on post-it notes affixed to computers plays as important a role in everyday practice as do the new information technologies. And that, they insist, is not resistance to change but effective adaptation to the capabilities and limits of each of the technologies available for us to use. Brilliant!

Yves Jeanneret's *Y-a-t-il (vraiment) des technologies de l'information?*[26] is simply stunning. In this book Jeanneret

---

[25] Ibid., from the online version, p. 4.
[26] Yves Jeanneret. *Y a-t-il (vraiment) des technologies de l'information?* (Villeneuve d'Ascq: Presses Universitaires du Septentrion, 2007). Unfortunately I took notes on the 2000

shows how radically Harris's integrationist semiology can transform our understanding of communication technologies. In addition to Harris, his bibliography includes references to Souchier, David Olson and Alessandro Zinna, three other scholars who draw upon Harris's work. His book includes numerous discussions of library catalogs, databases, search engines, metadata for image retrieval and the use of documents in archival research, as well as asking some very important questions about digitization, interactivity, intuitive design and transparence. His discussion of the semiological differences between library catalogs and search engines on pages 68-70 is excellent, and a later discussion of the communicational presuppositions of databases is wonderful.

Written under the direction of Jeanneret, Dominique Cotte's thesis *Des médias au travail* deals in part with one of the great problems that RDA has attempted to address: the separation of form, content and context in digital documents. In traditional semiology, signs and messages are considered a unity of form and content; this is in contrast to digital documents which are commonly understood in information science to involve a content—a "work" in FRBR terms—that can be packaged, formatted, displayed or realized in any number of forms (manifestations, expressions, items). On this matter Cotte finds Harris's work of considerable importance:

> That question of the document in itself raises in turn a methodological problem to which we shall return. Even though it does not deal with documents as such, the integrational semiology of Harris is of great interest in so far

---

edition borrowed through interlibrary loan but the copy I now have available, like the copy available in part via GoogleBooks is the 2007 volume. Because my notes are in English and the pagination in the two editions differs, apart from the one section on cataloging and search engines, I cannot now relocate all the passages I wanted to discuss. The topics are in there, but you will have to find them yourself.

as it considers the material support/form as being an integral part of the message and of the object of study. Harris thus opposes a semiology that would "understand [writing] simply as the expression of a message" to "a semiology in which writing is conceived as the textualisation of an object".[27]

To this Cotte adds that it is also "a textualisation of practices (but aren't the objects also the petrified remains of preceding practices?)". He quotes Harris:

> From the integrational point of view, the second option is necessary since it is impossible to analyse the integration of a message by itself in social life. In fact, the "message itself", the pure message, the message stripped bare, without material support, without author and without intended destination does not exist except as the product of an intellectual operation which makes of it an abstraction, ignoring everything pertaining to human communication.[28]

Cotte finds that Harris's understanding of the context of a message as including its integration into social practices "resonates greatly today with the disarticulation of the document in what we call digital documents. The question ... of the 'separation of form/context' in XML could be fruitfully studied from the perspective of Harris's contextual semiology."[29] That, in fact, is what I have been saying—and doing—for the past de-

---

[27] Dominique Cotte. *Des médias au travail: emprunts, transferts, métamorphoses*. Mémoire pour l'habilitation à diriger des recherches. Université d'Avignon et des pays du Vaucluse. 5 ovembre 2007: 69.
[28] Roy Harris. *La sémiologie de l'écriture*. (Paris: CNRS, 1993): 370 (quoted in Cotte, *Des médias au travail*, p.69).
[29] Cotte, *Des médias au travail,* p.69-70.

cade. For readers unfamiliar with Harris's semiology, let me add that his perspective is that of the speaker/writer, the one communicating in the act of communication using any of the available resources and means of communication; it is not the perspective of language, information or documents as systems of signs existing in themselves, whether mashed up, linked to or floating freely in the noosphere. And the semiology of human communication using technical systems has everything to do with FRBR, RDA and library catalogs of this, the next, or any other generation.

Harris's influence appears in a number of papers written or co-written by Emmanuël Souchier, such as "Citer, indexer ou cartographier" co-written with I. Garron and J.-L. Minel, in which the central topic is the question of citation in the logic of internet writing.[30] In "Les medias informatises comme organisation des pratiques de savoir" three professors of information science—Tardy, Davallon and Jeanneret—argue that the process of computer mediated communication constantly transforms what it is supposed to represent and therefore we must not think about knowledge organization using digital media as the simple production and use of an unchanging object understood as the content of communication: assumptions regarding possible use and effective utilization shape the whole of the communication through its transformations in use.[31] Laurence Schmoll discusses

---

[30] Isabelle Garron, Jean-Luc Minel, Emmanuël Souchier, "Citer, indexer ou cartographier? De la circulation et de la lecture des textes relatifs à une œuvre littéraire sur internet," in: *Indice, index, indexation : actes du colloque international organisé les 3 et 4 novembre 2005 à l'université de Lille-3 par les laboratoires CERSATES et GERICO* / Ismaïl Timini, Susan Kovacs (coordinateurs). (Paris : Association des professionnels de l'information et de la documentation (ADBS)) , v. 1 (2006): 163–174. Available at:
http://hal.archives-ouvertes.fr/docs/00/08/28/52/PDF/ArticleFinal_IG_JLM_ES.pdf
[31] Cécile Tardy, Jean Davallon and Yves Jeanneret, "Les médias informatisés comme organisation des pratiques de savoir," in

user models of readers revealed in pedagogically oriented internet sites, looking specifically at sites oriented towards teaching French as a foreign language,[32] and Nathalie Noel-Cadet offers a sociological view of usage of museum multimedia internet sites, examining three types of mediation: interactive, simulated and virtual.[33]

Jacques Perriault has been around a long time; his book *Éléments pour un dialogue avec l'informaticien* was published in 1971 and in it are references to even earlier publications. Of particular interest to me for this column are two papers published in the journal *Hermès* published by CNRS in 2004 and 2006 respectively[34], and his 1989 monograph *La logique de l'usage: essai sur les machines à communiquer*.[35] The two papers deal

---

Organisation des connaissances et société des savoirs : concepts, usages, acteurs. 6e colloque international du Chapitre français de l'ISKO, 7-8 juin 2007 (2007): 169-184. Available at: http://www.isko-france.asso.fr/pdf/isko2007/Actes%20ISKO%20FR%202007%20p%20169-184.pdf

[32] Laurence Schmoll. "Le lecteur modèle des concepteurs de sites Internet pédagogiques" *Revue des Sciences Sociales*, no.36 (2006) (Écrire les sciences sociales): 68-75. Available at: http://www.theleme-lejeu.com/news/_uploads/scient-schmolll-2006-lecteursitespedag.pdf

[33] Nathalie Noel-Cadet. "La médiation comme mode d'approche des usages de l'Internet" In: *X° Colloque bilatéral franco-roumain, CIFSIC Université de Bucarest, 28 juin–3 juillet 2003*, (2003) Accessed 19 October 2011 at:
http://archivesic.ccsd.cnrs.fr/sic_00000737/fr/

[34] Jacques Perriault, "Le numérique: une question politique," *Hermès*, nr.38 (2004): 183-189; Jacques Perriault, "La norme comme instrument d'accès au savoir en ligne," *Hermès* nr.45 (2006):77-87.

[35] Jacques Perriault. *La logique de l'usage: essai sur les machines à communiquer*. (Paris: Flammarion, 1989).

with norms and standards in a global and digital information system as political issues, with particular reference to online education and online access to knowledge. Short, critical discussions of metadata standards among others, by someone who understands that technological issues in a global system are always political issues. Regarding the earlier book, I shall here limit my remarks to a translation of an excerpt from the publisher's blurb on the cover of the book:

> Inventors have never ceased to imagine machines for producing artificial objects to listen to and view. Such were the magic lantern and the phonograph. Such are today's high definition television and compact discs. Faced with these discoveries, the public is always disrespectful. They rarely respect the intentions of the technicians and often divert the device from its original (intended) function.
> Precursor of what is now called ethnotechnology, Jacques Perriault narrates here the history of these practices and demonstrates that the manner in which communication technologies are used is in fact progressively constructed. In opposition to the logic of the technician, users are nevertheless not incoherent. Beyond the rejections and diversions, they follow and produce a singular logic: the logic of use.

This is Scardigli before Scardigli, or perhaps Scardigli's mentor; in either case his book, like Scardigli's and Le Marec's, will hopefully become part of the discussion on the future of our library catalogs, digital libraries and all future technical developments.

Another book with considerable interest for those interested in library users is the collective monograph *Premiers usages des*

Cédéroms de musées.[36] Joëlle Le Marec is one of the authors of this study, and as one might expect, it includes comparisons between the use of CDRoms in museums and online library catalogs. Some of their findings and conclusions were:

- The relations that the users establish with the CD means it is used differently—not instead of—other media such as books, videos, etc.;
- Of the first time users who tried out the CDs in the museum NONE wanted to buy the CDs after using them. Why? Access too complicated, too difficult, the structure of access was not transparent, the significance of the order or organization was not evident and gave first time users the impression of incoherence, CDs were more time consuming than a book, both to use and to consult. The authors suggest that this reveals a complete disconnect between the advertised and commonly believed image of CDRoms as easy, interactive and with greater content and the reality as the users described it.
- The practice of not using a CD "comes with" the technology itself, for all usage is constructed by the users.
- When the user has an actual project (rather than being a casual or merely curious visitor to the museum), the intentions of the designers and the assumptions about the future users and the structure of the contents are simply ignored or circumvented/surmounted by the user who makes it do what he or she wants to do. On the other hand, for users without a specific project the structure of the CD—aleatory, non-linear, unconnected bits of information—defeats the user. The technical difficulties are

---

[36] Jean Davallon, Hana Gottesdiener, Joëlle Le Marec, avec la collaboration de David Cohen, Loïc Étiembre, Natacha Godrèche. *Premiers usages des Cédéroms de musées: pratiques et représentations d'un produit innovant.* (Dijon: OCIM, 2000).

irrelevant to the user with a project; they are insurmountable for the user with no real purpose.

- The users were nearly unanimous in complaining about the lack of information about the content of the CDRom, what kind of usage it was made to support, what you could do with it (print, etc.), how to navigate, etc. The information that was there was information intended to promote sales, not to inform the potential users.

I began with Le Marec, and I would like to close with further remarks on her 2007 monograph *Publics et musées*,[37] followed by brief notes on a number of other papers by her, Igor Babou and others. *Publics et musées* takes us well beyond the concerns of *Dialogue ou labyrinthe?*, discussing the educational role of museums, popularization and communication in science. In putting these concerns together she puts back together the fractured world perspectives arising from the social and cultural divisions created and fostered by science and professionalism. This is a matter of extraordinary importance for me as a librarian; this was in fact an early intuition of mine that studying the works of Carlo Revelli suddenly made clear: cataloging is not an autonomous activity. Librarians often appear to think—at least they often speak and write—as if what they are engaged in is simply providing access to information, as though the information itself is no more their concern than why library users want it and what they do with it once they have it. In contrast, museums have always had an educational mission and hire scientists to work in them and not just people with museum studies degrees. She explores museum users in relation to those social practices, frequently relating her discussion to libraries as well. Unlike her 1990 book, this book is *au courant*; like her earlier book it is brilliant. Let me demonstrate.

---

[37] Joëlle Le Marec, *Publics et musées: la confiance éprouvée*. (Paris: L'Harmattan, 2007).

User surveys, she complains on page 110, often seem to ask questions as though the practices being investigated are autonomous, i.e. going to the library has no necessary relation to the fact that libraries already exist. The purpose of the institution is sought through the survey questions when in fact it is the existence of the institution and the purposes for which it was established that creates the practices associated with library use. Studies of library and museum use almost always forget that.

If that did not make you cry for joy, the last paragraph in her book ought at least to make you cry in despair:

> Throughout all the surveys, those in the past as well as the present, the publics surveyed expressed a faith in the museum as an institution and in the quality of what they could expect, and that result contrasted strongly with the disenchanted visions circulating among the musem professionals.[38]

The disenchanted visions she mentions occupy a large part of the discussion in her book, and they are, to state it briefly, that museum administrators think of their institutions as players in a market and library/museum visitors as consumers (sound familiar?). Yet none of the users Le Marec's team interviewed thought of themselves as consumers. They did not come to buy, they came to learn.

Between her 1990 and 2007 monographs Le Marec published a number of papers devoted to library and museum use,[39]

---

[38] Joëlle Le Marec, *Publics et musées*, p. 204.

[39] Joëlle Le Marec, "L'usage et ses modèles : quelques réflexions méthodologiques," *Spirale* n° 28 (2001): 105-122; Joëlle Le Marec. "Imaginaire d'usage et informatique: le public de la bibliothèque publique d'information du centre Georges-Pompidou," in Alain Gras, Bernward Joerges and Victor Scardigli (eds.), *Sociologie des techniques de la vie quotidienne*, (Paris: l'Harmattan, 1992): 227-232; Joëlle Le Marec, "Le public : définitions et représentations," *Bulletin des Bibliothèques de France* n° 46, v. 2 (2001): 50-55; Joëlle Le

including four papers on the topic of interactivity.[40] With Igor Babou she has published a paper on librarians at work[41] and several papers on communication in science in the context of libraries, museums and their publics.[42] Two other items that I

Marec, "Le musée à l'épreuve des thèmes sciences et société : les visiteurs en public," *Quaderni* n° 46 (2002): 105-122; Joëlle Le Marec, "Usages: pratiques de recherche et théorie des practiques", *Hermès*, nr.38 (2004): 141-147.

[40] Joëlle Le Marec. "L'interactivité, rencontre entre visiteurs et concepteurs" *Publics et musées*, no. 3 (1993) (Du public aux visiteurs): 91-109; Le Marec, Joëlle, "Interactivité et multimédia : lieux communs revisités par l'usage," *Rencontres médias 2: Aspects des nouvelles technologies de l'information* (1997-1998), Editions du centre Georges Pompidou, Paris; Jean Davallon and Joëlle Le Marec, "L'usage en son contexte - Sur les usages des interactifs et des cédéroms de musées," *Réseaux* n° 101 (2000): 173-196; Le Marec, Joëlle, "Dialogue interdisciplinaire sur l'"interactivité", *Communication et Langages* n° 128 (2001): 97-110.

[41] Joëlle Le Marec and Igor Babou. "Transformation des pratiques de lecture, écriture a l'heure des reseaux: objets, relations et normes dans le travail des bibliothécaires" in: Emmanuel Dreyer and Patrick Le Floch (eds.), *Le lecteur: approche sociologique, économique et juridique*, (Paris: L'Harmattan, 2004): 113-122.

[42] Babou, Igor et Le Marec, Joëlle, "Nova Atlantis - Manifeste pour une utopie baconienne en sciences humaines et sociales," *Alliage* n° 47 (2001): 3-10; Joëlle Le Marec and Igor Babou, "Sciences et médias : le champ « STS » à l'épreuve de la banalité," *Actes du colloque Sciences, médias et société*, (Lyon: ENS LSh - Laboratoire Communication, Culture et Société, 2005). http://sciences-medias.ens-lyon.fr/IMG/pdf/LeMarec_Babou.pdf; Joëlle Le Marec and Igor Babou, "Words and figures of the public: the misunderstanding in scientific communication," in: D. Cheng et al. (eds.) *Communicating Science in Social Contexts*, (Springer Science+Business Media, 2008): p. 39-54; Joëlle Le Marec and Serge Chaumier, "Évaluation muséale: Hermès ou les contraintes de la richesse," *La Lettre de l'OCIM*, nr.126 (2009): 7-14.
http://hal.archives-ouvertes.fr/docs/00/47/22/83/PDF/20100217122351447.pdf

want to mention are Cécile Derioz's thesis on the role of the public in organizational change in libraries and museums, a thesis directed by Joëlle Le Marec, and a special issue of the journal *Culture et musées* edited by Le Marec: *Évolution des rapports entre sciences et société au musée: dispositifs, discours, énonciation, publics.*[43]

All of the work discussed in this column is remarkably consistent in its focus on users and uses of information technologies; I could add quite a few more items if I thought the editor would let me get away with it. Reflections on Souchier's work on writing alone could bring some startling insights into the theory and practice of cataloging. But I could not cram everything interesting into one column—that is why it is a continuing column.

Scardigli's work in particular has an extraordinary importance for understanding current debates regarding cataloging because of the attitudes towards the users of technologies in libraries held by many of the important voices in the cataloging community. Exactly like the engineers whom Scardigli interviewed, many in the library cataloging community have a faith in computers that goes hand in hand with a devaluation and contempt for human abilities. Intner, for instance, wrote the following in 1990:

> I believe the fullness and accuracy in records produced by machines will far outstrip those in records produced by humans in most library cataloging departments ... If cataloging were removed from the hands of well-

---

[43] Cécile Dérioz. *Les publics: facteurs d'évolutions? Changements organisationnels dans les musées et les bibliothèques.* Diplôme de conservateur de bibliothèque. École nationale supérieure des sciences de l'information et des bibliothèques, Mémoire d'étude, mars 2008. http://www.enssib.fr/bibliotheque/documents/dcb/derioz-dcb16.pdf; Joëlle Le Marec (ed.), *Évolution des rapports entre sciences et société au musée: dispositifs, discours, énonciation, publics* (*Culture et musées*, no. 10) (Actes sud, 2007).

meaning but unschooled library staff and put into the realm of automatic computerized production, it would improve immediately. Between trusting a host of different humans with different educations, backgrounds, biases, and capabilities or a host of different computers all running the same expertly-programmed system to do the best job of cataloging, I'll bet on the computer every time.[44]

Intner's antihumanism of the early 1990's is not an embarassing relic of past ignorance but may be found throughout recent discussions of metadata, linked data and the semantic web which, we are told, is the future for library resource discovery. Certainly linked data and the semantic web will have some part in our future if for no other reasons than that they are being promoted to the exclusion of all other possibilities by most of the professionals with any power to influence local decision making and national policy. The question is whether those planning our organizational structures and designing our technical systems see themselves like the designers of airplane cockpits as designing systems that will in and by themselves produce perfect results through the elimination of the unpredictable and variable human actors who have been the primary forces behind the working of libraries and their catalogs to date. Another question is whether these systems being planned and designed are being designed for the real users studied by Scardigli, Le Marec and their colleagues, or whether they are being designed according to some user model as out of touch with reality as were the technicians and administrators interviewed by Scardigli and Le Marec. We do know that the system of bibliographical control advocated by the Library of Congress Working Group on the Future of Bibliographic Control is one in which machines are expected to be the "primary users":

---

[44] Sheila S. Intner, "Copy Cataloging and the Perfect Record Mentality." *Technicalities*, 10: 7 (July 1990): 14.

Further development of standards will be based on evidence arising from changing use patterns. The library community will realize that bibliographic data need to support a variety of user, management, and machine needs. In particular, it will be recognized that human users and their needs for display and discovery do not represent the only use of bibliographic metadata; instead, to an increasing degree, machine applications are their primary users. Data will be designed and developed with this in mind.[45]

To claim that machines are users is simply to ignore the fact that people are using those machines to do something: the machines follow instructions according to their human user's purposes, and those humans are living and acting in the real world, not the world of any user model or semantic web—unless, of course, we are designing for the semantic web's perfect user, the spammer. Judging from the report's bibliography none of the members of the Working Group read anything discussed in this column nor anything published in French (or any language other than English); whether they could or not therefore being a moot point. Is there any excuse for such an ignorance on the part of American library leaders? Of course anyone who thinks that the whole world is following their lead has no need to read English, much less French.

The cultural conflict examined throughout all of the publications discussed above is that between two clearly defined and extraordinarily homogenous social groups that deals with models and simulacra and an ever increasing power—programmers and managers—and another extremely heterogeneous group—more exactly groups—of persons who for diverse

---

[45] *On the Record: Report of The Library of Congress Working Group on the Future of Bibliographic Control, January 9, 2008.* http://www.loc.gov/bibliographic-future/news/lcwg-ontherecord-jan08-final.pdf

reasons wish to or are obliged to use the tools developed and imposed by the first two groups and who are all of them increasingly losing control over their own activities as giant corporations and institutions determine what tools will be designed and how and for what purposes. It is not just class antagonism and the expropriation of the means of production that is evident in this move to eliminate freedom—sorry, I mean fallibility—but an ideological project for the development of a clockwork world that the theists once imagined God had created. The theists were confronted with the real world thereby necessitating the invention of theodicy, an explanation for why such nasty things happen in God's perfect world. Today's believers in the superiority of their own creations, like the theologians of yesterday, are sure to blame Adam and Eve—and catalogers—for any and all problems that follow upon the implementation of the Next Generation Catalog. That much is entirely predictable.

XIV

Technology waits for no one? Thinking about technology, progress and responsibility in academic librarianship[1]

Not long ago a computer scientist associated with the Bamboo project gave a talk at the University of Chicago in which he described that project. He proudly noted that while many of the professors who had heard him describe the project had initially been sceptical, after viewing his demonstration they had fervently embraced—and I use his own words—the "magic" and the "miracles" that flow from Bamboo.

I have long thought that one of the persistent problems in librarianship is a widespread misunderstanding of information technologies. The discourse surrounding library technologies reveals desires and expectations appropriate to the marketing associated with them but rarely the critical reflection appropriate to an academic institution. In the library literature critics are either ignored, footnoted but not discussed, or attacked as being conservatives, luddites or Don Quijotes.

Computer scientists and information scientists are those who ought to have the clearest understanding of computers and information technologies; when we find them

---

[1] From a talk at UIUC Progressive Librarians Guild, 21 April 2008.

engaged in the marketing of magic and miracles we know that they are intellectually on the same level as Jimmy Swaggart. I do not exagerate: to speak of magic and miracles is to proclaim one's incapacity to understand, or, in the case of the salesman, the will to mystify and deceive, like the proverbial hucksters and charlatans dealing in snake-oils and psychic or religious healing. Unfortunately our Bamboo salesman was not an isolated freak; he seems to be representative not only of salesman-engineers like Bill Gates, Nicholas Negroponte and David Weinberger, but of many librarians as well.

Andrea Mercado's hoped-for library school assumes that neither I nor George Steiner are capable of using the library, much less helping others use it. Her library will be run by tech-savvy marketers, not scholars. This is the heart of my interest and I have stated it before: the divorce between the practices academic libraries are supposed to support, and the widespread attitude that librarians are professionaly occupied with knowing how to use information technologies, or worse, they (we) are simply information providers. I begin with a basic assumption: given a particular practice such as research in the sciences or humanities, the development and use of tools to support those practices requires a knowledge of those practices, not simply familiarity with the operating manual of some tool, whether online catalog, printed index or a Web2.0 application.

George Steiner recently argued that progress in the "hard" sciences and technology (technosciences, Hottois would say, since he claims they are now inseparable) opens new paths into the future, while progress in the humanities and social sciences leads to deeper understanding of the past, which is to say of ourselves. Part of that work of understanding must be understanding technology, not just past technologies, but today's and our imaginations for tomorrow's as well. Only when we understand can we decide whether or not some change is progress or regress. Yet our understanding of what happens today will certainly change as the consequences of today's actions gradually unfold. Like the inventors of DDT, the inventors of information technologies have almost no grasp of what they are actually doing and what these technologies will mean to future generations. Our understanding can never be "once and for all" because the future will reveal what we could not imagine, much less know, today.

Both the development and use of technologies require some understanding of technologies, human beings, human society, nature and how all these jointly shape and change the world. Most of those understandings are unconcious, unstated, unexamined and immensely consequential. To leave those assumptions unexamined simply means that we can never speak of progress, nor of regress, but only of change, stripped of all evaluation and interpretation. The practices of philosophy, the social and ecological sciences and humanistic scholarship are oriented towards bringing to light those assumptions, examining them, and criticising them in light of the philosopher's, the scientist's and the scholar's theories. These in turn are undeniably shaped by desires, hopes, ethical, political and metaphysical assumptions, commitments and intellectual or pathological orientations. Dissent and debate arise more often out of these latter desires and orientations than out of theory because our lives matter to us in ways that theories never can.

For Hottois, Virilio and Ellul the development and use of technologies of any sort must be accompanied by critical examination from as many perspectives as life provides. Without that critical activity, we shall be submitting ourselves blindly to a truly archaic servitude; technology as a "god" is far more cruel and inhuman than the divinities, priests, kings and tyrants of the past precisely because of the power and efficacy of our technologies. It is not by accident that this activity—critical inquiry in pursuit of understanding—happens to be—or at least formerly was—the *raison d'être* for the existence of the academic library. And I argue and urge that librarianship be firmly rooted in that activity and not simply a chase to learn how to use the latest or the most popular technologies on the market. As Andrew Abbott put it, " the future of serious library scholarship lies in a critically constructive and intense engagement with technology, not a running from it or a welcoming embrace." Librarianship always involves an interpretation, a symbolic accompaniment of technologies, not simply their use.

"Technology waits for no one" Ms. Mercado claims, but technology is not going anywhere. WE are going somewhere, even if we do not know where, and we make technologies to aide us in doing what it is that we want to do. It is that "we" that we must not forget, for it is that same "we" that brings us both GoogleBooks and the Gulag. Among librarians, discussions of the Internet, the Semantic Web, Library2.0 and so on are all too often evidence that we are not engaged in the lucid, critical examination of our ideas and their incarnation in technologies and techniques, but rather irrationally and archaically enslaved to the magic and miracles hawked in the marketplace.

[The following passages were handed out prior to the meeting to serve as the basis of discussion.]

I

Vico: De antiquissima Italorum sapientia ex linguae latinae originibus eruenda libri tres

Verum et factum convertuntur. (The true and the made are convertible)

Verum esse ipsum factum. (The norm of the truth is to have made it, or: The true is precisely what is made)

[Commentary by Verene: The true for Vico is something that is made by mind, the principle of human or divine knowledge. Making, for Vico, is combining elements into a whole. the whole may be a word, an idea, or a thing. As legere (to read) is to combine written elements into words, so intelligere (to understand) is to combine in mind all the parts of a thing in order to express the most perfect idea of it. ... God knows completely because God's mind reads and combines all the elements of things in terms of both their inner nature and their outer appearance. The human mind, because it does not make the actual nature of the things it knows, never can understand things fully. What is true for the human mind is made by combining the elements of things in their outward existence.]

II

Marx: Thesen über Feuerbach, #11
Die Philosophen haben die Welt nur verschieden *interpretiert*; es kömmt darauf an, sie zu *verändern*. (The philosophers have only interpreted the world, in various ways: the point, however, is to change it.)

III.

Ellul: Changer de révolution
Automation, cybernetisation and informatics: these aspects of technical progress carry to the extreme the contradiction, i.e. the fact that these means are now leading to an absolute concentration, a control of all, a determinism, an impossibility for a human being to remain a free individual. But perhaps also to present the contrary. Microcomputers, videos, etc. are extraordinarily individualising instruments that would permit the diffusion of tasks and independence... But here again this is not possible under capitalism: it must come about that social structures change, the interests of money eradicated, founded upon the free speech of the individual...

IV

Illich: Computer literacy and the cybernetic dream
For S., a statement is an utterance; behind each utterance there is somebody who means what she says. ... For F., words are units of information that he strings together into a message. ... As the two mind-sets confront each other, both can harden into ideologies. ... For the anti-computer fundamentalists a trip

through computerland, and some fun with controls, is a necessary ingredient for sanity in this age. Those of you who study computer literacy sometimes forget its importance as a means of exorcism against the paralyzing spell the computer can cast. But I know many F.s who, under this spell, have turned into zombies, a danger Maurice Merleau-Ponty clearly foresaw almost thirty years ago. He then said—and I quote—that "cyberneticism has become an ideology. In this ideology human creations are derived from natural information processes, which in turn have been conceived on the model of man-as-a-computer." In this mind-state, science dreams up and "constructs man and history on the basis of a few abstract indices" and for those who engage in this dreaming "man in reality becomes that *manipulandum* which he takes himself to be."

V

Steiner: My unwritten books.

It is the seemingly wasteful plethora of languages which allows us to articulate alternatives to reality, to speak freedom within servitude ... Without the great octave of possible grammars such negation and "alterity," this wager on tomorrow would not be feasible. ...

The true catastrophe at Babel is not the scattering of tongues. It is the reduction of human speech to a handful of planetary, "multinational" tongues. This reduction, formidably fuelled by the mass market and information technology, is now reshaping the globe. ...

The most compendious of dictionaries is no more than an abridged shorthand, obsolete even as it is published. ... speech is molded by gender. Women and men often do not purpose or signify the same thing when uttering or writing the identical word. Not taking "No" for an answer is a symbolic pointer. Shifts in meaning and intentionality within and across generations are constant. ... This looks to be so in our accelerated present, between age groups separated by the very mechanics of

information. Thus different levels in society, different localities, genders, age groups can come close to mutual incomprehension. The fountain pen does not speak to the iPod. ...
In essence the political is the negation of the private, although it may well be its enabling framework. ... Questionaires, officious documents to be filled out, the rampant vulgarities of interviewers and inquisitors, the "candid camera," and the yapping of the phone seem to me to be the nightmare unleashed by the technologies of information. Bear in mind the meanings of the term "informer." In the name of clinical efficacy, of national security, of fiscal transparency our private lives are scrutinized, recorded and manipulated. Concomitantly, the arts of solitude, of guarded discretion, of that inviolate silence which Pascal placed at the heart of true civility and adulthood have withered.

VI

Virilio: Un paysage d'événements.

Here we see the shift that happens, in a liberal state, from direct political responsability to "substitute agents", first bureaucratic substitutes, then technocratic, and finally techno-managers in a system of experts; and ahead, 5th generation computers, AI and the installation of *expert systems* in Japan and the USA capable of themselves making the decisions required in certain urgent situations where time for responsible human reflection (civil or military) is lacking.

[I read and translated this from the French version because this and several other chapters were omitted from the English translation. As is so often the case, this was nowhere indicated, not in the book nor in the publisher's information nor in the bibliographic record in OCLC. Only the last of these problems was I able to do anything about.]

VII

Breton: Le culte de l'internet: une menace pour le lien social?
The advocates of "Internet-for-everything"

The first position is defended by those who employ all their energy in developing the Internet and trying to apply it to every aspect of our lives, private, public and professional. These are the prophets of "Internet for everything". They have only one vision of the future: a world in which the new information technologies will be the new center, an invasive center since it will be everywhere. The Internet is the object of a true cult in this circle.

As one of them enthusiastically said, "cosmic history [...] is oriented, it possesses a completely discernable meaning, which is the intensification of the virtual character of the world. [...] The borders of the world will become more permeable, malleable, interactive, they will burgeon in every sense. Cosmic and cultural evolution today culminate in the virtual world of cyberspace"[2].

They do not hesitate to speak of a "new world" which they oppose to the old that will disappear. This virtual world, that of the network, also called "cyberspace" due to its origin in cybernetics, will progressively displace the archaic "real world". Still the defense of "Internet for everything" can be made in the name of many sensibilities.

At the center one finds those that often have a prophetic style and give the movement its meaning. It is often from among intellectuals of the lineage of McLuhan that the militants of the information society, and then the Internet have arisen. Their position is impregnated with religiosity. For example, one finds in this camp the Frenchmen Pierre Lévy and Philippe Quéau. It is among the ranks of these that one finds the fundamentalists of the Internet.

---

[2] Pierre Lévy, *World philosophie, op. cit.*, p. 160.

The first is the author of a number of works in which the mystical accents are increasingly evident. His influence on the Internet milieu is important. His last book, a passionate argument in favor of a "world philosophy"[3] is a good synthesis of certain beliefs of that milieu.

The second is supported by his position as director of the informatics and information division of UNESCO in his attempts to convince the fools who "still have not seen" that a "new metaphysical revolution" is in progress, where "the real becomes completely language", therefore information, and where, thanks to cyberspace, "a perfect identity of map and territory" will be achieved.[4]

These two authors crystallize what is thought in general in new information technology circles, by those who often see themselves as the bearers of values and a mission vis-à-vis the rest of humanity. If all the enthusiastic advocates of the Internet do not feel themselves invested with such prophetic visions, these two offer nonetheless a philosophical background accepted and assumed by many in more or less vulgarized forms. They constitute the "Internet worldview".

Many of the advocates of this new cult are convinced in every way that these techniques are by nature bringers of progress and that the more our world commits itself to new information technologies, the better it will be. Many information scientists subscribe to this view. Thus the American Nicholas Negroponte is the author of a celebrated essay on "being digital" in which he defends the idea that "informatics is a way of life" in which the ideal is henceforth to be able "to meet one's neighbor in the realm of number"[5]. Robert Caillau, information scientist at CERN (Centre européen de recherches nucléaires) in Geneva and one of the principal inventors of the "Web", also claims that "the computer is not a machine" and that after the

---

[3] *Ibid.*
[4] Remarks by Philippe Quéau at the colloquium "De Gutenberg ao terceiro milénio", Universidad autonoma de Lisboa, 6-8 avril 2000.
[5] Nicholas Negroponte, *Being Digital*, Knopf, New York, 1995.

culture of the hunt and physical force, of agriculture and money, will come the world of networks and information[6]. Bill Gates, the very mediatized founder of Microsoft, old libertarian and new liberal, ardently defends a world in which information absorbs all our activities.

Besides the prophets and the technicians one finds all those who for one reason or another have an interest–or believe they have an interest–in the development of the "Internet-for-everything". This is notably the case of the gurus of the "new economy" who see in the maximum development of the network the occasion to multiply profits or even rapidly build fortunes.

This is also the case with politicians, often surrounded by ardent counselors on these matters, who feel it is an occasion to fulfill their political program by riding a wave that they judge to be popular. In particular one thinks of the American vice-president Al Gore, or of all those like Lionel Jospin in France who are tempted by a "society of information solidarity".

Most of all, the Internet can be a formidable career accelerator. Whatever they do or do not believe, a certain number of persons ardently campaign in favor of overthrowing the values of our society and a rapid passage to a "global information society" regardless of the consequences, provided that it serves their individual destinies. How many have also made a rapid career by being led voluntarily, by an enterprise or an institution, to develop the new tool for those who little understand it or mistrust it? They have not done bad work but since the power that they can attain is proportionate to the importance of the place which the tool attains, the temptation to find oneself a advocate of "Internet-for-everything" is strong.

Prophets, technological optimists, or simply professionals driven by the Internet, all understand and mutually support one another in order to bring about a new "revolution", hardly ever asking themselves about the social and human consequences of such a belief. These people find the justification

---

[6] Remarks by Robert Caillau at the colloquium "De Gutenberg ao terceiro milénio", Universidad autonoma de Lisboa, 6-8 avril 2000.

for their real life actions in the writings of the "prophets" of the global information society who proclaim the arrival of a "new world", and these latter support their remarks with the many examples taken "from real life".

[...]

The advocates of rational use

Between technophiles and technophobes a third way is possible. Regularly throughout the history of the development of new technologies during the second half of the twentieth century, voices have arisen to criticize too great an enthusiasm as well as too great a pessimism. Norbert Wiener himself, after having contributed so much, in his own words, to "liberating the bad genie from the bottle", at the end of his life in the 1960's made a leap towards humanism.

In the world of informatics some of the most important names have had to speak out in favor of a reasoned, humanist use of information technologies, against the mad rush and excess to which they have given place. As early as the "information revolution" of the sixties and seventies when a better world through computers was promised, one of the most important AI (artificial intelligence) researchers, the American Joseph Weizenbaum, questioned the complete power accorded to computers in our societies.[7]

In France Jacques Arsac, holder of the first chair of informatics in the faculty of sciences in Paris, took up his pen in 1968 to denounce the belief according to which informatics has anything to do with "meaning": for him, that discipline, which he knew well, had to be restricted to the "treatment of form"[8]. His position, even though it was not so explicitly stated, was inspired by a religious point of view; his Catholicism would hardly accept that the realm of meaning proper to the spiritual world should be invested in technique.

---

[7] Joseph Weizenbaum, *Computer Power and Human Reason: from Judgment to Calculation*, W.F. Freeman & Co., San Francisco, 1976.

[8] Jacques Arsac, *Les machines à penser*, Seuil, Paris, 1987.

For these two specialists, the cause is understood: tools are just tools, all incursion into other domains such as the pretension to make a lever for "social revolution", goes contrary to the humanist ideas which place man–and not technique–at the center of the word.

The critique of the "ideology of communication" urged by Lucien Sfez [9] and the analysis of the "utopia of communication"[10] carried already, each in its own manner, the seeds of the beginnings of a reflection on the reasoned use of techniques in a context already largely technicized.

In spite of their own presuppositions, the current "anti-globalization liberals" appearing in Europe and elsewhere in the late 1990's contain a potential rational critique of the Internet. In France, the movement spurred on by *Le Monde diplomatique* and its network of friends played an important role in contesting the Internet, perceived by liberalism to be an entirely instrumentalized tool. This point of view, expressed for example by Ignacio Ramonet in *La tyrannie de la communication*[11] permits the analysis of the discourse accompanying the new information technologies to be in harmony with the philosophy of liberalism.

According to another perspective, the partisans of "regulation"–juridical and otherwise–of the Internet played a great role in defense of the controlled usage of the new technologies. This is the meaning of the remarks by the French media sociologist Dominique Wolton who, in *Internet et après?* tried to restrict the reach of the new technologies and argued for their regulation "so that the freedom of communication may not become synonymous with the law of the jungle"[12].

---

[9] Lucien Sfez, *Critique de la communication*, Seuil, Paris, 1988.
[10] Philippe Breton, *L'utopie de la communication*, La Découverte/Poche, Paris, 1997.
[11] Ignacio Ramonet, *op. cit.*
[12] Dominique Wolton, *Internet et après? Une théorie critique des nouveaux médias,* Flammarion, Paris, 2000.

Among the most active partisans of a "reasoned usage" today, especially in France, are people involved with teaching. This is undoubtedly why they have been made the butt of irony, even slander, from the most heated advocates of the information society: they are reproached for their apparently well known "resistance to change". It must be said that they are not well disposed to it. Since the sixties the information scientists of IBM, promoters of new "pedagogies" of mostly compartmentalized inspiration, confidently announced the end of "human" teachers and their impending replacement by "teaching machines"!

This is the same discourse which one sometimes finds today, where the Internet, allowing "access to the world's knowledge" dispenses with human mediation reducing it for the first time to a lesser position, making the professor the students' "assistant". Such an attitude hardly predisposes one to accepting the new techniques. Nevertheless, many teachers have attempted a pedagogical reflection on the rational use in the service of pedagogy and of the necessary teacher-student relation (we shall return to the arguments in this debate).

In the current climate, the advocates of rational use meet in every case with a strong tendency, that of "Internet-for-everything" and the cult which permeates it. Whatever may be their points of view or motivations, their position in effect implies a partial renunciation of the power of techniques and the establishment of strict borders between the world of technique and that of the human.

They extol in some fashion the inverse of the religiosity which bathes the Internet world: a "lay" usage of techniques, a sort of separation of the Church of Technique and the Human State. That explains why they have the greatest difficulty in leaving their isolation and sharing their experiences. Their actions are often confined to something quasi-clandestine, in the face of very strong social pressure.

The difficulties of this "third way" are such that, in spite of strengthening certain intellectuals little suspected of hostility to technique, every critical position or even a simple call for debate about the Internet and the discourse that flatters it is reduced more often than not by the media to the second term of a terribly simplified "for or against". How often it is said to those who express any kind of reservation regarding the "Internet-for-everything": "But that is so bizarre; you use e-mail all the time!" The cult of the Internet is so widespread that many cannot imagine that the Internet could serve simply as... a tool.

There is certainly a place for critique, but it is clearly demarcated within the boundaries of what appears to be a false debate: either you are a "technophobe", i.e. one who loves neither technique nor change nor anything modern, or else you are entirely "in favor of the Internet". Either you are closed up within yourself or you are open to the world and its fantastic new world of techniques. Either you are "young" advocates of the "new world", or you are "an old poker".

Technophile or technophobe, these are the only positions allowed in the discussion. Such a simplification obviously cannot pretend to have the status of social debate. There are many other trails to blaze toward the beginnings of a "laicization" of techniques, paths that are at an equal distance from the quasi-religious beliefs with which techniques are often ridiculously clothed and the hostility that is provoked in response.

In order to leave behind this false debate it is necessary to better understand the position of the advocates of "Internet-for-everything". What are their arguments, how does their discourse spread, what are the underlying values? Why speak of a "cult"? The following chapters attempt to bring to light what is sometimes only implicit in the discourses that valorize the new information technologies. We begin with that recent poster child of the Internet cult: the promise of a better world thanks to the establishment of a global information society.

VIII

Rosamond Rhodes: Genetic links, family ties and social bonds: rights and responsibilities in the face of genetic knowledge.
No one has a right to genetic ignorance.

IX

An old French peasant (quoted in Virilio: Un paysage d'événements).
Asked about what, in his opinion, had been the greatest modern calamity, an old peasant of the Île de France responded without hesitation: "the news [les informations]." And when he was asked to elaborate: "The war of 1914 came out of nowhere on me, from one day to the next no one had foreseen what would happen. The evening of the general mobilization we were peaceful, no one here dreamed of the war and yet we were not even 100 kilometers from Paris. ... But later with the radio and then television, we felt like we were always on the eve of a war or some catastrophe, and that was unlivable."

X

Gras: Grandeur et dependence: sociologie des macro-systèmes techniques.
Technique imposes itself as a manner of thinking the world, it is a system of the production of ideas and representations of nature far more than a system of actions on that nature.

XI

Hottois: Essais de philosophie bioéthique et biopolitique.

It is techno-science, or more exactly techno-scientists and those who collaborate with them, who will invent and produce the future in a dominant manner. It is no longer symbolic creativity, such as the interpretation of traditions, that will lead the way in creating the future. ... Symbolization will accompany the technosciences... Spontaneously savage and irrationally technophobic or technophilic, but more and more often informed and rational... That accompaniment is not passive: it orients, restrains, encourages and prohibits. ... This means that the symbolic cannot serve technoscience, nor can the latter serve the symbolic. The first form of domination engenders theocracy, the second technocracy. Both are extremely dangerous precisely because of the technical developments themselves. Both are deadening because they conceive, reproduce and understand by putting the symbolic and technoscience in the service of a particular form which cannot evolve.

XII

Rawlinson: Reibadailty

Aoccdrnig to a rscheearch at Cmabrigde Uinervtisy, it deosn't mttaer in waht oredr the ltteers of a wrod are, the olny iprmoetnt tihng is taht the frist and lsat ltteer be at the rghit pclae. The rset can be a toatl mses and you can sitll raed it wouthit porbelm. Tihs is bcuseae the huamn mnid deos not raed ervey lteter by istlef, but the wrod as a wlohe.

XIII

DeLillo: White noise.
You could put your faith in technology. It got you here, it can get you out. This is the whole point of technology. It creates an appetite for immortality on one hand. It threatens universal extinction on the other. Technology is lust removed from nature.
(Quotation courtesy of M. Lindner)

XIV

Bade: The social life of metadata
The characteristic trait of the "information society" of the early 21st century is exploitation and its overt desire theft. Mechanical *re*production rather than production predominates, as this is the *modus operandi* of information technologies...
Technologies are also the embodiment of ideas. As ideas, they must be totalitarian since they have no human capacities for judgement, change or forgiveness; as implemented, they are characterized by accidents and unforeseen outcomes, for what they produce when employed by human beings depends not only upon the designer's specifications but also upon all those factors that human action brings into play: psychological, economic, social, intellectual, legal, political and religious as well as the physical environment itself. The intelligent use of technologies in any social setting requires attention to all of the environmental factors that may influence or be influenced by the technologies.

Part Three

Library Science:
Ethics, Language, Management, Philosophy

XV

What Happened to Politics and Ethics? Seven 21st Century Library Philosophers on the Epistemological and Ontological Foundations of Library Science

Abstract
Seven recent monographs on the philosophical foundations of library science are discussed in light of the questions the authors ask and the assumptions that underlie the questions asked. The author finds that epistemological discussions frequently identify epistemology with philosophy of science while ontological discussions rest upon reifications, and in both cases there is an absence of attention to ethical and political questions. The author's critique links the absence of ethical and political dimensions in several of the works discussed to an approach to philosophy that offers the reader answers rather than questions.

1. Philosophy in the Library: A Healthy Debate or a State of Confusion?

Lately there seems to be considerable debate—or confusion, depending on how you understand it—as to what libraries are, what is the proper object of study for library science, and even whether or not library science is really scientific. Enter the philosophers, and who knew there were so many among us! Although Zwadlo (1997) cited a 1934 paper by Danton in which it was reported that only 1 to 5% of library publications have any philosophical discussion, the debate about philosophy for libraries renewed in the 1990s, and Danton would be astonished at the number of publications appearing since the year 2000. One of the most noticeable aspects of this renewed interest is a focus on epistemological and ontological issues, a focus that can be traced back to a series of papers published in *Library Quarterly* in the 1990's (see Radford (1992), Budd (1995), Zwadlo (1997) and Dick (1999)). That debate was largely an Anglo-American academic debate (Dick writing in English from South Africa). The task I set myself in this paper was to look at the debate during the past decade, and especially to consider views from beyond the Anglo-American universe. I chose seven books to examine, looking at them in particular for the political and ethical dimensions of the discussion.

2. The Library: A Radically Political Institution

I shall begin with Serbian librarian Željko Vučković's 2003 monograph *Javne biblioteke i javno znanje* (which could be translated in English as: *Public libraries and public knowledge*). Like the other authors discussed below, he focuses on epistemological issues; more than any of the other authors he is concerned with the potential of libraries for political life. The hypothesis the author wishes to explore is the following:

> Public libraries are the most open and most democratic form of the institutionalization and use of public knowledge. Hence their key role in designing and building a

library information system and infrastructure and their strategic importance in economic and social development. Providing free, equal and unrestricted access to the achievements of culture and civilization, to knowledge, ideas and information, the public library contributes to the development of a democratic public and the quality of life in the community, and the practical realization of the concept of rational communication. (Vučković, 2003, p. 7)

Jesse Shera's *social epistemology* is a guiding theoretical and methodological orientation in the first half of this work as the author proceeds through a discussion of terminology, chapters on the function of the library, public librarianship as a social institution, the development of the idea of public librarianship, the legal foundations and history of public libraries in Serbia. The second half of the book looks at public librarianship in the context of international legal regimes, UNESCO declarations and IFLA, the public library as part of postmodern culture and the changes and challenges of public libraries in the information society with its digital libraries. A short chapter on the development of technical information systems for public libraries in Serbia is then followed by an even shorter chapter on the philosophical and axiological principles of public librarianship. It is those few final pages that are chiefly of interest to me, since the discussion within the book assumes these principles rather than argues them.

The final chapter begins with the question "Why philosophical considerations in an area that is primarily practical and pragmatic, in a service- and client-oriented activity?" (ibid., p. 174). It is a question that nearly every one of the authors discussed below asks. The answer, he suggests, depends on the definition of philosophical inquiry but even more importantly on whether one thinks that librarianship needs a systematic theoretical foundation. In the author's view, systematic theory "is an indication and measure of professional responsibility... responsibility towards library patrons and society as a whole" (ibid. p. 174). Theory in librarianship is evidence of self-awareness and critical self-reflection for a librarian responsibly engaged with the society that creates and sustains libraries. This perspective focused on social responsibility distinguishes Vučković from all of the other writers discussed here, for they all address the question in relation to another issue, namely whether or not library science is a science. He quotes with approval Michael Gorman's statement that librarians must defend the purpose of libraries, which is "the collection, storage, organization and dissemination of knowledge and the recorded information of humankind, and the services based on these records" (ibid., p. 180), and he continues with the assertion that the philosophy of librarianship should remain unchanged no matter what technological changes take place, for it is rooted in "the support of humanity and the democratic development of society, through free access to public knowledge" (ibid., p. 180) rather than in any particular set of technological conditions.

The practices libraries engage in and support certainly will change with changing technologies, but the philosophy of libraries as institutions serving political life through making knowledge public will not. In a later article Vučković listed the three "primary tasks of the public library in the era of electronic media": 1. making the right to information a reality; 2. helping ordinary people orient themselves in the information chaos; 3. actively participating in solving educational problems (Vučković, 2008, p. 25). In this formulation of the work of public libraries, even the tasks are understood to be independent of the technologies involved. With his philosophy and his understanding of the tasks of libraries, Vučković puts himself above the chief criticisms leveled against the field by several of the authors discussed below, namely that librarianship has been oriented towards following techniques and tools rather than towards social purposes or a theory driven orientation.

There are similarities to this perspective on libraries in Osburn (2009) and Heber's (2009) emphasis on stewardship of the cultural record, and Salarelli's remarks on technological change, but it is surprising that in Vučković alone the philosophy of librarianship is rooted in the political dimension of libraries, their connection to democratic, civil society rather than in some objective and apolitical abstraction such as information, access services or library collections. Stewardship is not the same thing as politics, information can be disinformation or in the service of an oppressive regime, and cultural preservation is not the same thing as "the support of humanity and the democratic development of society". Public libraries, for Vučković, are fundamentally and radically political institutions, *not information services*! Of course they are *also* information services, but public libraries do not exist simply because information exists but rather because political life demands information, knowledge about one's situation. The political dimension of libraries is therefore not an incidental side effect resulting from the establishment of public libraries for other reasons, rather it is their fundamental reason for being.

As I understand Vučković, it is only because public access to information is important for political life that we need public libraries. None of the other authors discussed below even come close to that understanding of libraries, but then Vučković is writing of public libraries, not an ideal library conceived of as independent of or even pre-existing political life. Alfaro López (2010) does discuss the origins of library science in conjunction with the establishment of public libraries, and a reading of Vučković with Alfaro López in mind or vice versa could be a very productive exercise indeed. The web of interrelationships encompassing political life, public institutions and science seems often to be avoided by a too narrow focus, though of the authors discussed below, neither Heber nor Osburn are guilty of such narrowness.

While Vučković's orientation was an unexpected surprise, what was not so surprising was that those authors who orient their philosophies toward information and technological developments are the furthest removed from libraries as both social and political institutions. Books by Rendón Rojas (2005) and Morales López (2008) provide examples of discourses centered on information that avoid the ethical and the political, an avoidance that in itself has ethical and political ramifications.

3. ((P(x)&¬Q(x))&R(x)&S(x)&T(x)&U(x)&¬V(x))
Bases teóricas y filosóficas de la bibliotecología by Rendón Rojas is "an epistemological reflection on library science" (Rendón Rojas, 2005, p. 3) organized into five chapters, the first devoted to epistemological foundations. Epistemology, he claims, is a word frequently found in the library science literature, but often used imprecisely. For Rendón Rojas, epistemology is a synonym for philosophy of science, so the big question is whether or not library science is a science. Philosophy as he understands it is "a process of seeking and a doctrine that reflects some results of that search; an interrogative attitude before reality together with the answers to those questionings" (ibid., p. 4). In the first chapter we are led through a bit of formal logic and discussions of positivism, Popper's notion of falsification, an extended explication of Kuhn on scientific revolutions, a brief note on Feyerabend's epistemological anarchism, and another long section on Lakatos. Finally Dilthey, Gadamer and company provide him with a hermeneutic, dialogical approach appropriate to a humanistic discipline for which the methodologies of the hard sciences are just too hard. He then identifies his philosophical premises: a realist ontology and a dialectical methodology: dialectical cognitive realism.

The book proceeds in the second section "The foundations of a discipline" to indicate what foundations library science requires, namely philosophical, theoretical, extratheoretical, methodological and logical foundations. The third chapter goes into some detail concerning the ontological foundations while the fourth treats the theoretical foundations and the final chapter returns to the philosophical foundations again, this time the gnoseological foundations.

In the chapter on the ontological foundations of LIS, Marx, Husserl and Heidegger are brought together to demonstrate the necessity and objectivity of informational relationships that arise from the activities of human existence as authentic being and form the basis of libraries and library science. The ideal and abstract but authentic human being accomplishes his projects involving things in the world via language which is the "house of being" (Heidegger); language requires an interlocutor, and therefore relationships of a linguistic and informational character arise from the nature of our being (*Nota bene*: it is out of language rather than social life that these relationships arise). Libraries and librarians facilitate those informational relationships, presented by the author as conversations among authentic human beings, and library science studies those conversational relationships. An interesting but difficult chapter that ought to have had considerably more social and political import but one can hardly expect a political ground for libraries arising from Heideggerian being. What is more surprising is how Marx seems to have gotten neutered by Heidegger somewhere within the walls of the "house of being".

The author's desire to present a necessary and objective object for the discipline of library science—as opposed to the arbitrary and historically contingent objects of actual practice—leads him always and everywhere to deal only with very abstract ideal objects: being, activity, informational relations. Whereas traditionally other writers on library science (he cites Setién and Gorbea) describe the activities of librarians as a list of things that they *do*, Rendón Rojas wants us to think of these as things that we *are*. We can think of these informational relations as a matter of our being because "they arise independently of the will of individuals" (ibid., p. 76). Human beings are informational beings and therefore all the activities involving informational relations arise necessarily and objectively from that generic condition.

The activity of the librarian, the archivist, the information scientist, the bibliographer are phenomena of a superstructure that rests upon a base of informational relations. Beyond these activities one can search for intentional meanings ... but here we are dealing with an intentionality not of individual subjectivity but of a generic subjective intentionality (ibid., p. 76)

Whereas Salarelli (2008) begins with the observation that libraries do not spring up in the empty desert but amongst concrete human beings in specific historical and social conditions as the foundation of his philosophy of library science, Rendón Rojas founds his philosophy of libraries on ideal being, ideal authentic human beings, ideal activity, ideal informational relations, ideal library users and ideal libraries. What is the difference between an ideal object and a reified term? Apparently nothing at all, as the next chapter demonstrates.

Everything becomes clear (or gets worse, depending upon your philosophical inclination) with the analysis of terminology in the fourth chapter. Definition number one informs us that

x is information $\equiv$
$((P(x)\&\neg Q(x))\&R(x)\&S(x)\&T(x)\&U(x)\&\neg V(x))$

and this is followed by similar definitions for documents, users, actual users, potential users, information institutes and other concepts and objects, including the following definition of *libro* (book) on page 133:

$x\{P(x)\&Q(x)\&R(x)\&S(x)\&T(x)\&U(x)\&V(x)\&W(x)\&P_2(x)\&(P_1)\&(Q_1)\&Q_2(x)\}$

Now we formally understand not only what a book is, but also what everything else in the informational universe is from users to archives.

In this ideal informational universe the dilemma facing Rendón Rojas and the unmentioned target of certain passages is the notion of libraries as autopoietic, autonomous and self-referential systems, that is, libraries understood according to the social systems theory of Niklas Luhmann, the subject of the book by Heber. Rendón Rojas pointedly addresses the issue on page 137 and I translate the entire first paragraph:

> A first characteristic that stands out in analyzing the institution of documentary information is that it is an organism created by the society and that fulfills a social function (P), from which we have chosen the term institution and not followed the general consensus in calling it an information unit. The fact of being a social institution signifies that its existence is due to a social necessity and that—like political institutions (the state, or others that have arisen historically: parties, ministries or secretaries of state, presidencies, congress, in the case of representative democracies) or juridical institutions (the police, public prosecutor, judges, supreme courts of justice)—are inserted into the structure of society for its proper functioning, independently of the persons that occupy a particular position in the institution. But that institutional characteristic does not absorb the subjective element of the individuals that give it life, and need not turn into an autonomous and self-referential system despite the ends for which the institution was created. (ibid., p. 137).

He refers the reader at this point to an earlier paper of his, Rendón Rojas (1999), which is in fact a critique of Luhmann's theories with reference to library and information systems. The question for me was, just how different is Rendón Rojas's understanding from Luhmann's? Luhmann does not deny the existence of human actors outside the system, he simply finds them uninteresting and ignores them, whereas

Rendón Rojas does not deny the existence of actual individuals creating and utilizing the system, he simply rejects them in favor of their idealizations! The good news here is that he has noted the problem and makes the reader aware of it. It may in fact be the most important discussion in his book.

The final chapter is devoted to the "gnoseological foundations" of library science, "that is to say, it deals with the problematic of the object of study of the discipline and the specificity of that study, as well as its relation to and differences from related disciplines" (Rendón Rojas, 2005, p. 149). The object of his monograph is, he announces, "to demonstrate that the traditional focus has been superseded by the evolution of the objects with which library science must deal, but this does not mean that it must be completely abandoned, only that it must adopt a new, more abstract vision that can adapt to and explain these changes without definitely renouncing the past and with-out abandoning itself to technology and the market" (ibid., p. 149).

Rendón Rojas insists that a scientific revolution has taken place in library science, and the old objects of our attention—books, libraries—have been replaced by new objects: documents, databases, networks, digital libraries, etc. Library science has, as the scientific consensus reveals, changed its object of study and is now focused on the concept of information. The author then takes us through a brief exposition of the semiology of information, i.e. the traditional triad of syntax, semantics and pragmatics of information. We get more equations, such as $H=-P(1)\log(P(1))-P(2)\log(P(2))-\ldots$ and diagrams

Source→encoder→sender→medium→receiver→decoder→destination

and still more complicated diagrams, with the chapter ending on a note regarding the library as educational institution.

The conclusion: Library science studies an ideal object —information—that has a reality independent of human beings (and therefore independent of ethics and politics), but it studies this object as it functions in relation to another ideal object, the human user. That is a rough simplification, for Rendón Rojas has more than just this to say in his conclusion, but he has failed to convince me with his arguments. There may be more to the formal definitions and diagrams than I realize (I am not a logician), but they seem to me to be attempts to hide the indeterminacy and reified nature of the terms discussed with the appearance of scientific method and rigor. This may indeed be library science and even philosophy, but all I could see in this book was an elaboration of abstractions based on commonplace answers to questions that I would not ask. How a logician or a more mathematically competent information scientist would evaluate Rendón Rojas's interrogative attitude before reality together with his answers to his questions, I cannot say. It is an interesting book to consider in light of Heber's book, and the book has sold out of three printings in two editions, so there must be others who appreciate the book in ways that are beyond my capabilities. But I think the anonymous reviewer on Google Books (viewed 30 August 2011) was onto something when s/he wrote "Este libro es muy útil para escribir justificaciones a proyectos de investigación", which translated into English means something like "This book is very useful for writing justifications for research projects."

4. An Exercise in Authority: Defining Library Science
Valentino Morales López follows no particular philosophical orientation explicitly but follows the general path of the analytical philosophers (Wittgenstein, Russell and company) by focusing on terminological clarification. The issue he addresses is the language of science:

> One of the main issues is that the language used by scientists must be uniform in the use of terms as much as in their meaning, since this prevents communication and the transmission of information among the members of an epistemic community from becoming full of noise

that would impede correct understanding among its members. (Morales López, 2008, p. 11)

The science he has in mind is "the science of recorded and organized information" and its associated terminology. The author claims that none of the authors that he has consulted "have made an integral study of the terms and concepts that have been proposed for naming and defining" that science. He offers what he describes as his contribution to the "epistemology of library science" by describing the history of terminology, and seeks to find some clarification in etymology. It may seem a bit odd to try to understand the proper meaning of terms like "library science" and "information science" as well as the proper domain of those disciplines in the 21st century by investigating whether or not "there exist correspondences with Latin or Greek roots" (ibid., p. 14) for the terms, but it is true that some terms in Spanish certainly look like Latin or transliterated Greek.

At first glance, Morales López appears to set a rather modest goal: proposals for the proper definition of the terms *bibliografía, bibliología, bibliotecología, documentación,* and *ciencia de la información*. Yet that is a far more difficult and consequential task than writing an entry in a dictionary, and his is in fact a very ambitious project. It reminds me of one of the books listed in his bibliography by a philosopher among information scientists who attempted to define information and misinformation. He concluded his lengthy examination of the term misinformation with the pronouncement that misinformation was a form of information that was always false. Etymological researches have a way of putting the conclusions into the assumptions upon which the whole investigation is based. This is one of the most common problems with etymological research and speculation, and it is also the chief failure of Morales López's book.

In this book Morales López does not limit his study to just those five words/phrases in Spanish, but includes the related words in several European languages spanning the centuries from Kallimachos and the library of Alexandria to Michael Buckland in 1999, comparing the definitions given in the past with the associated practices then and now and evaluating them all in light of his assumptions about what library and information science is and ought to be. This of course raises the question of whether all those authors in all those places across all those centuries were all writing about the same thing: library and information science as the English speaking world understands it today. Can people in fact mean different things when they write what appears to us now to be the "same" word, or must we conclude that most if not all of them were using a word incorrectly if their definition does not agree with what we think the word ought to mean? Clearly the definitions discussed show that they did not all conceive of the object of their study in the same manner. And Morales López appears to understand this when he remarks that "on occasion the use of *biblioteconomía* and *bibliotecología* has led to difficulties in communication between the members of those two communities, since the discussion is not about a simple linguistic difference but reflects different conceptions about the discipline" (ibid., p. 76). Yet throughout the book Morales López proceeds to seek the right definition as though he thinks that if he can match up the right word with the right concept we will finally all know what we have been talking about all along. He analyses and evaluates etymologies, terminologies and concepts, sometimes quoting the definition one author gives in order to demonstrate that our current concept did not yet exist even though the same word was used, and at other times arguing as though the authors ought to have meant the same thing but offered the wrong definition.

In Chapter one "Bibliografía" we read that although the term *bibliografía* "in its formal structure contains Greek and Latin roots, that does not mean that in its semantic aspect there is any continuity with the meaning that one could attribute to it in that classical past" (ibid., p. 20). The proper etymology of the meaning of the (current?) term "we find not in classical etymology but in the language of the 17th century" (ibid., p. 20). He follows this with several pages of discussion of the practice of bibliography in the ancient and medieval worlds, presenting arguments about whether there was any continuity between the lists of Kallimachus, Galen and medieval library catalogues. After a discussion of the origin of the term bibliography amongst the many similar and competing terms "such as *bibliotheca, cathalogus, corpus, elenchus, flores, inventarium, index, nomenclator o repertorium, thesaurus*" (ibid., p. 25) the author turns in section 1.3 to the history of the term "*bibliografía*" which he notes first appeared in the title of a work consisting of a list of books in Naudé's *Bibliographia politica* of 1633. We have already been informed (on page 20) that the word *bibliographia* appears in many variant forms in different languages— *bibliografía, bibliographia, bibliography, bibliographie* and *bibliografija* (in Russian)—but that the meaning of all these terms in the modern age is the same and "is accepted without discussion, even though the meaning is the subject of debate" (ibid., p. 20). Our philosopher must have written that passage during a siesta.

Morales López notes that "The first formal definition of bibliography appeared in 1704 in the *Dictionnaire universel françois et latin*, in which bibliography was defined as "knowledge and interpretation of ancient manuscripts" (ibid., p. 29-30) and he compares that definition to one found in a 1774 dictionary: "knowledge of ancient manuscripts". Contrasting those two definitions he remarks:

> The contradiction between the two earlier definitions is notable since the first states that bibliography is the interpretation of manuscripts and the second asserts that bibliography describes the manuscripts. Possibly the author of the first definition considered not only the descriptive aspect but also that concerning the intellectual content of the manuscripts, while the authors of the second definition took into account only the descriptive labor. Certainly both of those two aspects form part of

bibliographical work, so that an adequate definition should include the description and the interpretation of manuscripts." (ibid., p. 30)

Note what Morales López is doing here: two definitions describe two different activities, one that involves interpretation (perhaps along with description), and one that does not. Since the two definitions are for the "same" word, one of them must be wrong. Says who? Says Morales López. Why? Because—claims Morales López—the work of bibliography ought to include both description and interpretation. This is not an exercise of clarification, it is an exercise of authority, the authority of the philosopher to tell the scientist (or anyone) what they should mean by their terms. Morales López apparently knows what *bibliografía* really means and is therefore able to evaluate both definitions for adequacy. And not only those two, but all those to come.

We are still at the beginning of the author's discussion of the first of his selected terms, but before we are finished with *bibliografía* we will know the rest of the book in advance. Definitions of bibliography "are abundant, many of them too general to be mentioned, or merely repeat other definitions in different words" (ibid., p. 48). Schneider's 1934 definition of bibliography is dismissed as a tautology, and Maclés's definition is deficient because "it assigns to bibliography a task impossible to accomplish: the knowledge of all texts" (ibid., p. 45). Yet the author accepts Maclés's definition "as the best definition of bibliography" (ibid., p. 48) in spite of its deficiency "because it reflects the current situation of bibliography up to the 1950's, ... and coincides with the historical development of bibliography, which with the passing of time has ceased to be an independent science and become a branch of other sciences" (ibid., p. 48).

Morales López argues against the definition of *bibliotecología* as "the study of libraries" on the basis that a focus on libraries is no longer possible since "this discipline covers ...

areas that have little relation to libraries" (ibid. p. 111), yet, impossible as it may seem to be, we shall find Alberto Salarelli arguing for just that in the next book discussed. Morales López also criticizes the first edition of *Bases teóricas y filosóficas de la bibliotecología* by Rendón Rojas, remarking that "his definition has the weakness of centering the nucleus of library science in the process of documents, but not in recorded and organized information" (ibid., . 113) because, he insists, it is the latter that is the "hard nucleus" of library science. Throughout the book the argument against every definition proposed is always that x cannot be y as this author claims, because x is z, and z is everywhere supplied by Morales López.

The only significant exception to the above manner of dismissing definitions is the case of *documentación*. Those scientists who proposed and defended the term "involved themselves in absurd discussions about what the term documentation should mean" (isn't the pot calling the kettle black here?) and succeeded only in laying an untenable foundation for "a science that would have to be developed later" (ibid., p. 124) but never was. Morales López dismisses the term, declaring it to be a dead name for a science that never existed, and anyway no one but the Spaniards are still using it (ibid., p. 144).

We should not be surprised then that the author declares in his conclusion to the book that exactly as Lakatos demanded, the hard nucleus of that science which all these terms attempt to name is present throughout the entire history of that science, and it must not be changed because it is its proper object. That hard nucleus is "the study of recorded and organized information" with which the book began. It "corresponds to a single discipline ... that must have a single and recognizable name" and "the English speaking world has found a certain solution in the use of the term *library and information science*" (ibid., p. 219). He suggests the term "bibliotecología y estudio de la información" for the Spanish speaking world in imitation of the successful English term. For the first time now we know what we really should be studying and what to call it. And with that name what appeared at first glance to be a multilingual and historical approach to a number of related topics turns out in the conclusion to be another affirmation of academic territorial politics in an Anglo-American universe.

Morales López's book was fascinating in its detailed descriptions of how past writers have understood the terms investigated and the associated questions regarding whether the field denominated was a technical practice or a science. His remark "it is notable that while in France [bibliothéconomie] was understood as a technical field, the Germans considered [Bibliothekswissenschaft] a science, which later led to different developments in each country" (ibid., p. 82) pushed me towards an entirely different line of questioning than that which he followed, and section 3.3.4 "Reflexión sobre los diferentes orígenes de la bibliotecología" ought to have led the author to exactly the kinds of considerations evident in the books by Vučković and Alfaro López—but he leaves the matter with no further comment. To his credit, in this case as in many others Morales López offers enough detail that one can think both with and against him while reading; at many points the reader is likely to be provoked into reflections that move well beyond the narrow purposes for which Morales López wrote his book and the conclusions he offers. And indeed, rather than reading the book for his conclusions, I recommend reading it for the historical discussion of the terminological debates that have literally defined and redefined the field from the beginning. Certainly everyone involved in ontology development or pinning great hopes on the latter should read this book carefully as the histories narrated put that entire project into question.

Unfortunately the philosophy that underwrote his book did not permit the author to ask any truly interesting epistemological questions; his is a philosophy of words doing double duty as concepts without an adequate semiology or philosophy of language. All the author really wants to teach us is that our field of intellectual efforts is really a science or at least a unified single discipline, and that we should call it *library and information science* or an equivalent phrase in another language. For me at least, those are answers to questions that are of very, very little interest.

5. Libraries Are Not Essential for Human Life

Alberto Salarelli's recent book *Biblioteca e identità* is as different from Morales López (2008) as the latter is from Rendón Rojas (2005). Philosophy for Salarelli is apparently something far more engaging than trying to identify the proper meaning of some disciplinary terminology and provide those terms with formal definitions. And at his best—and I mean when he stops telling us what others have written and puts his own mind in motion—Salarelli is awesome, although I suspect that is at least partly because he has read so widely. Many of his citations are to translations into Italian of works in other languages, but just as many are to publications in Italian. The book was worth reading for those Italian references alone. How often can you say that about a book? The book is also worth reading for his discussion of what other people have written about technological change in libraries, knowledge management, cultural memory, and identity, ethics, ontology and epistemology for library science. However, the real pleasure in reading his book comes when his own mind jumps into action.

Consider this passage in chapter two, his critique of Knowledge Management (Informazione e conoscenza: contro il "Knowledge Management"):

> Their [Davenport and Prusak] words, nevertheless, sound like a desperate defense:
>
>> the conventions of language force us to discuss knowledge as a "thing" that can be "managed". We want to emphasize again, however, that knowledge is as much an act or process as an artifact or thing.

It is not true that this is a matter of a mere problem of the use of terminology, but rather a clear conceptual difference that they continue to want to ignore in perfectly bad faith, since—as is demonstrated in that *excusatio non petita*—the authors know very well that knowledge is not a "thing" and that for that reason cannot be managed at all. (Salarelli, 2008, p. 49)

If we compare this approach to language, terminology and definition in library science to what we find in the book by Morales López, we can see clearly two profoundly different conceptions of language, of philosophy and of science. Salarelli lets the KM crowd have it again a few pages later with more remarks on their language:

Knowledge Management has based its success upon the systematic disinterest in the meanings of words: here we find ourselves faced with an extraordinary example of how, in contemporary society, labels can conceal the absence of any real content: antithetical terms are juxtaposed deliberately ignoring what one wants to say in order to increase the explosive affect of harmonizing opposites: of an oxymoron is made a conquering slogan. (ibid., p. 63)

Salarelli's book is a collection of essays rather than a monograph working towards a conclusion like the books by Vučković, Rendón Rojas, Morales López, Heber and Osburn. As such it gives not just one climax but several, and each of the eight papers includes comments that jolted me into thinking about connections and possibilities that Salarelli himself only hints at or points to. One example appears in the first essay on technological changes in our time ("La Grande Trasformazione"). Quoting the Grand Inquisitor's vision of the future in *The Brothers Karamazov* Salarelli remarks:

the extraordinary success of networked tools for information management has led to the imposition of this as the only plausible macrovision of the world, containing everything and excluding nothing: the network society. (ibid., p. 36)

The networked society as totalitarian society: how often have I not seen evidence of the attitude that "if it isn't on the web it can be ignored" or even "if it isn't on the web it does not exist"? (In a discussion page on Wikipedia one can find the argument made against a Wikipedia author (not me) citing one of my books because the Wikipedia editor, unable to find my book online, declared that it did not exist and therefore could not be cited.) It is a practice of social exclusion that is enforced not by a malign state but by that much extolled wisdom of the crowd, one person at a time. Salarelli's critical remarks in this chapter on how technology is defining our debates are well worth reading, and he is not alone in seeing a technical focus as detrimental for the development of the field; the same topic appears in the book by Osburn and is a major focus of the book by Alfaro López.

Salarelli's third chapter concludes with a concise but marvelous critique of the rhetoric of conversation in connection with our information technologies—a matter to which he returns in the sixth chapter—and the serious matter of cultural memory so important to libraries (which is the main topic of Heber's and Osburn's books), while the fourth chapter looks at the connection between boredom, reading, sex (!) and information overload. Not your typical philosophy of library science!

The fifth and sixth chapters deal with library angst and ontological questions associated with technological changes of the past couple decades: What is a library? What is a digital library? In the brief fifth chapter he urges us not "to forget that the purpose of librarianship is to put the reader in the best condition to transform *information* into *knowledge*" and acknowledges that

Libraries are not essential for human life: they are social institutions historically inserted into a precise moment in the history of human communication, and may not even be considered useful in tomorrow's society and, therefore, eliminated. Or simply ignored. (ibid., p. 107)

The much longer sixth chapter, like Morales López's book, takes an etymological approach, but the similarities end there. Whereas Morales López understands libraries in terms of indexing and organizing information, Salarelli understands "the essential element in which the entire field of library science is founded" (ibid., p. 131) to be a cultural project of *collecting*, not just organizing documents. He pursues this line of thinking in connection with digital libraries, arguing that "digital libraries are not search engines (even though they use these powerful means in the activity of information retrieval). Digital libraries are collections of organized documents" (ibid., p. 136). The contrast with Rendón Rojas is sharp enough to cut the reader's fingers.

Chapter seven, on the ethics of librarianship, follows this acknowledgment of the library as collection with a discussion of the reverse side of collection, namely selection, deselection, exclusion, censorship. Salarelli puts together aspects of librarianship usually discussed separately, and in doing so very pointedly makes them ethical issues.

In the final chapter—Library science as a science? Epistemological considerations—Salarelli argues that library science cannot be considered a science in the same fashion as the "hard sciences" but can best be understood as a discipline. On this point Rendón Rojas and Salarelli are in general agreement. Salarelli's starting point for reflecting on library science is that society comes first, not the library: "Libraries do not spring up in the middle of the desert, but among human beings" (ibid., p. 185). *Pace* Rendón Rojas, Salarelli insists that individual human beings—not an abstract and indefinite universal

Humanity—"people who live their lives in a definite place and time" constitute the social basis of libraries and hence the theoretical basis of library science. What gives rise to librarianship and library science is the existence of libraries as social institutions—not the existence of an abstract ideal, whether information or the ideal human user—and "every society ... has definite characteristic modes of institutions for documentation, the library not surprisingly being only one of the possible results of this process" (ibid., p. 186). Librarianship and library science must therefore "put the library at the center of its epistemological question because the library is the foundation object of the discipline itself" (ibid., p. 187-188). Again in sharp contrast to both Rendón Rojas and Morales López, Salarelli refuses to conflate library science and information science:

> [I]n the moment in which library science is included in information science it irrevocably loses its own epistemological basis. In fact the horizons of reference for library science and information science differ not only in their objects of study but also in the specific characteristics of their methodological approaches. (ibid., p. 189)

If there is a fault with Salarelli's writing, it is a fault that I and Osburn (see below) share: many references, many quotes. I appreciate the references and the quotations rather than him trying to pass off the ideas of others as his own or misrepresenting their thought. But he writes well enough and brilliantly when he writes in his own voice, and I would be more than happy to let him take off on his own and write what he thinks for himself; he does not need to lean on the authority of others. If philosophy is the practice of thinking clearly and questioning assumptions in any arena of thought or practice—as I would like it to be—then Salarelli is certainly a philosopher, and the essays in *Biblioteca e identità* deserve to be read far beyond the borders of Italy.

6. Why Did Public Libraries Thrive in Nazi Germany?

Like Salarelli, Tanja Heber understands libraries as collections, specifically as repositories of cultural heritage. This approach is very different from understanding libraries as repositories of information, but has similarities to Osburn's understanding of libraries as "stewards of the social transcript". The philosopher to note here is Luhmann, and the orientation, systems theory. In fact, if you are familiar with Luhmann (or even Maturana and Varela), from that knowledge and the title of the book alone you can guess the main outlines of the book and its conclusions.

Luhmann's social systems theory is one that I know chiefly through secondary literature, so I am unable to evaluate Heber's presentation of his theories and her use of them for understanding libraries. However, the consequences of understanding the library as an autopoietic system are not difficult to grasp, particularly if one is already familiar with the chief sources of Luhmann's theory in systems theory and cybernetics. Bateson's "difference" that makes a difference appears throughout, and Maturana's notion of structural coupling is repeated like a mantra:

> The publishing industries and book trade are particular examples of the structural coupling between libraries and other systems. The particularity of this relation is that through the evolution of media a mutual evolution takes place. ... The structural coupling between publishing/book trade and libraries demonstrates how far the systems can be dependent upon the exchange relationships among them. By means of the structural coupling both systems react to the environmental changes and adapt their structures accordingly. (Heber, 2009, p. 61)

The first section of the book (chapter two) is comprised of an analysis of the different systems of libraries in Germany, the national, public, religious, scientific, educational, and special libraries. The third chapter discusses the library specifically as a storage system analyzed through the Luhmannian lens, while the fourth chapter discusses the significance of technological changes for libraries, the big change being the change from collections to service institutions coinciding with the development of communications technologies in the modern period. Chapter five discusses libraries and cultural memory through three theories: Luhmann's concept of memory, Maurice Halbwachs' notion of collective memory, and the related theories of Jan and Aleida Assmann. (I admit unfamiliarity with all of these authors and their theories of collective and cultural memory.) The final chapter puts chapters three and five together: the library as storage system for cultural memory.

The library as a social system is the result of a difference that made a difference: the establishment of libraries in antiquity was the formation of a new social system for transmitting the cultural memory of society. Once differentiated, the system has maintained itself through further evolution of the difference that it takes to differentiate it from a simultaneously evolving environment, i.e. it is an autopoietic or self-organizing system. Thus the several thousand year history of libraries reveals an evolution in which what differentiates the library from other social systems—the political, religious, scientific, economic, and educational systems—has evolved in such a manner as to maintain the library system in its relations with those systems rather than being absorbed into one of them or disappearing. "From a self-contained circle of knowledge, the library has become a network-like system of knowledge, which is reproduced from complex structures and organized programs to underpin the cultural memory of society" (ibid., p. 206).

The relation between the library systems and other social systems includes "zones of interpenetration" as is the case of public libraries which are both state-supported and a political resource for the citizenry:

> Libraries, which are borne by the public administration are, therefore, dependent upon the political system. ...

However, they also have a political role in contributing to the political opinion of citizens and enabling government authorities as well as the members of a society to have access to information and knowledge. The structural coupling between libraries and the political system characterized by supply and allocation of resources and information is so fundamental that one can speak of an interpenetration zone. (ibid., p. 43)

Yet it is difficult to see anything political in this relationship when it is immediately characterized in the very next paragraph as a programmed input-output:

> The relationship of a library to its support/sponsor [Träger] is also characteristically an Input-Output relationship. On the one hand, the sponsor provides the means, through the program, to control the functioning of the library, while on the other hand the library is able to organize the services that are necessary for achieving outputs to satisfy the interests of the sponsor. (ibid., p. 43)

Luhmann's Input-Output is in fact brought in to explain too much. We read that the library "transforms an input such as financial means into a goal, such as investing its means to acquire a new database license, producing thereby an output, namely increased possibilities for literature searching and information seeking" (ibid., p. 63). How a description of libraries in these terms increases our understanding of libraries I was unable to discern.

Heber does us the favour of explaining Luhmann's terminology in his own words in quotations, something I cannot do in English. Although there is a certain attraction in describing and explaining matters in terms of evolution, autopoiesis, and the familiar language of computer processes, I wonder whether these terms explain too much at the same time as they fail to explain crucial matters, i.e. the proffered explanation simply hides the real issues. Acknowledging zones of interpenetration among autonomous systems still leaves you and me entirely out of the picture.

That absence—of responsible agents—was nowhere more disconcerting than in the author's description of the "problem" that arose for German libraries in the first half of the 20th century.

> With National Socialism began the new era that had more consequences for the public library system than for the academic library system. At this point it should be pointed out that "the organizations based their decisions in alignment with the majority of the functional systems in the society," and in this period the political system now had an extraordinary authority....
>
> Due to this ideology, the number of public libraries almost doubled in 1933-1945, especially in rural areas. (ibid., p. 101)

If Luhmannian sociology can comfortably describe the "problem" of the changing library environment between 1933 and 1945 as one to which the library system adjusted with great success, then we are presented with an "understanding" of libraries that grotesquely misunderstands and misrepresents both libraries and their political environment under National Socialism.

Heber's book demonstrates one thing fairly clearly, namely that Luhmann's theory can explain anything so long as one lets Luhmann pose both the questions and the terms of the discussion. Like many other European scholars Heber obviously finds Luhmann's theories illuminating, particularly in addressing the question of what libraries should become. Given the changes in the systems comprising the environment in which the library system operates, Luhmann's notions of structural coupling and differentiation together predict that either the library system intensifies the difference and hence the complexity of its relationships with other social systems, or the functions of the library system will be absorbed by those other systems, the library ceasing to matter for its former supporters and users. Heber's book is thus intended as a challenge to librarians while being presented within a theory that ignores human agency. Any attempt to understand libraries autopoietically leaves human agency outside of the system, and that is not a move towards understanding libraries but towards their mystification. It is a pity that Heber did not read (or at least she did not mention) Rendón Rojas's critique of Luhmann applied to libraries; dealing with a critical perspective might have made her book much more interesting.

7. Re(a)d in Tooth and Claw: The Library as a Manifestation of the Nature of Humanity
If Heber shows us Luhmann as one extreme in the rigorous development of systems theory, Osburn shows us the opposite extreme, the rigorless variety of his own making. In *The Social Transcript: Uncovering Library Philosophy* Osburn offers a functional interpretation of the library and presents it in terms of cultural evolution. The titular emphasis on the social in Osburn's book predisposed me to pick it up over a number of other recent volumes in English for discussion in this essay. I skimmed through a couple sections to try to see whether Osburn offered something to complement the other viewpoints discussed here, and the first paragraph of Chapter One made me decide in his favour:

> Concept of and practice in the library so often are confused in the mind of both the public and the scholar that fundamental misunderstandings easily arise about what the library is and why it exists. This situation emanates primarily from the strong image of practice, which is what the public sees and what most of the professional and scholarly literature addresses. As a consequence,

image of practice almost invariably overshadows concept of function. In concept rather than in concrete, however, the library is a matter of rational social process, a process far more fundamental to humanity than isolated procedures and transactions could possibly suggest. (Osburn, 2009, p. 3)

This picture of the state of library theory and philosophy and the objections raised against such a state appear again and again in the literature, and with his different approach to the matter the book seemed to be a good choice for discussion here.

I then read the final few paragraphs. Osburn's next to the last paragraph in the final chapter (before the Epilogue, that is) was almost enough to discourage me from reading the book at all:

> With the ultimate purpose to define a library philosophy, this book has proceeded to describe library function in society, reasoning that philosophy flows most naturally from function, rather than from the actions involved in fulfilling that function. (ibid., p. 262)

Philosophy flows from function? I had no idea what that might mean (it became a little clearer when I returned to the beginning). Philosophy begins in wonder, Plato declared, and that means in questioning. Osburn continues:

> Owing to the longevity of the library, which has existed since the earliest stages of written language and, in concept, even before that in the oral tradition, its function is determined to be related closely to cultural evolution. (ibid., p. 262)

The concept of the library preceded the origin of writing? This is certainly a semantic innovation, but perhaps he is only reprising the argument in a book he cites but which I have not read,

Wright's *The Oral Antecedents of Greek Librarianship*. But we are not finished yet.

> When understood from the library perspective, this synthesis of research and theory relative to cultural evolution sheds much light on the basic function of the library and leads to the conclusion that the library is sufficiently integrated into cultural evolution, in fact, for it to be considered a cultural technology and, therefore, a manifestation of the nature of humanity. (ibid., p. 262)

Again, I am not sure I can make any sense of this claim, but I would bet Osburn has read neither Salarelli nor Gilbert Hottois (neither appear in his bibliography). Has it not proven difficult enough to determine "the nature of humanity" without making libraries a manifestation of that humanity? Whatever he means by this statement, he seems to be in disagreement with the viewpoint expressed by Salarelli concerning the non-necessary nature of libraries. These objections notwithstanding, I returned to the beginning—the very beginning, i.e. the Prologue —and began to read.

The first sentence of the Prologue was, like the final paragraphs quoted above, incomprehensible:

> This book introduces a philosophy for the library in cultural evolution, specifically for its role in the integration of mind and society. (ibid., p. xi)

I honestly cannot make any sense out of the notion of "the integration of mind and society". He apparently means by mind something very different from my mind, perhaps something on the order of Teilhard de Chardin's "noosphere" for he mentions Boulding's reference to the word.

This is followed by a sentence that is repeated as the first sentence in Chapter One and was already quoted above, namely "Concept of and practice in the library so often are confused in the mind of both the public and the scholar that fundamental misunderstandings easily arise about what the library is and why it exists" (ibid., p. xi). Clearly in Osburn's mind "what the library is and why it exists" is something that the philosopher (Osburn, not Aristotle) is going to explain to us from his unconfused vantage point. He continues:

> In concept rather than in concrete, however, the library is a matter of rational social process, a process far more fundamental to humanity than isolated procedures and transactions could possibly suggest. (ibid., p. xi)

Remember that passage? Yes, it is also in the first paragraph of Chapter One, and the objections to this appearance are the same in the Prologue as to its appearance in Chapter One, namely that Osburn appears to believe that there exists a "concept" of the library that is the real and true concept and that all differing concepts of the library are simply wrong. Moreover, his statement that "Survival of the library concept through the millennia poses a curious mystery" (ibid., p. xi) is astonishing, since he is claiming in this book to have been the first to formulate it. We can perhaps understand what is going on when he remarks two pages later that the library philosophy (concept?) that he is going to reveal to us

> is there, having been deeply embedded in the social function of the library throughout the millennia, continuing still today and every day. ... The subtitle of the present book indicates that there really is a library philosophy to be uncovered from deep within the age-old layers of library function as a uniquely human creation. But that philosophy remains to be uncovered, rather than created or invented or even discovered... (ibid., p. xiii)

This one and only true library philosophy is not one that Osburn is going to create but one which is already there waiting to be uncovered? And what is the difference between uncovered and discovered?

Osburn wants a philosophy appropriate for all libraries everywhere for all times, including, apparently, future institutions that have yet to exist, whether or not we would or future beings will call them libraries. Osburn will therefore define the Library in such a way that for all eternity any institutions fitting his definition should be called libraries, and all institutions that do not fit his definition must be called something else. Define it yourself and insist that everyone accept your definition: it is as easy as that to bind the future to your way of thinking. It is so simple one wonders why the founders of the library of Alexandria did not think of doing it way back then and saving Osburn the trouble of having to uncover all this, not to mention saving Morales López the trouble of arguing with 2000 years of definitions that history unfortunately proved deficient.

That is not the only example of practical or theoretical fictions reified and human agency denied. Osburn's reification of terms goes hand in hand with his denial of the librarian's role, responsibility and activities in the making of all of the libraries that have ever really existed. The "social" in Osburn's book is an abstraction that he mistakes for an eternal verity; it is a theory of the social without social actors (shades of Luhmann, though Osburn apparently did not read him since he never quoted him). On page xiv we read that "the library maintains its essential dimension ... through the assurance it instills in society ... In fulfilling its function in society, the library enables... the library fosters mental integration... the cultural technology called library produces both a capacity and an environment". The library, it seems, may have been "a uniquely human creation" as he wrote on page xiii, but according to Osburn it is the library—not its human creators or librarians—which maintains, instills, fulfills, enables, fosters, produces, etc.

This is clearly the legacy of cybernetics with a vengeance: the library as self-organizing system. Ethical and political dimensions of librarianship are unthinkable because the library is understood to be something existing in itself, something which we must correctly understand for what it is rather than something we can fashion and direct as we see fit according to our ethical concerns and political situation. In concept, of course, for what do we find "in concrete"? Vučković's library is a political institution because Vučković makes it one, Western Washington University Library supports Mongolian studies like no other institution in the Americas because Henry Schwarz and Wayne Richter have devoted fifty years of their lives to making it just such an institution, the University of Chicago Library serves an educational function because generations of librarians have dedicated themselves to making it just that kind of an institution, and the Rudy Lozano Branch of the Chicago Public Library system is a community meeting place and haven for the youth of the Pilsen neighborhood because generations of librarians have joined together with community activists and chess players to make it that way. These actual concrete facts about real libraries have arisen not from some eternal concept of the library but "depend upon the liberty and will of men"—those are Hannah Arendt's remarks on salvation, but they fit the case of libraries too, so long as we remember to include women.

On page eight I stopped reading Osburn's book. Since I found in both the Prologue and the concluding chapter the same reifications, the denial of the political and the pompous attitude of the philosopher who claims to know the proper meanings of words and the proper concepts associated with them, why keep reading? I dipped in here and there, looking at some sections where I thought I would have an adequate background to evaluate the discussion to see if perhaps Osburn actually came up with something worth reading, but what did I find? "The three chapters comprising Part Two of this book are dedicated to demonstrating that the library is, indeed, the product of natural selection for the purpose of adaptation to environmental change..." (ibid., p. 165). Is there a more scientifically incompetent way to deny the ethical, political and the social dimensions of libraries than an appeal to natural selection? And will the survival of Osburn's philosophy also be a matter of natural selection rather than the critical intelligence of current and future librarians?

On page ninety eight we read "Language has played the central facilitating role in cultural evolution, and by most accounts also is in large part a product of evolutionary forces." Here we go again: evolution (biological?) explains the existence of language, not social relations. His appeal to "most accounts" indicates—as does his bibliography—that he has not read Rudi Botha's searing critique in *Unravelling the Evolution of Language*.

Osburn has read widely, and that is something I appreciate. Unfortunately he has not read well, much less critically. In Chapter Four—Communication—Osburn throws together incompatible and contradictory theories to make his "synthesis": Schramm, Whorf, Plotkin, Vygotsky, Dawkins, Leroi-Gourhan, Chafe, Tomasello, Bergson, Dennett, Goody, Dobzhansky, Sapir, George Steiner, Pinker, Searle, John Maynard Smith... and many others from every imaginable discipline are strung together like they were all leading up to Osburn's conclusion. Unlike natural or everyday language, scientific terminologies have their meanings only in relation to the theories in which they are embedded. Evolution and natural selection for instance are not at all the same thing in Darwin, social darwinism and Dawkins. Yet Osburn proceeds in this chapter and all the others by serially connecting jarring juxtapositions of theoretically incompatible statements held together only by the common occurrence of certain words (communication, language, memory, knowledge, etc.) which seem to make them all relate to the same thing, although only to those unfamiliar with the larger theories from which the quotations have been extracted. His treatment of Dawkins is typical of his failure to grasp the importance of theoretical differences and debate: Dawkins' cultural memes are brought in to elucidate the notion of the natural selection of libraries, while objections to Dawkins' theory of memes—he does acknowledge that the theory is not accepted by all—are simply dismissed with the remark that "Genetics and memetics also differ in matters of degree of precision and regularity" (p. 102). With that critical loss of precision and regularity as his driving license, Osburn can drive through intellectual history any way he wants to, and he does.

The real clincher I found in his reference to R.G. Collingwood, one of my favourite writers in any field, and someone whom I have been reading and rereading for thirty years. Osburn quotes 10 lines from a two page fragment published posthumously in Collingwood's *The Principles of History* describing "distinctions traditionally drawn between philosophy and history on the bases of their method and the objects of their study" (Osburn, p. 43). Osburn proceeds to base his philosophy on Collingwood's description. But what is Collingwood's very next sentence following what Osburn quoted?

> This way of contrasting history with philosophy cannot survive the study of historical thought already made in the earlier chapters of the present book. (Collingwood, 1999, p.114)

Is this fragment of Collingwood's the only writing by Collingwood that Osburn has read? Whether or not that is the case, Osburn has not understood Collingwood's philosophy at all. Collingwood was the philosopher of questioning, not the philosopher of answers, much less answers offered as timeless truths and eternal verities. It is hard to imagine a philosopher further from Collingwood than Osburn.

8. The Dictatorship of Theory

In contrast to the dialectical realism and logic of Rendón Rojas, the analytical philosophy underpinning Morales López's study, and the evolutionary functionalism presented by Osburn, Alfaro López (2010) explicitly adopts the constructivist epistemology of Gaston Bachelard and his fellow travelers (Koyré, Piaget, Althusser, Canguilhem, Foucault, Morin and Bourdieu). The history of science is understood as a practice that develops through stages, from a prescientific empirical stage to the stage of full-fledged theory-driven science. He uses Bachelard's key notions of "epistemological obstacle" (*obstacle épistémologique*) and "epistemological break" (*rupture épistémologique*) to explain the historical trajectory and current dilemmas facing library science.

The three essays in Alfaro López's book take up Bachelard's notions one at a time. The first chapter "The library as epistemological obstacle" is an interesting reflection on a common theme: the practical and technical aspects of librarianship as an obstacle to theoretical engagement and development. This is one of the themes in Salarelli's and Osburn's books as well, but here the the problem is discussed in terms of Bachelard's understanding of science. According to this interpretation of the development of library science, since its establishment in the 19th century the field has been in its prescientific, empirical, constitutive phase. The focus on practical, empirical issues—the collections themselves, their users and the technologies involved —has kept the field as a whole from moving on to a theory driven stage as a mature science. He expresses this notion succinctly in the opening sentence of the first chapter: "The library has kept us from thinking the Library" (Alfaro López, 2010, p. 3). Being still in the constitutive phase of their development, library science and librarianship together are stuck "in the concrete, the immediate, the factual" and in order to become a mature science it will be necessary to begin thinking the library "in the order of the abstract, the intellectual, the conceptual" (ibid.). That movement from the constitutive phase of a science to the mature phase is accomplished through an "epistemological break" or rupture, which is the subject of the second chapter. In its constitutive phase library science has changed gradually. Now however that gradual change has become an obstacle to change, since these gradual changes are made in order to avoid radical change (ibid., p. 46). Alfaro López argues that library science needs to achieve autonomy, that is to become a mature science rather than a practice for which science is an "ornamental accessory" (ibid., p. 47).

> Those fields which have achieved truly scientific status quickly and in the best manner assimilate everything that information technologies generate, which in turn impels that science further. In order to find its autonomy it is necessary to deal with the cognitive, that is to say theoretical, substrate in order to comprehend and assimilate the changes produced by information technologies. On the other hand those fields which have not advanced to scientific autonomy are confronted with uncertainty in this situation. (ibid., p. 63)

A clear case of the latter situation is that of library science, "its foundations in question, so that uncertainty before an unstable and incertain future has marked it from one end to the other with doubts and uncertainty... Its current cognitive functioning does not deal with the elements and adequate categories for a global understanding of the radical changes that are taking place" (ibid., p. 64). The question he puts to the field is this: Mere technique or science? (ibid., p. 68). What will bring us from mere technique to science is the epistemological rupture brought about by theory construction, the topic of the third chapter.

Library science in its constitutive phase relied largely on positivism as its epistemological basis. Positivism "served to justify and consolidate its technical orientation ... and led to improved efficiency in library services" (ibid., p. 93). The next question the author poses is why did the positivist epistemology paralyze library science? (ibid., p. 94). The short answer is that the formalization and operationalism associated with positivism marginalized the imagination and creative cognitive processes that alone move science forward. It is through theoretical innovation, not empirical facts, that science progresses.

At this time the subjection of theory to the technical is no longer the appropriate response (the error arises from continuing to work according to the same positivist schema: to keep theory under the subjection of technology); the response to this challenge is to turn our thinking around: technology must respond to theoretical dictates. (ibid., p. 99)

A constructivist epistemology would construe the field as "a system of relations, in which practices and objects form a complex totality of interaction" (ibid., p. 106). This would bring library science into its mature, autonomous phase "as a distinct field of scientific knowledge determined by theory" (ibid., p. 108).

The last chapter deals with research and teaching in library science. In the author's treatment of the subject, this is understood to be the connection between society and techniques: "Society requires concrete and practical knowledge and the technical search for solutions" (ibid., p. 125). Yet this connection is slighted in an orientation towards technique:

The technical foundation on which library science was based during its constitutive phase led to widespread illusions concerning that foundation, separating it from the social world. Analyzing this situation in greater detail we can understand that it arose in large part because its origin in that technical foundation led to a knowledge that closed in on itself. Technical standards impose the production of schematic knowledge; the scheme of technical knowledge seeks practical solutions, that is, answers, that are already known, which can then be reiterated, thereby avoiding the asking of new questions that require theoretical support, which in turn would work towards renewal by refusing that reiteration and seeking new avenues for the production of knowledge. (ibid., p. 129)

In conclusion, the author claims that library science has thus far failed to fulfill its social function because it continues to isolate the field from the social by focusing on the technical, and, I would add, of conceiving of the social solely in terms of the technical.

Without the final chapter on research and education, the book's arguments could easily lead toward that kind of theoretical speculation divorced from all engagement with the real world that was so common in the 1980-1990s. In fact while reading the first chapter of the book I could not help thinking of the graduate student I met in the early 1990s who complained about having to read a novel in one of her English literature classes. "I am fascinated by theory" she remarked, "but I have no interest in literature and no desire to read it."

The theory that drives Alfaro López is not a theory of library science but Bachelard's theory of science. There is not really any philosophy or theory of library science in this book; rather a philosophy and theory of science by means of which the author examines, interprets and criticizes library science. It is a theory of scientific development which, like that of Lakatos drawn upon by Rendón Rojas, is interesting and sure to provoke many readers, but in the end fails to convince me, primarily because of its lack of interest in human agency and the ethical and political issues which that would entail.

Whether it comes from Alfaro López or Bachelard, the theory that a mature science must be an autonomous science is one that I reject for the simple reason that the world is not divided up into autonomous objects unrelated to any others, just sitting there waiting to be investigated in isolation. And if the objects of a science are not autonomous, then the science also cannot be autonomous. Furthermore, I am not sure why library scientists (and information scientists, computer scientists, management scientists, linguists...) feel that they ought to be scientists engaged in an official science to justify the moniker. Thinking clearly about what I as a librarian am doing, why I am doing it, and how my activities as a librarian relate to other practical, social and intellectual activities going on in the world is sufficient; I at least do not need the mantle of science to justify my life's work any more than I need a philosophy or a theory in order to think. Too much harping on science (and Alfaro López is not alone in this) makes me suspect that science in this case has some rather unscientific emotional and ideological friends (or are they enemies?) hiding in its pocket. At any rate, let us hope that others who read *Estudios epistemológicos de bibliotecología* have more interest in libraries than the above-mentioned student had in literature.

9. Philosophy Without Ethics and Politics, or Why Easy Answers Are Too Easy

Seven very different books, and several different philosophical orientations—social epistemology, dialectical realism, phenomenology, analytical philosophy, hermeneutics, systems theory and constructivist epistemology—referring to philosophers including Marx, Heidegger, Husserl, Lakatos, Luhmann, Boulding, Bachelard and not a few others. I am very happy about all that. But I am not very happy about a philosophical orientation towards answers rather than questions, and many of these books enact just such a philosophy. What is information? I know! What is a library? I know! What do we call the study of libraries and information? I know! What is science? I know! Are we scientists yet? I know! A question oriented philosophy "answers" every question with more questions and acknowledges that the answers we give to ourselves and act upon constitute our acting in the world, not the eternal essence of things. What we think and what we do as librarians make libraries what they are, moment by moment; librarians, not some platonic form, eternal concept or self-organizing system, determine the shape and future of our institutions. And any philosophy that takes that into account will require an ethics and a political philosophy from the beginning.

The publications I have discussed here represent not only contrasting views of what libraries are, but of what libraries ought to be and may become, as well as radically divergent philosophical orientations. Nearly all of these authors discuss one issue that seems to be an obsession among librarians (or rather the philosophers among librarians) as much as it was an obsession among linguists when I was a graduate student in linguistics thirty-five years ago: Is our science a real science? Have we had our scientific revolution and arrived at scientific maturity? The question arises because for nearly all of these authors epistemology has been understood to be synonymous with philosophy of science, so unless library science is a science it has no knowledge to offer. None of the answers to that question convinced me, for the question itself does not interest me in the least.

The association of philosophy with foundations and answers appears throughout these seven books, as it did in the papers by Radford, Budd and Dick. Those earlier authors also offered various philosophical orientations that they thought could provide epistemological foundations for library science. Zwadlo responded by rejecting the very idea of choosing "a philosophy", arguing instead that "We don't need a philosophy of library and information science: we're confused enough already". Yet somehow I managed to end up agreeing with Zwadlo as well as his opponents. Zwadlo is right that the last thing we need in LIS is "a philosophy", but both he and his opponents are in fact doing what librarians desperately need to do: they are questioning the way things are or at least appear to be, thinking carefully about libraries and librarianship using any and all philosophical approaches that seem to them to provide us with some insight into what libraries have been, are now, and may become. That is philosophy as I would have it, philosophy as a mode of thinking, not something one *has* (or does not have). We do not need to be told what to think (science, positivism) nor how to think, but we certainly do need to think! The result of those papers in the 1990s has been vigorous debate, which some would like to equate with confusion. Yet while the political dimension has not been lacking in that *Library Quarterly* debate begun by Radford, it certainly has not taken root in the epistemological and ontological foundations proposed by the participants. It is a pity that too many of the books and articles published during the past twenty years—like some of those discussed above—fret obsessively about science but forget about all things ethical and political. What is philosophy without ethics, without the political? As we have seen, all too often it is nothing more than science deified. Whenever epistemology is synonymous with philosophy of science, ethics and politics seem to vanish.

What all of the publications discussed above do demonstrate clearly—even those with which I have strong and deep disagreements—is that bibliotecología, bibliotekarstvo, biblioteconomia, Bibliothekswissenschaft, biblioteksvidenskab, kütüphanecilik, tushuguanxue, library and information science or whatever you call it, is definitely not an eternal verity that we can somehow discover if only we have the right philosophy of libraries and an appropriate terminology. It is an open, historically varied, indeterminate, contested, passionately disputed, often intelligently argued, politically important and socially vital topic of interest to people of different perspectives in different social situations. If it is or isn't science, I personally do not care. Libraries, librarianship and information science are clearly live issues that people can and do argue about, rather than eternal verities or closed systems running on automatic in which we have no involvement.

What is a library? What do you want it to be? Does the future of libraries and library science depend upon someone defining both in words? Or upon those who make a library and a library science what they will be here and now, in a particular space in a particular time? Must the Library be an eternal ideal or can libraries be different things to different people in different places at different times, oriented by and understood according to different philosophies? Investigate the matter, state your case, say what you mean, argue with me: if that is not science and philosophy at the same time, I do not know what is, nor does anyone else.

References

Alfaro López, Héctor Guillermo (2010). *Estudios epistemológicos de bibliotecología*. México: Universidad Nacional Autónoma de México. (Colección Teoría y métodos)
Budd, John M. (1995). "An epistemological foundation for library and information science" *Library Quarterly* v.65 nr.3 p.295-318.
Collingwood, R.G. (1999). *The Principles of History*. Oxford: Oxford University Press.
Dick, Archie L. (1999). "Epistemological positions and library and information science" *Library Quarterly* v.69 nr.3 p.305-323
Heber, Tanja (2009). *Die Bibliothek als Speichersystem des kulturellen Gedächtnisses*. Marburg: Tectum.
Morales López, Valentino (2008). *La bibliotecología y estudios de la información: análisis histórico-conceptual*. México: El Colegio de México. (Biblioteca Daniel Cosío Villegas)
Osburn, Charles B. (2009). *The Social Transcript: Uncovering Library Philosophy*. Westport, Connecticut and London: Libraries Unlimited. (Beta Phi Mu Monograph Series)
Radford, Gary P. (1992). "Positivism, Foucault, and the fantasia of the library: conceptions of knowledge and the modern library experience" *Library Quarterly*, v.62 nr.4 p.408-424.
Rendón Rojas, Miguel Ángel (1999). "El sistema de información documental ¿Un sistema autorreferencial y autopoiético?" *Revista Interamericana de Bibliotecología*, vol. 22, n. 2. (julio-diciembre), pp. 51-65
Rendón Rojas, Miguel Ángel (2005). *Bases teóricas y filosóficas de la bibliotecología*. México: Universidad Nacional Autónoma de México. 2a. edición corregida y aumenta-

da.(Colección Sistemas bibliotecarios de información y sociedad)

Salarelli, Alberto (2008). *Biblioteca e identità: per una filosofia della biblioteconomia.* Milano: Editrice Bibliografica. (Bibliografia e biblioteconomia. Argomenti, 1)

Вучковић, Жељко [Vučković, Željko]. (2003). *Јавне библиотеке и јавно знање.* Нови Сад: Библиотека Матице српске, Футура публикације.

Вучковић, Жељко [Vučković, Željko]. (2008). „Библиотеке, знање, демократија" *Панчевачко читалиште,* број 13, p. 22-25.

Zwadlo, Jim (1997). "We don't need a philosophy of library and information science: we're confused enough already," *The Library Quarterly*, v. 67 nr.2, pp.103-121.

XVI

Se vogliamo che tutto rimanga com'è, bisogna che tutto deva essere scritto in inglese[1]

The splendid isolation of American library science

> In brief, splendid isolation, freedom from entanglements with European nations, was the dominant ideal to the end of the nineteenth century and was an integral part of the American ethos. (Morris Raphael Cohen and Felix S. Cohen. *American thought: a critical sketch*. New York, Free Press, 1954)

Looking at library science in the United States we are confronted with an ostrich, its head buried in English. Yet in its use of English, library science in the United States is little different from any other American science, and the situation apparently

---

[1] Originally published in Italian under the same title in *Biblioteche oggi* 2012, v.30 nr.4, p.20-24.

has roots that go back a long way. If "splendid isolation" was a dominant ideal in 19th century America, it seems to have survived into 21st century American academic if not economic life. Here in the United States we often hear that the language of science is English (or at least Broken English), and it seems that many scientists in Europe share that understanding—or at least they desire an American readership enough to write in English. For it is true that any scientist who writes in a language other than English will be ignored here. In this land rightly proud of its constitutional guarantees of academic and religious freedoms and a general freedom of speech, the online databases and bibliographical references accompaning articles in the major professional journals all tell a different and disturbing story: if it is not published in English, it does not exist. There may be freedom of speech here, but if you are not speaking in English, no one is listening. What does not exist has no right to a hearing.

Is this linguistic picture of contemporary American library science at all accurate or is it a misperception? One could treat this as an empirical question to be resolved by counting citations or surveying 17.4% of the faculty of 28% of the library schools in the United States, with a few European faculty thrown in for good measure. However I do not think there is any need to engage in a quantitative study of who cites publications in what language and how often, nor even a survey of faculty attitudes towards the literature beyond English, though that might make interesting reading. If you want you can pick up any journal published in English—even one published by IFLA—and count the references to non-English publications, repeating this for as many English language journals and journal issues as you like. This simple exercise ought to convince anyone of the accuracy of my portrayal. I do this often, but I do not keep count.

I do not keep count because I do not need to. It is quite clear that there is a literature of library science not in English—a substantial literature, a good literature and an irreplaceable literature—and the absence of attention to it by American librarians and library science reseachers can only be explained by American attitudes and aptitudes. I do not need to measure any surrogates for American attitudes because I live with them, because I have been reading for years without finding references to those who do not write in English but whom I have come to appreciate. I do not find non-English publications by following citations in articles by my American colleagues. I look for them. I look very hard. I read everything I can find that is not in English. And I am grateful for those European scholars who cite the non-English publications of their European colleagues. They have been my best guides.

Is English *the* language of library science or rather one among many? The answer to that question depends of course upon whom you ask: asked of a monolingual English speaking librarian or professor of library science, the answer is unequivocably yes, even when that person reads publications in translation. "If it is not in English it does not exist" is not so much a lie as an excuse—a convenient fiction—to mask an ethical refusal. Science-not-written-in-English does in fact exist, but many English speakers choose to ignore what they cannot or do not want to read, and blame instead the foreign authors for not writing in the only language the provincial American chooses to read.

What is the significance of this situation, of this linguistic attitude? Does it matter in which language we write and read? Should we accept the notion of one single language for library research and scholarship? If so, should we be promoting the learning and use of that language, and which language should that be? If not, how do we understand our current situation and what should we be doing in response to it? I have encountered five explanations of the current linguistic situation; I offer my own interpretations and responses.

Explanation number 1: English is the international language of science
Is English currently the international language of science? Suppose we assume that it is. What does it mean? Does it mean that if anyone wishes to publish research on any topic it must be published in English? That is clearly not the case and *Biblioteche oggi* is sufficient proof of that. So whatever the reason may be for lack of attention to non-English publications by American librarians and professors, it is not that there is no research published in languages other than English.

Explanation number 2. Research published in the English language is good enough, comprehensive enough in scope, and so vast in its quantity that we can safely assume there is nothing "out there" in some other language that we cannot ignore. If it is important, if it is worth reading it either is or soon will be available in English.
Anyone who looks at the non-English literature of library science can see that this is no explanation at all but merely a poor excuse for shallow literature searching. Limiting myself just to what I have found of interest in the field of library science, I can list many writers who have published little if any in English and yet have been immensely valuable for my understanding of libraries and information technologies: Isabelle Boydens in Belgium, Peter Janich and Uwe Jochum in Germany, Joëlle Le Marec, Yves Jeanneret and Emmanuël Souchier in France, Mirosław Górny and Jacek Wojciechowski in Poland, Carlo Revelli and Alberto Salarelli in Italy, Rosa Nehmy and Isis Paim in Brazil, Željko Vučković in Serbia, Valentino Morales López in Mexico—to name just a few. The crucial point is that what I found in the non-English publications of these writers *cannot be found anywhere in English*. There is an engagement with Anglo-American scholarship *and a response*, this latter rarely taken into account in the Anglo-American world. And of course there are also unique ideas and perspectives that are not responses to American challenges but arise

from a different knowledge, experience and point of view. It is these latter that are of the utmost importance to me.

Explanation number 3: The whole world looks to American science as the leader, so why should those who are expected to be the leaders follow anyone else?
This is actually—honest to God I will swear on any Holy Book you put before me—the explanation offered by a professor in one of my graduate seminars in 1983. The seminar was on 20th century theories of poetics (!!!) and the professor offered the above explanation in answer to a question about the absence of Heidegger in the syllabus.

Personal horror stories aside, is there any substance to this claim? Yes, in fact there is: much of the world does look to the United States (and the English speaking world at large) because of the wealth of ideas, the quality of research, the wide distribution of that research and the successes and reputation of American science and technological developments of the past. Yet the fact that librarians and others around the world are interested in research published in the United States does not mean that a reciprocal interest is unwarranted or unnecessary—quite the contrary, as I indicated in my comments on Explanation number 2 above.

I am in the habit of searching an EBSCO database or browsing E-LIS (this being a multilingual gold mine in comparison to the extremely anglocentric EBSCO database of library science literature) when I want to catch up on the field at an international level, but I often feel that I am nearly alone in my desire to attend to ideas not expressed in English. In the current issue of *Library Resources & Technical Services* (April 2012) there is a review of the literature on cataloging and classification for 2009-1010. Like all other reviews of the literature published in American library science journals, "only English-language literature is reviewed" but the author does acknowledge (apologize?) that "not all of the literature covered is U.S.-

based."[2] If Americans wish to continue thinking of themselves as those to whom alone the world looks to for leadership, they need at least to keep one eye upon what the rest of the world is publishing to see if indeed there is not some professor at the Sorbonne or a librarian in Bandung, Brno, Dakar, Kaunas, Ljubljana or even Hamelin running away with the field behind our American backs.

Explantion number 4. Keyword searching
This is indeed an important aspect of our current situation. Search by English language keyword and you can expect English language results. Set your Google parameters to English results only and you will get even more isolated from the wonderful diversity of the world's voices. This technical explanation, important as it is for our time (and likely to become even more important with the development of greater customization as a feature of more and more systems) cannot account for the phenomenon as I encountered it during my student days, nor even in the 1990s as a not so young librarian. The early dominance of English in the world of information technology is itself related to a long history of American disinterest in the world beyond English. Keyword searching arose among a group of monolingual Americans, and its successes in America for too long diverted attention away from efforts to seriously consider constructing information systems for a multilingual world.

Explanation number 5. Attitude: hubris and willful ignorance
I understand our current linguistic situation to be rooted in attitudes and orientations, our ethical relations with the world. Since we think of ourselves as the greatest nation on earth, the home of the free where everywhere else people are in chains, it should come as no surprise that we are not disposed to learning

---

[2] Sue Ann Gardner, "Cresting toward the sea change: literature review of cataloging and classification 2009-10" *Library Resources & Technical Services* v. 56 nr.2 April 2012, p.64.

anything from the rest of the world. If we go elsewhere it is to teach, to engage in research, or to "liberate" the less fortunate; we do not go to listen and learn in another language unless we want to install ourselves there to take your money.

Whatever the real explanation for the current linguistic situation may be, it is in any case necessary to examine some of the more complex aspects of the languages of science in the 21st century. Where does language learning and teaching fit in? Translation? The semantic web and other promised or promising multilingual technical solutions? Library education and employment?

Language Learning
In my cold war era youth language learning was important to the United States government, its intelligence agencies and its armed forces, and therefore language teaching and learning were a part of nearly every degree program in every university (I am not sure this is the case anymore; the University of Chicago currently requires only one year of foreign language). Surely every American librarian my age had to have four years of high school or two years of college language instruction. The trouble is, few of us ever had a need in our everyday life or in our professional activities for any language other than English. When languages are not used, they are lost. Perhaps this explains in part the failure of Americans to engage non-English scholarship: they were never interested enough in the world beyond their home to use the language of elsewhere, and whatever they may have learned in their youth, they lost it long ago. Do we have an influx of immigrants? Teach them English—why learn their language? Does the library need to catalog something in Albanian or Dutch? Search OCLC and take what you find. Is there something important in my field that was not published in English? Get a grant to have it translated. Yet there are problems with translations, and getting grants to fund them is the least of them.

Translation
A decade ago I purchased Paul Virilio's *Un paysage d'événements* but before I sat down to read it, the English translation appeared in the book store. I noted that the English version was a much slimmer volume and compared it to my French edition. With no statement to inform the reader of the English version, six out of eighteen chapters of Virilio's French had dissappeared. I read the French version and finally understood why many of the friends and teachers of my youth had urged me to always consult the original text, relying on translations only when I could not read the original.

Getting grants to fund translation can be difficult enough; getting good and complete translations even more difficult. But none of this even gets a chance to happen if no one is aware of what the rest of the world is writing, much less evaluating it for possible translation. The greatest obstacle to getting translations made is finding someone who will push such projects forward. We definitely need more translation into English, but I do not believe that translations will ever change the attitudes which I regard as the crucial factor, and in fact more translations may simply reinforce the intransigence of those who believe everything worth reading is or will be available in English. Translation is not enough.

Linguistic limitations of bibliographic tools and technical systems
Another revelation came to me after reading a paper by Isabelle Boydens and Seth van Hooland published in the *Journal of Documentation* in 2011. Looking for more by Boydens I discovered to my astonishment and dismay that her 1999 monograph was in only one library in the United States, and none of her dozens of published papers were in EBSCO's databases. The lesson I took from this incident was that I would have to look for good work myself since our bibliographic information systems suffer from severely distorted coverage of non-English publications.

Similarly one can look at the coverage of OCLC and Google Books. If either of these tools are to become the *de facto* catalogs and online libraries for students and researchers, their linguistic limitations, not only in their coverage and searching systems but in their algorithms for ordering the display and ranking by relevance need to be carefully scrutinized. Fortunately English speaker-readers can read Jeanneney's recent book related to this problem since it has been translated into English. Jean-Noël Jeanneney is horrified when he imagines how our children might come to see the world: Will future generations think no great books have been written in a language other than English? And even worse: Will they see history only through American eyes?

> The president of the French national library has made himself the frontman in what he sees as a struggle to save cultural diversity. In the postmodern world, the battleground is the internet. Here, search engines determine what tomorrow's generations will click on, learn and think. (*Financial Times*, quoted from the University of Chicago Press website)

Differences that make a difference
Personal experience has been the catalyst for much of my research and my attitudes, and here I will offer yet another tale from life: my discovery of the writings of the Italian librarian Carlo Revelli. Revelli is one of those librarians who does not write in English but who has been fortunate enough to have two of his books reviewed in the American library literature. As I read his work it slowly dawned on me that his approach to cataloging was profoundly different from any that I had previously encountered. I quickly turned to a number of treatises on cataloging to see if I had merely missed something in my earlier reading, but no, everywhere the difference was pronounced. I had learned something in Italian that did not exist in English. Yet it was not the case that I learned from my encounter with

Revelli that I could probably experience the shock of the different in every language I chose to read. Rather it was that expectation of finding something valuable that led me to his books in the first place. And that is what I would like to see in America: an expectation that reading the world beyond English would be more than worthwhile, that it would be a continual revelation.

Just today I ran accross an essay by Georg Arnestad in the Norwegian journal *Bok og Bibliotek*. Here are Arnestad's concluding remarks:

> In the "Library of Babel," as Jorge Luis Borges describes it in his famous short story, all the world's knowledge was collected. But access to it was impossible. In the commercially operated public library without books as the Danish researchers describe it, it's even worse: You can access everything. But there isn't anything.[3]

Doesn't that make you want to read the rest of Arnestad's article, as well as the article on the future library described by the Danish librarians? That Danish-Norwegian debate was not published in English, and probably never will be; yet now is the time to read it, not after the library in which nothing exists has signed an exclusive contract with ALA or IFLA. How many American readers will look for this Norwegian debate? How many will read it? How many can?

Monolingual libraries in a multilingual world
Perhaps the most important experience for me has been to observe over the course of many years how inattention to the actual linguistic situation of science and scholarship—and hence of libraries—distorts library policies in ways detrimental to the development and use of the literature produced beyond the con-

---

[3] Georg Arnestad, "Biblioteket i Babel", *Bok og Bibliotek* 2012 nr. 1, p.65.

fines of English. Americans do not read the foreign language materials, and libraries like to withdraw funding from unused collections—you can guess the result. And with diminished acquisition of non-English materials, the need to employ librarians with non-English linguistic abilities decreases. And with the unemployment possibilities for linguistically competent librarians, it is unlikely that library schools will attract or teach to those for whom the world beyond English matters. You have to be able to write in HTML in order to get in library school, but if you cannot read Dante in Italian, it does not matter. There are no jobs that require Italian, and if one should arise, the library will hire somebody who knows Spanish instead and expect them to just do their best with the Italian dimensions of the job descriptions... and in all likelihood add Scandinavian and African studies to their responsibilities should the need for a librarian in those areas arise later. Better yet, drop these difficult language materials and let students use the internet. There is an irresponsible idea whose time has come!

In conclusion: English only, Babel or Pentecost?
We have, it seems, at least three options. The first, which has been the situation against which I have set myself, is a world in which all communication not in English can be ignored, and ignorance of anything not published in English can be excused. This is the situation in the United States today. This alternative is nothing other than a justification for dismissing the rest of the world. For anyone who acknowledges the existence of the world, it is untenable.

The second option, Babel, is the world in which there are no Carlo Revellis, no George Steiners, no Ramon Lulls, and of course no David Bades. It is a world in which everyone writes and reads only in their mother tongue and ignores the rest of the world. It is the world in which everyone ignores everyone who does not speak and write the same language. It is an option open only to nationalists and fascists. For anyone who delights in the differences the world makes, it is untenable.

The third option is like Pentecost, where everyone speaks in their own language and in spite of that every voice gets heard and and every language is understood. Yet not exactly like Pentecost, because we cannot rely on the third member of the Trinity to do the work for us since he is not everywhere welcome. The task of communication and understanding is up to us—and all of us—because Carlo Revelli cannot do it alone. As an American I am trying to follow the Italians who are leading in these efforts with *Osservatorio internazionale* and E-LIS. I read what I can and write what I can, even though I can write well only in English.

And why write this lament devoid of any empirical foundation nor even dressed up in statistical authority? If no one writes of these matters then library scientists will have nothing to count and therefore declare that the problem does not exist. So I have written to add my voice to those voices already on record in order that science will have something to study. But alas! I am publishing it in Italy and in Italian, so no American librarians or professors will ever read it. For of course anything worth reading would be published in English. Capisce?

XVII

Thinking About Efficiency in Libraries

Reading the final report of the Library of Congress Working Group on the Future of Bibliographic Control I could not help but notice that efficiency as a value that trumped all others was evident throughout the report. In Bade (2009) I remarked "The demand for efficiency begs the question of what we are trying to do in our activities of bibliographic control, i.e. efficient at doing what?" (Bade, 2009, p. 1). This question prompted me to set out to look more broadly and more carefully at the discourse of efficiency in LIS. One of the first items I located was a 1913 essay by a cataloger at the John Crerar Library named Aksel G. S. Josephson. He offered the following definition of efficiency:

> Efficiency exists when we achieve the desired results with the least expenditure of effort and the smallest amount of resultant waste. ... When our task is accomplished in such a manner that every step counts directly toward it, when every effort results in a corresponding accomplishment, when the amount of resultant waste is a

minimum, then we have before us the results of efficiency. (Josephson, 1913, p. 7-8)

Josephson put this in the context of a library by asking whether or not "the present bibliographical condition" is efficient. In more concrete terms he asked "Can we gather together anywhere in this country a complete series of bibliographical records of any subject that anyone wishes to investigate? Are the existing and available records adequate? Is the material referred to in the records available?" (Josephson, p. 9). While his apparent desire for "a complete series of bibliographical records of any subject" ought to raise plenty of objections, for the purpose of investigating our understanding of efficiency the passage—including this assumption—is instructive. Anyone familiar with the library literature of the late 20th and early 21st century will note the sharp contrast between Josephson's association of efficiency with completeness, adequacy and availability *from the viewpoint of one using the library*, and the reduction of efficiency to matters of cost *for the library* that characterizes the literature of our time.

In the library management literature efficiency has come to mean economic efficiency, often simply cost-cutting, and has frequently been discussed as something separate from effectiveness. There have been voices of caution such as Hernon and McClure (1990) who wrote at the beginning of their book

> Attention to efficiency rather than effectiveness fails to consider the likely tradeoff relationships between the two types of measures. Efficiency of an activity or service cannot be improved past a certain "critical point" without injuring the effectiveness of that activity or service, and vice-versa. Thus, continued attention to increasing the efficiency of various activities and services may become dysfunctional or counterproductive to effectiveness criteria. (p. 8)

More recently Marc Storms made the same distinction in his complaint about "too many managers running around libraries in the Netherlands":

> Management that focuses only on making sure that everything keeps running efficiently is not a path I would recommend. Everything needs to work effectively. ... Efficiency means the right cost and employing the right means, but effectiveness means getting the job done. (Storms, 2003, p. 9)

Unfortunately the majority of references to efficiency in the literature of library management are not so carefully considered, and nowhere have I found any detailed discussion of the nature of efficiency. Efficiency is either defined to fit the writer's purposes or simply assumed to be unproblematic. The literature on efficiency in relation to information technologies suffers from the same kind of treatment.

Outside the boundaries of LIS there is a literature relating efficiency to time, technique (a concept broader than technology), cooperation, competition, justice, and many other matters. The year 2009 has already produced a bumper crop of studies from diverse theoretical perspectives and from these I have selected four for review. They present four very different approaches to understanding efficiency, but provide complementary rather than conflicting treatments of the topic. Rather than reviewing each of these books in terms of their own disciplinary orientations—management, ergonomics/reliability engineering, law, and environmental economics—I propose to review them with an eye on the LIS discourse of efficiency: just what is meant by "efficiency" in LIS? Is efficiency a technical issue? An ethical issue? A necessity? Economic sense or nonsense? Managerial propaganda or just a word we use to justify organizational changes? These are precisely the kinds of questions raised and discussed in the books reviewed here, and in fact the meaning of the word *efficiency* in managerial discourse is the main topic of Callender's *Efficiency and Management*.

Callender remarks in his preface that his experiences in the business world and government led him to try "to better understand the management use, even worship, of the term *efficiency*" (Callender, p. xiii). The method he chose was to examine the use and varied meanings of the term efficiency in the literatures of engineering, management, economics, accounting, Human Resources Management (HRM) and the procurement profession, adding case studies of economic commentary in the mass media, and of the railroad and procurement industries. What he argues is "the demise rather than the rise of efficiency" (Callender, p. xiii), suggesting that unlike the industrialized nations of the west, the "rising economies in Asia and other parts of the world ... seem to possess a concept of how to enact efficient practice" (Callender, p. xiii). His principal objective is, he writes,

> to demonstrate that, despite the historical management support for the notion of technical *efficiency* until the middle of the twentieth century, the notion of efficiency now has a limited impact on contemporary management practice despite its constant usage in management discourse. (Callender, p. 3)

and what he finds confirms

> that the notion of descriptive efficiency has been developed as a populist concept in managerial discourse and is typically interpreted in simplistic, normative terms and thus has limited technical meaning in management practice. In the hands of plausible management commentators who have seemingly assumed that management efficiency will emerge from the adoption of their various prescriptions, the term provides status without necessarily creating substance. (Callender, p. 3)

What his study revealed and what he is arguing is not an objection to efficiency but to the meanings that the term has come to have in the fields investigated and the way the term is used. Efficiency has become, he argues, "an ideological statement of support for any management intention, rather than a practical means to inform a range of management actions" (Callender, p. 3). As a wonderfully humorous example of this he remarks that

> it is unlikely that Chief Executive Officers (CEOs) would wish their remuneration to be linked to *least cost* concepts even though their rhetoric concerning *corporate efficiency* and shareholder Return on Investment may often promote such views (Callender, p. 19)

Defining efficiency in terms of least cost is an example of what he calls *economic efficiency* (abbreviated in the book as EEec) which he distinguishes from other meanings of efficiency such as *descriptive efficiency, allocative efficiency, technical efficiency* and *dynamic efficiency*. (The multiplicity of meanings and the terms he provides for them are confusing enough; his resort to abbreviations makes reading very difficult.) The problem with understanding efficiency in terms of an economic definition like 'least cost' or 'greatest benefits relative to cost' is that these terms

> may be quantified when applied to a single situation, but both terms suffer the legacy of the descriptors *least* and *greatest*, both of which are subject to individual interpretation. How does an organization know that it has achieved its least cost goals? Can the term least ever imply an absolute value, or is it subject to change over time? What are the measurable greatest benefits relative to costs for an organization? Are these values ever finite or will greatest benefit vary as the nature and value of costs change over time? (Callender, p. 20).

Callender traces the history of the term 'efficiency' in the management literature, revealing a move away from the use of efficiency to mean *technical efficiency* (maximizing performance) towards *economic efficiency* (least cost, etc.), a shift away from the engineering perspective focused on what one intends to achieve, to the managerial perspective narrowly concerned with cost cutting and profit. His case study of the railroad reforms of the 1990s in the United Kingdom and New South Wales is a narrative of the triumph of economic efficiency over technical efficiency among those responsible for the rail system "in an environment where system design and operation requires the maintenance of quite rigid professional operating standards" (Callender, p. 146-147). The new policies adopted were service-based models that sought "to improve general levels of customer service, reduce the cost to the state of operating the public rail network and increase the efficiency of labour" (Callender, p. 146). The officers of the State Rail Authority of New South Wales were committed to "the competitive outcomes-focused ideology of Economic Rationalism" and assumed that "better service was the path required to rejuvenate rail, with safety and operating efficiency being somehow looked after by the myriad of [outsourced—DB] contractors that now undertake rail maintenance." These new managers, he writes, "seemingly believed that a laissez-faire approach to technical efficiency (TEmp) would not have any significant consequences" (Callender, p. 168).

Within a decade of the railroad reorganization in New South Wales judicial inquiries into accidents led to recommendations to reverse most of the policy changes of 1996. Callender writes that the primary achievements of those policies—made in the interest of achieving greater efficiencies—have been an intense media scrutiny of the practical results of policies, a judicial review of an accident that "linked a decline in safety standards in the interest of on-time running", a major reduction in staff, "a limited improvement in financial performance" and new regulatory bodies that increased operation costs (Callender, p.

167). And although the New South Wales system is almost back to where it was before, the rail system has "yet to deliver either technical efficiency (TEmp) by demonstrating higher output from existing resources or ... by delivering rail owners least cost outcomes" (Callender, p. 171). The government promoted efficiency and a competitive structure "without regard to the history, culture and technical consequences of such a change" (Callender, p. 168). The price of this "efficiency adventure" Callender writes, "of lives lost, careers destroyed or damaged, and political credibility and money will never be known" (Callender, p. 169).

Callender's final chapter opens with a concise summary of the results of his study:

> The evidence gathered in this study suggests that the management discipline has drifted into allowing the notion of efficiency to be typically defined within the confines of the economics discipline as any activity that results in a lower or least-cost outcome, whether or not this outcome can be demonstrated. If this is the case, then the evidence also implies that efficiency has come to be seen as an ideological expression rather than one that defines standards of management or organizational performance. In short, the word efficiency has become a meaningless figure of speech in the vocabulary of managers. The exact meaning implied by the management user is almost unimportant, as the mere use of the term suggests that the outcomes being reported are justifiable. (Callender, p. 182)

One need only look into the literature of library management to verify Callender's conclusions for LIS. Yet what of those of us who really do sense the need to discuss matters related to efficiency, those for whom it is not an ideological weapon or propaganda? For such readers Erik Hollnagel's book is a perfect complement to Callender's.

The first thing to note about *The ETTO Principle* is that unlike Callender's book it is a breeze to read. Hollnagel writes well and writes for "people who, for one reason or another, are reluctant to start on a conventional textbook or work of science" (Hollnagel, p. iv). Rather than offering the reader a dense, terminologically complicated text filled with references and scholarly apparatus, he has chosen to write for the lay reader and to conclude each chapter with some notes on the literature, there for your interest, to be pursued or skipped over at will.

The second thing to note is that Hollnagel writes from the perspective of one of the world's leading researchers on why things sometimes go wrong (cf. the subtitle of the book) in the operation of technical systems. His definition of efficiency is neither ideological nor economic but practical. The first discussion of efficiency appears in his remarks on the Stop Rule:

> Since the purpose of an accident investigation is to find an adequate explanation for what has happened, the analysis should clearly be as detailed as possible. This means that it should not stop at the first cause it finds, but continue to look for alternative explanations and possible contributing conditions, until no reasonable doubt about the correctness of the outcome remains ...
> Ending an analysis when a sufficiently good explanation has been found, or using whatever has been found as an explanation when time or resources run out, even knowing that it could have been continued in principle, corresponds to a criterion of efficiency.
> We shall call the first alternative *thoroughness*, for reasons that are rather obvious. And we shall call the second alternative *efficiency*, because it produces the desired effect with a minimum of time, expense, effort or waste. (Hollnagel, p. 12-13).

315

That is a pretty simple definition and one upon which Hollnagel will expand a few pages later where he also offers an expanded definition of *thoroughness*.

The third thing to note is already in the passage just quoted: efficiency is defined in relation to its opposite. The main point of the book is that efficiency and thoroughness are *both necessary but rarely simultaneously possible*. This is what the ETTO Principle states:

> In their daily activities, at work or at leisure, people routinely make a choice between being effective and being thorough, since it rarely is possible to be both at the same time. If demands to productivity or performance are high, thoroughness is reduced until the productivity goals are met. If demands to safety are high, efficiency is reduced until the safety goals are met. (Hollnagel, p. 15)

Hollnagel then expands on the definition of efficiency:

> Efficiency means that the level of investment or amount of resources used or needed to achieve a stated goal or objective are kept as low as possible. The resources may be expressed in terms of time, materials, money, psychological effort (workload), physical effort (fatigue), manpower (number of people), etc. The appropriate level or amount is determined by the subjective evaluation of what is sufficient to achieve the goal, i.e., good enough to be acceptable by whatever stop rule is applied as well as by external requirements and demands. (Hollnagel, p. 16-17)

Efficiency is necessary because time and resources are both limited; thoroughness is necessary "to make sure that we do things in the right way, so that we can achieve what we intend, and to avoid adverse consequences" (Hollnagel, p. 17) these latter being major producers of inefficiencies. Hollnagel's emphasis on time is particularly interesting; Callender also noted that demands for efficiency often went hand in hand with a failure to consider temporal developments and potential consequences, and Merlini (2009) puts our changing experience of time as a result of technological developments at the centre of his analysis. Classical economic decision theory, Hollnagel reminds us, assumes "that alternatives as well as criteria are constant while the decision is made, that hence time does not exist" (Hollnagel, p. 25). In the real world, however, when one wishes to do something

> there are always two options. One is to wait, to gather more information, to see how things develop, or just to hope for a greater level of certainty—or less uncertainty. The other is to go ahead on the assumption that the situation is known well enough and the alternatives are clear enough ... It is this dilemma between time to think and time to do that is at the heart of the ETTO principle. (Hollnagel, p. 28)

> The ETTO principle names a phenomenon or a strong characteristic of individual—and collective—performance, namely that people in dynamically changing, hence unstable and partly unpredictable situations, know that it is more important to do something before time is up, however imperfect it may be, than to find the perfect response when it is too late. (Hollnagel, p. 58)

This will remind many readers of the discussions in the library literature about rapid versus full cataloging, timely access versus "the perfect record" and so on. This is exactly Hollnagel's terrain and although librarianship does not enter the discussion, he does discuss the time sensitive data collection, analysis and dissemination work of the Canadian office of Aeronautical Information, Regulation and Control. This office is required "to produce a weekly report that is as accurate as possible" (Hollnagel, p. 73)—and it succeeds.

Of particular interest for library operations is Hollnagel's discussion of "collaborative ETTO" in chapter six. All actions and especially collaborative actions do not occur in isolation but follow from and influence the actions of others. We can think of our actions in the context of the actions of others either from the viewpoint of efficiency or of thoroughness.

> In such cases, thoroughness means that the person does not simply accept the input he or she receives from somewhere or from someone else, but instead makes an effort to confirm that it is correct. ... Similarly, thoroughness would mean that the person considers the possible side-effects and secondary outcomes of what he or she produces as output, in a sense adopting the mindset of whoever is going to work on the results. Similarly, efficiency means that the person trusts that the input he or she receives is correct, i.e., that the previous person was thorough. Efficiency also means that the person assumes that the next person, whoever is going to work on the results, will make the necessary checks and verifications, i.e., that the next person is thorough. (Hollnagel, p. 119)

Since there is never enough time or resources to check everything at each step of the way we have to trust what others have done, i.e. the choice for efficiency is forced upon us.

> It is as if everyone, including ourselves, reasons in the following way: 'I can allow myself to be efficient, because the others will be thorough.' If only some people do that, the system may be able to correct itself and to find a balance of functioning that is both reasonably effective and reasonably thorough. But if everyone begins to work in this way, for instance because of system-

ic pressures, the net result may be that something goes wrong. (Hollnagel, p. 120)

This describes the world of cooperative cataloging very well: its appeal, its necessity, its potential catastrophe. We are eager to enter into cooperative agreements and automate, and outsourcery has become our new religion because it means we will no longer have to perform the required labor nor deal with a staff but only pay the lowest bidder. And we sit and wait for someone else to do our work for us (cooperation), or we significantly limit our knowledge and control over the results (outsourcing and automation). How do we avoid this scenario in which we each expect everyone else to do what we do not have the time or resources to do? From the analysis of case studies of accidents, near accidents and successes Hollnagel concludes that socio-technical systems work only when and only because everyone makes "approximate adjustments to their work" (Hollnagel p. 123). We must understand, he argues,

> that what *anyone* does depends on what others have done, what others do, and what others are going to do— and that *everyone* is in the same situation. In order to be able to improve safety we must acknowledge that the most important part of the – dynamic and unpredictable – environment is what other people do. It is the ability of people to adjust their performance in response to the adjustments that others have made, make, or are going to make, that makes the social system strong. (Hollnagel, p. 123-124)

Technical systems are not like social systems, and socio-technical systems are not like either social or technical systems considered separately. If I may put my own interpretation forward, I would suggest that, following Ellul (1964), technical systems embody the search for efficiency, while social systems embody the search for inefficiency, i.e. freedom, for it is only in the space where anything can happen that the new and the unforeseen—the future—become possible. Any socio-technical system must seek a balance if we are to avoid the unbearable alternatives of a future that is totally controlled or totally out of control.

The ETTO principle describes that search for a balance which, because of our temporal and corporeal existence, is always a trade-off. Because both efficiency and thoroughness are necessary, we are left with a paradox:

> efficiency in the present presupposes thoroughness in the past, which paradoxically means that thoroughness in the present is necessary for efficiency in the future (Hollnagel, p. 149)

And that leads us back to Callender's question "Are these values ever finite or will greatest benefit vary as the nature and value of costs change over time?"

The recent literature discussed by Callender, like the library literature, views efficiency from a very narrow perspective: cost-cutting. The beauty of Hollnagel's book is that he looks at efficiency from the perspective of temporal processes within socio-technical systems, recognizing their dynamics and unpredictability in light of the full range of human interests, needs and susceptibilities. Mathis' *Efficiency Instead of Justice?* provides yet another complementary perspective, examining the meaning of efficiency in light of legal and economic justice.

Part One of *Efficiency Instead of Justice?* is devoted to understanding the economic analysis of law, in particular the notion of efficiency in welfare theory. Part Two discusses the philosophical foundations of the economic analysis of law, dealing with Adam Smith, Jeremy Bentham and John Rawls in order. In Part Three we move to the contemporary debate surrounding Posner's ideas, the author's critiques and his conclusion. The book is particularly relevant to recent debates in librarianship not only because of its discussion of *Homo economi-*

cus, but also because of its discussions of welfare economics and distributive justice, matters of significance to librarians dedicated to access to information and worried about the digital divide. There is also his critique of Bentham, whose utilitarianism was recently resurrected as a philosophy for librarianship precisely in the context of developing more efficient library operations (Banush and LeBlanc, 2007).

The second chapter, "Efficiency Criteria" presents two economic understandings of efficiency—Pareto efficiency and Kaldor-Hicks criterion—and criticisms of them. The criterion for Pareto efficiency is "any change that puts one member of a society in a better position without making somebody else worse off" (p. 33). The Kaldor-Hicks criterion states that "a change is an improvement ... if the gainers value their gains more highly than the losers their losses" (p. 39). I will not dwell on these theories nor on Mathis' criticisms, but one objection he makes to adopting a consistent policy following the Kaldor-Hicks criterion is that humans "need to have just treatment meted out—in specific cases and, most importantly, case by case!—to themselves and, indeed, to others" (quoted from the English edition, p. 49). This observation parallels my own understanding of the nature of bibliographic description (it is an activity of attention to the facts case by case), and is pertinent to discussions of automated systems of cataloging as much as the administration of justice. Summarizing the chapter Mathis writes that both Pareto's and Kaldor-Hicks' understanding of efficiency in economics

> contain not only weak, uncontested value judgements but also strong ones. Far from making analysis of normative questions superfluous, the demand for efficiency therefore has the opposite effect: it brings into sharp focus the need for closer scrutiny of the relationship between efficiency and justice. (p. 49)

That relationship he treats directly in Chapter Nine, to which we now turn.

Mathis first looks at the relationship between efficiency and justice in Hollnagel's terms as a "tradeoff." He rejects the economists' assumption that this relationship is one of conflict, assuming instead that "justice and efficiency are substitutable, up to a certain point" (p. 185) and proceeds to discuss them in terms of a trade-off on the values-level—how much justice a person or a society is *prepared to sacrifice* in order to achieve more efficiency (or vice versa)" (p. 185-186), and a production trade-off: "how much justice *must be sacrificed* in order to achieve a certain level of efficiency (or vice versa)" (p. 186). For these trade-offs we can substitute "thoroughness" for justice and get Hollnagel's ETTO, or "service to the users" and we get the debate in the library world. And here Mathis returns to the concept of efficiency, and asks the question "Is efficiency a goal at all?"

> Efficiency is far rather an instrument for achieving other social goals. According to Dworkin, a trade-off between means and ends makes no sense—unless efficiency is thought of as a 'false target' for other goals ... Therefore efficiency is only of limited use as a 'false target' for increasing social utility in the utilitarian sense." (p. 191)

Certain policies in the library world suggest that efficiency has indeed become a false target rather than a means to some other social goal, and as Mathis/Dworkin has argued, this makes no sense. In another recent and fascinating book (that perhaps I should also have included in this review) Merlini has argued that this "meaningless efficiency [efficienza insignificante]" is "putting the priority of the answer ahead of the question" (Merlini, 2009, p. 66) a way of stating the issue that I find particularly revealing. Ellul took a related approach to technical development, arguing that the chief aim of technique was efficiency, and that in the technical approach to any problem "The multiplicity of means is reduced to one: the most efficient" (Ellul, 1964, p. 21). Making efficiency the aim towards which we strive and determining the means towards that end solely according to criteria of efficiency leads to absurd decisions and just those conflicts that Mathis insists are not necessary. In the end we get injustice instead of efficiency, and, as Morel (2002) and Kerdellant (2000) have documented, business failures and technological disasters. None of these would any of us consider to be efficient.

Mathis does not leave us with a trade-off, however, since he argues that this is a one-dimensional approach. Instead, he argues, rather than a monocausal relationship "there are multiple interdependencies between the two goals, and while they conflict in some respects, in many other ways they actually stand in a harmonious or at least a neutral relationship to one another" (p. 198). And in his conclusion he argues that "the endeavour to realize both goals need not always be a competitive trade-off, and can in fact be undertaken cooperatively to a large extent. Piana (2008—yet another recent book that I could have included in this review) argues similarly in the context of globalization, insisting that "economic rationality and ethical rationality do not go hand-in-hand any more than they are in opposition, rather they converge in a common terrain" (p. 10). Piana in fact takes as his premise Mathis' conclusion and proceeds to discuss that cooperation in terms of the ethics of solidarity in a global economy in which information technologies "are no longer inscribed in the order of means, but are more and more acquiring the character of ends" (Piana, 2008, p. 5). The focus on cooperation and the recognition that efficiency as a means is not necessarily in opposition to the social ends which are our goals is all good news—and matters apparently not well understood among librarians—but we have not yet dealt with the Jevons Paradox.

The Jevons Paradox was stated succinctly by Jevon's as follows:

It is wholly a confusion of ideas to suppose that the economical use of fuel is equivalent to a diminished consumption. The very contrary is the truth. (Jevons, 1866, p. 123, quoted in Polimeni et al., p. ix)

In his introduction to Polimeni et al. (2009) Tainter spells out the consequences of this paradox:

It suggests that efficiency, conservation and technological improvement, the very things urged by those concerned for future energy supplies, may actually worsen our energy prospects. (Tainter, in Polimeni et al., p. x)

The Myth of Resource Efficiency has, apart from the introduction and conclusion, only three chapters. The first of these is a review of the classical and contemporary economics literature on the matter mentioned by Jevons in the passage quoted above. In the first chapter (by Blake Alcott) the question is put directly in the author's introduction: "is efficiency part of the solution or part of the problem?" (p. 13). Alcott follows this lead question with a discussion of the definition of efficiency according to the economists discussed:

Throughout the following examination of our author's definition of efficiency it is axiomatic that efficiency denotes a ratio. The numerator is output and the denominator is (energy) input. 'Efficacy', or 'effectiveness' or, more ambiguously, 'power' denote in contrast the causation of a given amount of output regardless of cost or input. Ontologically, the thing that is efficient is the input. ... We are not investigating consumption efficiency—for example boiling only the amount of water needed for the cup of coffee. (p. 13)

He then makes the interesting observation that it matters how we define an increase in efficiency, for understanding an increase of efficiency as "less input per unit of output ... biases our thinking by holding output constant and looking at what could be saved" whereas understanding the same process in terms of "more output per unit of input ... biases it by highlighting increased output with perhaps no saving" (p. 16). A good portion of this chapter is devoted to the literature on 'rebound' and 'backfire'. Rebound is when an increase in efficiency causes or contributes to an increase in resource use. Fuel efficient cars lead to (whether contribute to or cause is a key part of the debate) people driving more. When the gains in efficiency lead to so much more driving that the increase in fuel consumption is more than 100% of that "saved" by the efficiency measure, this is called 'backfire'. Although the authors do not make the connection explicitly, it seems that backfire is a phenomena associated with thinking of efficiency in terms of "more output per unit of input", much like we read in the library literature of "more, better, cheaper, faster."

The first chapter was fascinating to read, much more enjoyable than Callender's discussion of efficiency in the management literature (not the fault of Callender, but of the management literature). But as one might expect in a review of scholarly literature, scholars disagree. There are no answers, and those looking for answers rather than a good question (such as that posed by Alcott and quoted above) will have to pick up a less interesting book. That would however be a shame for the second chapter is remarkably appropriate for anyone working with information technologies. That chapter, by Giampietro and Mayumi, concerns the evolution of complex adaptive systems, both biological and socio-technical.

The authors begin with a statement of three conceptual problems for the study of the relationship between efficiency improvements and rebound effects. The first is how to define and measure efficiency, the second is how to distinguish efficiency improvements "due to a change in technological coefficients (when the system performs 'the same set of transformations'; but 'better')" from those improvements due to changing the nature of the task, "when the system finds more convenient methods to perform 'something else' instead of the original set of transformations" (p. 80). It was this second conceptual problem that particularly caught my attention because this is precisely the problem we are facing when we try to understand how to use and evaluate the new technologies and techniques available today. For example, is the automatic generation and exchange of metadata really more efficient than human created metadata, or are these two very different tasks producing two very different (though perhaps superficially similar) products which cannot be compared in terms of efficiency precisely because of the differences? If we choose the "more efficient" system we are in fact choosing a very different system and changing entirely the "complex adaptive system" that our current information infrastructure most certainly is. This is in fact the heart of Giampietro and Mayumi's topic, the purpose of whose chapter "is to provide a different perspective on the discussion about the link between increases in efficiency and sustainability" (p. 80) and it is a truly fascinating and provocative discussion.

"Living systems when evolving in time have the peculiar ability to 'become something else'" the authors remark and then extend the applicability of the statement to socio-technical systems with a discussion of technological change in agriculture. Technical innovation and efficiencies have eliminated animal power from agriculture but this, they note "implies that improvements in efficiency within a given context (in this case farming in the oil era) do imply a reduction of adaptability in the long term (if we will run out of oil)" (p. 80). They anticipate one of their conclusions in the comment "These theoretical issues imply, when dealing with evolutionary trajectories, that it is impossible to use the concept of efficiency for planning the best course of action" (p. 81).

At this point the reader may recall that both Callender and Hollnagel stressed the importance of time and temporal developments for understanding efficiency and the effects of efficiency measures. An ecological perspective cannot be narrowly bounded, whether temporally or geographically, but this kind of forward glance is not at all like the futurology and crystal ball gazing one finds among prognosticators of technological invention and library futures. If only the library world had prognosticators with the perspective of Polimeni et al.!

The critique of formal models for evaluating and planning for efficiency is a central element in this second chapter and provides an argument from evolutionary theory (and in English) to complement and strengthen Górny's (2008) argument (in Polish) on evaluating efficiency in libraries. The more useful that formal models are "for increasing improvements in efficiency, the quicker the status quo will change and the more likely it is that these formal models will become useless for making tong-term predictions" (p. 90-91). Continuing their discussion of efficiency in relation to temporal developments the authors note that "alternative (and also contrasting) assessments of efficiency can be found when considering simultaneously tasks referring to different temporal horizons" (p. 95). And those alternative and contrasting perspectives "are necessary to preserve diversity", for

> a successful surviving trajectory of evolution must result in the ability to establish an impredicative loop between increases in efficiency, an attribute very relevant in the short run, and an increase in adaptability, an attribute very relevant in the long run. If only one of the two strategies is adopted—increasing adaptability by reducing efficiency or increasing efficiency by reducing adaptability—a negative side-effect will show up either in the short or the long term. (p. 97)

The authors elaborate on this matter and the farming example above later on in terms that are strikingly reminiscent of the many calls for change in the library, yet at the same time just as strikingly different. They define adaptability as:

the ability to adjust our own identity in order to retain fitness in the face of changing goals and changing constraints. Fitness means the ability to maintain congruence among a set of goals, the set of processes required to achieve them and constraints imposed by boundary conditions. ... Therefore adaptability requires the ability to preserve diversity (an adequate option space) in terms of both possible behaviours and organizational structures. (p. 122)

When efficiency is "defined at a particular point in space in time, according to a particular interpretation of this term"—which it must be for practical action—then "in order to increase the efficiency ... we have to eliminate" less efficient activities and support the efficient ones—from the perspective of that temporally and spatially limited understanding of efficiency. And here they go back to the farm:

Driven by technological innovations tailored on this interpretation of efficiency—such as the green revolution or genetically modified organisms—agricultural production all over our planet is converging on a very small set of standard solutions (commercial seeds, technological packages, and economic demand heavily affected by transnational corporations and globalized markets). On the other hand, the 'obsolete' agricultural systems of production, those that are being abandoned all over the planet, may show a very high performance if a different set of goals and criteria—rural employment, ecological compatibility and preservation of biodiversity—were adopted" (p. 122).

In other words, the question that remains is the one I asked at the beginning of this review: efficient at doing what? It is here that efficiency becomes a political OR an ideological matter (and sometimes both):

> Any given perception/representation of the external world based on a particular formal model must necessarily reflect a set of choices made by a special storyteller about the selection of a relevant narrative for a given state of affairs in relation to a given set of goals. ... As Schumpeter aptly remarked, '[a]nalytical work begins with material provided by our vision of things, and this vision is ideological almost by definition'. (p. 129)

The final chapter by Polimeni provides an empirical macroeconomic analysis of rebound and backfire across a wide range of countries and resources. Although the whole book is devoted to the Jevons paradox in reference to energy resources, the authors stress that the paradox appears to apply to the use of any and all resources, including, presumably, information resources. Polimeni's general statement appears to describe exactly what librarians and other information professionals have experienced over the past decades:

> As a resource becomes more efficient to use, and more affordable, current technology will be used more or new technology will be introduced that contains more options and features. (p. 147)

Now however disconcerting this may seem in relation to oil and other non-renewable resources, the LIS profession has been dependent upon this "paradox" and in fact many information professionals are delighting in it and dreaming of a glorious future in which we will be the crown jewels of the information society. If improvements in efficiency are counter-productive and actually promote consumption, then the labour required in the future will increase rather than decrease. We immediately think job security, but perhaps there is more to it than that. What does this mean for the development of efficient search and research, web-authoring, publication and scholarly communication of any kind? In spite of my own interest in the matter of policies and organizational structures and scholarly communication in libraries, this book made me think that the arguments presented are probably more important for those whose interest is in the design of technical systems such as search engines. In the conclusion the authors mention Zhu Yuan-Chang's chessboard, a story illustrating a hypercycle. They remark

> Hypercycles, or positive autocatalytic loops, when operating without a coupled process of control (and damping), do not survive for long; they just blow up (p. 173).

I really wish the authors had discussed the production and use of information resources in relation to the Jevons paradox, but perhaps this review will inspire some reader to undertake the matter.[1] If the Jevons paradox pertains to information resources like all other types of resources, then does their warning that relying on "efficiency and technology as a solution is foolhardy" (p. 3) apply to LIS as well? For those not afraid to think outside the LIS box, this book is a challenge indeed.

Callender, Hollnagel, Mathis, Polimeni et al.—what has all this to do with the design and use of information technologies and the work that librarians do? For one thing it should make us see the insufficiency and even misleading nature of the greater part of the discourse on efficiency that we find in the LIS literature. We appear to have made little or no progress since Robinson (1920) stated "The measure of the efficiency of any library must be the measure of its usefulness, all else being plant and machinery and operators contributing to that end," for recent writers on efficiency treat the topic as an issue separate

---

[1] "Regarding your question relating to information, I do think the Jevons' Paradox holds as we can obtain answers quicker, but do not know how to analyze the answer. So we end up doing more searches looking for the answer. I think this is common in the new generation of students." (John Polimeni, email to David Bade, 28 August 2009)

from usefulness or effectiveness. Chen (1997) stated "efficiency refers to resource utilization efficiency, rather than an evaluation of effectiveness" and Shim (2000) similarly distinguished effectiveness (usefulness for the users) from efficiency (technical efficiency, or the ratio of outputs to inputs) and assumed that the latter can be evaluated separately from the former.

During the past few years innumerable references to efficiency have appeared in the literature of library management, system design (searching efficiency) and discussions of library legislation, yet a search of these literatures revealed that with few exceptions (such as Hernon and McClure, 1990) efficiency is assumed to be an unproblematic concept. Efficiency in the LIS literature is rarely defined, and when a definition is given, it is often reductionist and simplistic, such as Vitaliano's definition:

> Efficiency is defined as whether or not a library could reduce the inputs it uses equiproportionately and still produce the same output. Inputs are defined programmatically: holdings, opening hours, serials and new books. Output is internal and external circulation. (Vitaliano, 1998, p. 107)

Hammond (2009—in press) in an otherwise interesting article writes of 'efficiency' without any qualification throughout the paper, but also refers to technical efficiency—i.e. production efficiency, the object of his study—allocative efficiency and economic efficiency. Unfortunately he nowhere mentions effectiveness. (His article is a good example of the multiple terms and related problems noted by Callender.) He does however recognize the inadequacy of earlier studies, noting that "Efficiency is, as a result, a potentially more complex phenomenon than many earlier studies have implied" (p. 3).

With effectiveness eliminated from the discussion, many authors proceed to evaluate efficiency without any relation to other factors that determine the success of people's choices and actions (e.g. time, cooperation, competition, communication, learning). Efficiency as a value both unquestioned and in no relation to any other values appears in Barčkutė (2008) who was content to insist that the increased use of IT needs to result in a more efficient operation. Indeed many references to efficiency limit the discussion to the efficiency of the technologies in doing what they are designed to do, not the broader context of people in their various tasks and what they need to do. We find an example of this kind of treatment in Mansourian (2008). The author proposed a new conceptual measure (Web Search Efficacy, or WSE) to evaluate the performance of web searches, but as WSE is based on user expectations of "quick and easy" it is really a measure of user perceptions of how quick and easy searching is—which certainly has something to do with efficiency but is not the same thing as asking the users about whether the system was effective. Fischer and Schwan (2008) went a bit further, treating efficiency as synonymous with speed—the faster the results are obtained, the more efficient the system—arguing that what Microsoft engineers thought would make for more efficient use of their products (adaptively shortened pull down menus) actually resulted in an increase of inefficiency, i.e. a decrease in speed of obtaining results. Questions of ease and effectiveness in obtaining the desired results did not enter into their evaluation.

In one of the best articles on the topic Górny (2008) asked why our assessments of library efficiency have been of little use and suggested that our efforts have been devoted largely to methodologies and techniques, when our focus ought to be on library objectives. As mentioned above, Górny's remarks on the effect of rapid technological change on evaluation are similar to the criticism made in Polimeni et al. where we read "when trying to predict changes associated with evolution, any formal model is bound to become obsolete" (Polimeni et al., p. 110). Lazcano Herrera and Font Graupera (2008) criticize what they consider the misplaced emphasis on technologies and system performance, suggesting that we need to focus on library users' experiences with technologies, looking not at what technologies are designed to do (however efficiently) but at whether library users can actually use them to do what they want or need to do. When efficacy is understood to be central to the notion of efficiency, then to understand efficiency in libraries the first and most important task is to understand the goals of library users, goals that are largely related to social and normative practices. When we have made clear to ourselves why libraries exist, for whom and to serve what purposes and practices, then and only then may we determine what means (technical efficiency) will best serve the library's users, and how our policies (economic and allocative efficiency) will effect our service over time (dynamic efficiency).

The political and ideological character of the discourse on efficiency was noted not only by Callender for whom it was the central issue, but also by Mathis and Polimeni et al. The 2008 report of the Library of Congress Working Group on the Future of Bibliographic Control presents an example of that ideological discourse. We read therein that "Libraries must work in the most efficient and cooperative manner to minimize where possible the costs of bibliographic control," and throughout the document efficiency is equivalent to a reduction of cost or cooperation (the managerial euphemism for requiring that someone else do the work). It appears that the same ideology was at work in the drafting and passage of the German and Belgian legislation mentioned in "Rückenwind aus der Politik" and Cauwenbergh and Lekens (2009).

The advocacy of cooperation noted in the preceding paragraph points us to the most important issue of all for working with global technical systems: efficiency in relation to cooperative action, a topic that Hollnagel has discussed in more detail than the other authors. Some librarians have made a serious mistake in assuming that joint exploitation of a technical system is the same thing as cooperation. Indeed it is noteworthy that demands for efficiency are frequently coupled with an extravagant praise of cooperation—e.g. in Cauwenbergh and Lekens (2009) and the Library of Congress report mentioned above—perhaps because cooperation is misunderstood as being nothing more than letting someone else do the work—outsourcing under another name?

Sixty years ago Roethlisberger (1949) complained that the "striking contrast between technical efficiency on the one hand and matters of human cooperation on the other presents the number one problem of our present industrial civilization" (p. 233). His comments on efficiency and the relationship of technology to social structure are remarkably appropriate to today's "information society" as well:

> I find little justification for the prevailing assumption that so long as we turn out goods efficiently of good quality and of low cost, matters of cooperation can be left to chance. I find little evidence for the popular beliefs that cooperation is a matter of logical and technical contrivance or a matter of verbal exhortation—something that can be willed into being by verbal persuasion or efforts of personality. I find that there are just as brute and stubborn facts that determine matters of cooperation as there are brute and stubborn facts that determine matters of technical efficiency (Roethlisberger, 1949, p. 233)

Many of the changes modern technology originates can collide head on with the social organization of the company and its attempt to maintain internal stability—a necessary precondition, as we have seen for cooperative behavior. With the very best of intentions, modern technology can unwittingly foster the segmentation of the social structure of industry into groups with radically different points of view. It can unwittingly assist in the development of rigidities of relationship between segments of the structure that make cooperation difficult, if not in some cases impossible. The patterns of behavior produced by modern technology do not in and by themselves make for cooperation. (ibid., p. 237)

We continue to think of our use of technical systems as though the system itself enables not only the performance of the task but cooperation as well, as though our use of the system has no consequences for others elsewhere or in the future, as though efficiency is a purely local and private matter for us here and now, as though we live isolated within a world which we can exploit as we please rather than in a world in which all of our actions affect everyone everywhere else, including ALL future generations. This is a mistake with serious consequences, and Hollnagel's discussion of cooperation in socio-technical systems, Piana (2008) on efficiency in the context of globalization, and Polimeni et al. from their macroeconomic and ecological perspective have all provided evidence and arguments that help us understand efficiency, cooperation (and exploitation) in the context of shared and finite resources.

What the books reviewed above can do for us—if we read them carefully and together—is to lead us to see that the appeal to efficiency is not a simple matter at all, and that when efficiency becomes an end rather than a means we can easily get distracted from what it is we are actually trying to accomplish, and perhaps prevented from accomplishing it. We need to think ecologically, globally and ethically about efficiency (and economy, cooperation and technologies) in libraries and how our actions today are going to shape the world for our children and their children. For if Hollnagel is right that efficiencies tomorrow will require thoroughness today, our children are going to hate us for sure.

References

Bade, David. (2009). "Irresponsible librarianship: a critique of the report of the Library of Congress Working Group on the Future of Bibliographic Control and thoughts on how to proceed," paper presented at the Music OCLC Users

Group (MOUG) Meeting, February 17, 2009. Available at: http://eprints.rclis.org/15687/
Banush, David and Jim LeBlanc. (2007). "Utility, library priorities, and cataloging policies," *Library Collections, Acquisitions, & Technical Services*, v. 31 , pp. 96-109.
Barčkutė, Ona. (2008). "Vartotojas informacinių sistemų plėtros procese," *Informacijos mokslai*, v. 46, p. 57-66.
Callender, Guy. (2009). *Efficiency and Management*. London: Routledge. (Routledge Studies in Management, Organization and Society, 4)
Cauwenbergh, Johan and Nete Lekens. (2009) " En waarom niet wat meer samen?" *Bibliotheek- en Archiefgids* v. 85 no. 1 (January/February), p. 12-20
Chen, Tser-yieth. (1997). "A measurement of the resource utilization efficiency of university libraries," *International Journal of Production Economics*, v. 53, p. 71-80.
Ellul, Jacques. (1964). *The Technological Society*. New York: Vintage, 1964.
Fischer, Sebastian and Stephan Schwan. (2008). "Adaptively shortened pull down menus: location knowledge and selection efficiency," *Behaviour & Information Technology*, v.27 no. 5 (Sept.-Oct.), p. 439-444.
Górny, Mirosław. (2008). "Dlaczego oceny efektywności bibliotek są mało efektywne?" In: *Dokument, książka i biblioteka w badaniach naukowych i nauczaniu uniwersyteckim*, ed. by Marta Skalska-Zlat and Anna Żbikowska-Migoń (Wrocław: Wyd. Uniwersytetu Wrocławskiego), pp. 47-61.
Hammond, Christopher J. (2009). "The effect of organisational change on UK public library efficiency," *International Journal of Production Economics*, vol. 121, issue 1, pages 286-295.
Hernon, Peter and Charles R. McClure.(1990). *Evaluation and Library Decision Making*. Norwood, NJ: Ablex.
Hollnagel, Erik. (2009). *The ETTO Principle: Efficiency-*

Thoroughness Trade-Off, or Why Things That Go Right, Sometimes Go Wrong. Aldershot: Ashgate.

Josephson, Aksel G.S. (1913). "Efficiency and bibliographical research," *The Papers of the Bibliographical Society of America*, v. 7 (1912-1913), nr. 1, p. 7-21.

Kerdellant, Christine. (2000). *Le prix de l'incompétence, histoire des grandes erreurs de management*, Paris: Denoël.

Lazcano Herrera, Carlos and Elena Font Graupera. (2008). "Los hechos de información, un escenario para evaluar la brecha digital local del usuario/cliente en la sociedad del conocimiento" *Anales de Documentación* no.11, p.79-792.

Library of Congress Working Group on the Future of Bibliographic Control. (2008). *On the Record: Report of The Library of Congress Working Group on the Future of Bibliographic Control (January 9, 2008)*. Viewed online 15 April 2009 at: http://www.loc.gov/bibliographic-future/news/lcwg-ontherecord-jan08-final.pdf

Mansourian, Yazdan. (2008). "Web search efficacy: definition and implementation," *Aslib Proceedings: New Information Perspectives*, v. 60, no. 4, p. 349-363.

Mathis, Klaus. (2009). *Efficiency Instead of Justice? Searching for the Philosophical Foundations of the Economic Analysis of Law*. New York: Springer Verlag. (Law and Philosophy Library, 1572-4395 ; vol. 84)

Merlini, Fabio. (2009). *L'efficienza insignificante: saggio sul disorientamento*. Bari: Dedalo. (Strumenti/Scenari ; 77)

Morel, Christian. (2002). *Les décisions absurdes, ou l'analyse des erreurs radicales et persistantes*. Paris: Gallimard.

Piana, Giannino. (2008). *Efficienza e solidarietà: l'etica economica nel contesto della globalizzazione*. Cantalupa, Torino: Effatà Editrice.

Polimeni, John M., Kozo Mayumi, Mario Giampietro and Blake Alcott. (2009). *The Myth of Resource Efficiency: the Jevons Paradox*. London: Earthscan.

Robinson, Julia. (1920). *Library Efficiency Test*. Chicago:

American Library Association.
"Rückenwind aus der Politik," *BuB: Forum Bibliothek und Information*, v. 60, no.5, May 2008, p. 379.
Roethlisberger, F.J. (1949). "Efficiency and cooperative behavior," *The Journal of Engineering Education*, v. 40, nr. 4 (Dec.), p. 233-241.
Shim, Wonsik. (2000). "Assessing technical efficiency of research libraries," *Advances in Library Administration and Organization*, v. 17, p.243-339.
Storms, Marc. (2003). "Van de individuele gebruiker kan men toch geen leengeld vragen," *BibliotheekBlad: vakblad voor de openbare bibliotheken,* Jaargang 7, nr.16/17, 5 (september), p. 6-9.
Vitaliano, Donald F. (1998). "Assessing public library efficiency using data envelopment analysis" *Annals of Public and Cooperative Economics* v. 69 nr. 1 p. 107-122.

XVIII

Outsourcing and Cooperation: Questions of Flexibility and Responsibility[1]

For the past ten years I have been studying and writing about the problems of communication in libraries. My primary focus has been on library catalogs but my approach has grown out of two very different intellectual engagements. The first of these is my interest in language and linguistics. I began my academic life as a student of linguistics and maintain that interest to this day. The second formative influence may seem like quite a stretch for you, but it is perhaps even more important for understanding why I ask the questions that I do and why I press certain issues as strongly as I do. That second engagement is a long struggle to understand violence and justice, an intellectual struggle that goes back thirty one years and in large part has been a continuing tormented reflection on the incomprehensible actions of the men and women who enacted the shoah. It was in 1995 while reading Hannah Arendt's discussion of Eichmann's trial that I first put together the topics of efficient transportation systems and cataloging in libraries. By paying attention only to his job of keeping the system running efficiently and refusing to give any thought to why he was keeping it running and what were the results of his managerial decisions, Eichmann was able

---

[1] Remarks at the Northwestern University Library Assembly of Librarians, July 16, 2012.

to serve the system while committing crimes against humanity—with a clear conscience. Since that reading I have devoted a great deal of my energies towards understanding the relationships between the management of libraries as socio-technical systems and the goals and purposes which libraries serve.

Today I am going to speak of flexibility and responsibility as questions to consider when thinking about outsourcing and cooperation. I will be returning to topics that I have addressed a number of times during the past decade but my comments today will draw in large part on my own experiences in outsourcing and cooperation in library cataloging, including working with the Library of Congress cataloging in publication program ECIP and cataloging African, Southeast Asian, Mongolian, and other books for other institutions both as an individual and through an outsourcing agency. Beyond that it is also the case that rather than addressing library management problems as a library manager, I will be addressing these problems from four other perspectives at the same time: as a library employee, as an experienced outsourcing cataloger, as a library user, and as a linguist who has made problems of library management a primary focus for research on linguistic communication. Library cataloging will be the context of most of my remarks for therein lies my experience, but the questions to be asked and lessons to be drawn are more broadly applicable.

To begin with I should note that outsourcing and cooperation in libraries as in any other endeavor are neither simply solutions nor simply evils, an observation that I imagine few will find objectionable. Yet I often find that the problems that arise sooner or later after the introduction of outsourcing and cooperative programs are simply ignored or dismissed as insignificant in relation to the benefits realized. While I recognize the benefits of outsourcing and cooperation intelligently managed, I will argue that the benefits have never been fully realized *precisely because the problems involved have never been faced squarely and honestly.* By thinking critically about outsourcing and cooperation we ought to be able to come to a better understanding of how these organizational forms of working work and why they work when they do.

Referring back to the subtitle of my talk, I propose that librarians need to rethink the relationships between flexibility and responsibility. Outsourcing provides a certain kind of flexibility—for instance the ability to deal with unexpected changes in personnel or the kinds or amounts of materials received—yet always with a corresponding loss of responsibility, precisely because outsourcing is nothing other than making someone else responsible. Cooperative cataloging on the other hand may encourage the original cataloger to take responsibility, but policies often entail a corresponding loss of both responsibility and flexibility for all subsequent users of that work. Responsibility and flexibility vanish whenever catalogers are encouraged or forced by policy or automated processes to accept as found metadata created elsewhere in the chain of production rather than evaluate, rethink and learn from, or as it is often pejoratively described, to agonize over and tinker with the work of other professionals.

The nature and extent of the lessening of responsibility and flexibility do not occur predictably and necessarily as a result of entering into relationships of outsourcing and cooperation, but are largely determined by the library policies, organizational structures, workflows and technical implementations within which context outsourcing and cooperative activities are established. The task of management as I see it is to increase flexibility and maintain responsibility through the judicious use of outsourcing and cooperative cataloging among many other possibilities. All too often it appears to this observer that outsourcing and cooperation are imagined and embraced simply as means for speeding up workflow by reducing the flexibility of or even eliminating staff while at the same time placing all responsibility on others external to the organization.

The first question I will ask is: How does outsourcing enhance and how does it limit flexibility? I will limit my remarks to the most obvious benefit and limit. The most obvious benefit is that someone agrees to do the work. There may also be economic benefits and perhaps fewer headaches for the personnel department, but the really significant benefit is that someone agrees to do the work. In every case in which the library lacks the staff resources required to do the job, finding some means of getting the work done is the primary issue at stake. The availability of outsourcing options, whether in cataloging, selection, binding and labeling or any other process means that the library has options and the ability to respond to many changes in circumstances.

Immediately upon entering into such an arrangement, however, other kinds of flexibility vanish. Outsourcing usually involves legally binding contracts; what flexibility the library has in writing the contracts turn into rigid limits once the contract is signed. The limits of outsourcing are more intriguing than the benefits, and I shall discuss them in relation to two cataloging projects, the first being one which I found out about at its termination, and the second, one that I was asked to work on but in the end did not.

In the first project, a library in which I worked received funding for materials in a certain language, materials which were then regularly ordered and received. Yet no one in the library could even read the script in which the books were written, much less catalog them. So the primary vendor used for the acquisition of such materials was pressured for quite some time to provide MARC cataloging records with each item ordered, pressures to which the reluctant vendor finally succumbed. After signing the contract, everyone was pleased, including apparently the vendor. This idyllic arrangement in outsourcing lasted for some time until one day an observant copy cataloger noticed while cataloging a bilingual book—the second language of which he could read—that the subject provided did not match the apparent topic of the book. Upon further investigation the copy cataloger realized that all the books in that language had the same subjects and class numbers in the record. So the problem was brought to the attention of cataloging management.

The underlying problem was that none of the professional catalogers could read the language either, and in fact this was why the outsourcing arrangement was established in the first place. We were delighted with the flexibility outsourcing provided; we were for quite a long while delighted with the product received in exchange for a slice of the budget; we were happy to leave all processing to copy-catalogers with instructions to accept the record as it came since none of us could possibly criticise or improve the record; we were not so happy to realize we had received nothing of value; some of us were deeply troubled that something like this could and had in fact happened.

The question that needs to be asked is how often does this happen? And how could anyone possibly find out that such is happening if there is no one in the library who is paying attention or who can even recognize that there is a problem? One indication of how widespread this problem is can easily be found by looking carefully at bibliographic records in OCLC that have been created by outsourcing agencies or records which have been upgraded several times by more than one library. In my investigations of such records I have found incontrovertible evidence that for certain kinds of materials the persons responsible for creating records at certain outsourcing agencies at the time of cataloging could neither read nor understand at all the language of the material they were cataloging. Similarly with copy cataloging: in many cases bibliographical records in OCLC are upgraded or otherwise changed in many rather trivial ways while glaring errors in subject analysis, attribution of authorship and classification survive all efforts at correction, even when multiple institutions have left their signature on the record.

This should be a troubling situation to be taken seriously everywhere, but instead any inquiries are met with a response along the lines of "we can neither expect the lower level staff who search and upgrade copy to recognize these problems, nor can we ask them to do that because it is not in their job description." And of course if you do not route everything first through lower level staff who do not or cannot notice such problems and are in any case prohibited from correcting them, then everything would have to be routed through someone who could identify such problems and undertake corrective action. That, of course, would considerably slow down the system unless more persons were hired to perform that evaluation. Since well trained, thinking staff paid to take responsibility are more costly than untrained staff paid to obey orders, we get the latter, accept the consequences as inevitable, and do nothing to address the problems that follow. And the problems are far more serious than anyone admits: labor that is cheap, obedient and unquestioning is neither flexible nor responsible labor. For Norbert Wiener, the labor of human beings who are expected to work according to the same efficiencies operative in an automated process is the precise equivalent of slave labor.

The second project turned out differently. Not long ago I was contacted about the possibility of cataloging books for a library in need of cataloging books in "Azerbaijani, Bambara, Catalan, Fula, Hausa, Icelandic, Indic, Kazakh, Khmer, Kyrgyz, Latin, Mandingo, Moore, Niger-Kordofanian, Shona, Somali, Tajik and Zulu." Knowing as I did that the library in question had no one on the staff who could read any of these languages I was in the same position as the vendor mentioned earlier. I could agree to make some very easy money knowing full well that the paying library could not possibly evaluate anything I could provide them. Yet having written at length about bad cataloging and professional responsibility, I would be embarrassed to embark on such deception, no matter how well I was paid. So I replied by saying that I could work easily with certain of the languages, not at all with Indic and Khmer, and that while I had considerable experience with many African languages and would be happy to do the best I could, I knew none of them in the same way that I know English or Catalan, and could not even promise that I would be able to provide subjects for all of them. I never heard back about the project. Perhaps someone underbid me; if not, that raises some interesting questions.

Does any library that asks for a cataloger who knows "Indic" or "Niger-Kordofanian" even know what they are asking for? No one in the world "knows" Indic or Niger-Kordofanian. Does any library that collects in many African or Asian languages seriously expect that the cataloger—in-house or out-house—will know all the languages involved? Issues of flexibility and responsibility are inextricable here. Had the library in question agreed to let me work on the books, they would have received the same kind of attention to their collection that I have given to African collections at Urbana, Northwestern, the University of Chicago and the University of Florida. The cataloging would have been better I hope due to the experience gained, but at least no worse. And they would have paid dearly for my services for I know from experience that it could be a very time-consuming project which I could not afford to undertake at slave wages. Yet who can fault a library for responding with "No thanks" to a cataloger who admits "I don't really know how but I will try"? And this leads up to my second topic: much cooperative cataloging is done by catalogers like myself who do not really know all that we need to know but who do our best. Cooperation ought to mean that after some of us have done our best there are others to do their best by way of evaluation and correction as needed. But does it?

Cooperation is hardly new and hardly a result of managerial wisdom. At its best it arises spontaneously among persons working together towards a goal that they all understand in a similar fashion. At its worst, cooperation is an inappropriate word used as propaganda to hide the grim realities of wreckless irresponsibility, or to mask the grossest forms of exploitation and coercion. I will remain silent about the latter; I would like instead to focus on cooperation at its best. My architect friend Scott Francisco provided me with a quote from some anonymous person (an old European joke, it seems) that perfectly encapsulates cooperation at its best and at its worst:

> Heaven is a place where the cooks are French, the police are British, the mechanics are German, the lovers are Italian, and it's all organized by the Swiss. . . . Hell is a place where the cooks are British, the police are German, the mechanics are French, the lovers are Swiss, and it's all organized by the Italians.—Anonymous
> http://pilot-projects.org/wp-content/uploads/2010/06/The-Way-We-do-Things_Francisco_ABS2.pdf

Cooperation undertaken to increase the flexibility of all organizations involved requires that all involved accept responsibility for all others involved. This is the view of Erik Hollnagel, whose writings on complex industrial systems have been of immense importance to me in my efforts to understand both cooperation and the meaning of efficiency. This understanding of cooperation can be found throughout the literatures of ergonomics and high-reliability organizations and it differs markedly from the literature on cooperation that one finds in the library literature. As I have written about this matter numerous times and at length over the past decade, I hesitate to repeat myself, but repetition is unavoidable since the fundamental issues have not changed even though the technical situation has. As in the case of outsourcing, in the overwhelming majority of discussions of cooperative cataloging this has been understood to be and presented as a solution to the problems arising from uncooperative cataloging. That is, cataloging has been misunderstood in the first case as something that does not in and of itself involve cooperation, and then cooperation is touted as the means to solve the problems arising from cataloging pursued without the benefit of cooperation. Yet the cooperation advocated has been much more along the lines of "let someone else do the work"—which I call exploitation, not cooperation—rather than "let us all be responsible for each other." We need to back up and rethink cataloging as a practice and then think about what cooperation in cataloging means.

Cataloging as I was taught it, as I have observed it and as I have practiced it, has always been a cooperative effort involving long dead scholars who compiled bibliographies and catalogs, correspondence with living authors, and conversations with colleagues on- and offsite. Yes, in the old days I retyped information found in printed indexes of Mexican legal literature whereas now I download or copy and paste information from OCLC, VIAF or an online bibliography or catalog. That cooperative activity in which I and many other catalogers have engaged for decades has always had its origin in our understanding of what it is that we are doing and for whom we are doing it. In the best cases—and I think that is the majority of cases—it is undertaken with a sense of responsibility, the conviction that what we do matters not just for our personal sense of pride in a job well done—the pernicious old stereotype of catalogers who catalog only for themselves—but for any and all future users of the library who want to find and use the resources that we are cataloging.

Unfortunately, cooperation in cataloging has often been promoted at the managerial level on an entirely different basis, as an activity to be undertaken in an entirely different frame of mind, and an irresponsible frame of mind at that. In those perspectives cataloging information or metadata is something that one should find and use; any time spent evaluating or altering what already exists is unjustifiable—a duplication of effort — and only slows down the system. Flexibility is achieved by relying on the work of others, and the burden of responsibility is left squarely on *their* shoulders. This, I argue, is not flexibility in achieving a certain goal but a radical redefinition of the goal of our efforts. The redefinition of our goal is clearly spelled out in many documents: according to those documents we are not concerned primarily with communicating anything to library users, but with the most cost-efficient organization of a technical system. With that redefinition of copy cataloging—turning it into a simple matter of metadata reuse—we are no longer even talking about cataloging or scholarly communication but only about the functional parameters of a technical system, a system for which all human uses are understood as externalities rather than as its teleological foundation. And one can indeed talk of technical systems in that fashion, but no cataloger or catalog manager should ever *think* of them in that manner.

I would like to describe one case of cooperative cataloging that illustrates much of the potential and many of the limits of cooperation in libraries. The case involves the collection of books in African languages here at Northwestern. It began a long time ago and is still in progress.

I met Mammadou Niang in 1991 in Urbana while he was studying linguistics and I was in library school. Fifteen years earlier I had studied African linguistics with the same professor under whose direction he was then writing his dissertation. I ran into Mammadou again a few years later after coming to Chicago and he asked me if I had visited the library at Northwestern, and if I knew why they had so few books in Pulaar or Fula in their collection of African books: he could find almost nothing in the online catalog. I told him I would find out. I found out. And I found out that there was an incredible collection, access to which was available only through a card catalog onsite or directly browsing the shelves. I wrote to Mammadou and he asked what Pulaar books they had. Long story short: I decided to let him know about everything in the collection.

The University of Chicago Library allowed me to visit Northwestern every week to work on the collection: that was cooperation number two (the first being my decision to help Mammadou). Northwestern University Library provided me with a photocopy card, a book truck and free access to the collection to make copies of front and back matter in order to use as surrogates for cataloging: cooperation number three. *Long before I needed them*, the national libraries of Nigeria, South Africa and a few other libraries had provided printed bibliographies indexed or arranged by language for my use: cooperation numbers 4-15. Also many years earlier Michael Mann and Valerie Sanders had provided me a catalog of texts in the

SOAS Library in order to confirm language identification: cooperation number 16. Some young Shona speaker on the Ashland bus one evening proofread the Shona section while riding between Garfield Avenue and Pilsen: cooperation number 17. Ramdane Achab and others on Amazigh.net, Valentine Vydrine, Mamady Doumbouya and many others helped out, some on one single item, others on whole sections. Of course at this point numbering the instances of cooperation is ridiculous: there were at least a hundred people directly involved, and I have no idea how many more were indirectly involved, including the many past staff members and visitors to the Herskovits Collection who were involved in describing and organizing the collection before I set out to compile a catalog of it. Then along came Gary Strawn who unlike David Bade actually has some technical knowledge and skill. He was certain that he could go further and put the printed catalog on the web if only he could get my original MSWord file. He got it and he did an amazing job: cooperation number 1273?

In that brief history I see cooperation at its best, each person doing what they could do, each of us relying on the others to do what they each could do. Throughout the project questioning, evaluation, checking, cross checking and correcting directed the work. In spite of that, there were mistakes that remain. In his remarks on the catalog in a 2001 essay published in *Annales Aequatoria* Honoré Vinck pointed out that catalog number 5268 was in Boloki, not Selenge. The error remains in the printed catalog but with a little further cooperation it could easily be fixed in the online catalog. That was one indication of my limits: some languages I could not identify at all and simply reproduced what some unknown person had previously recorded (i.e. copy-cataloging). Some sections were proofread by more than one specialist while I alone proofread others while half asleep. There were technical limits too: the main font used (the only good font available at the time) was proprietary and did not cover all characters needed; other fonts I used proved to be trouble when bringing into the Northwestern online catalog;

even though the fonts display in the catalog, I do not know how to search with special characters. The subject descriptions that I did not provide were added to the records through harvesting such information as could be found in OCLC using automated means, and that process of course had its technical limits just as the value of the subject data populating those records in OCLC was constrained by the limits of the catalogers who originally cataloged those records.

Over the course of time the goals of the project changed according to the possibilities and limitations that became clear as I proceeded: my own linguistic limitations (I decided early on no subject analysis), the opportunities provided by people I met on the bus or in a coffee shop, software updates (I lost all of the Amharic entries with the upgrade to Windows 98, on which system I could no longer even open my files: where were you when I needed you, Mr Strawn?), and more recently the decision to add the entries I prepared to the online catalog. The main goal, however, did not change: Mammadou Niang now knows what Pulaar books he can get at Northwestern. It is for the Mammadou Niangs in the world that libraries exist, and for whom we cooperate in the preparation of our catalogs.

The African languages project is, I think, more representative of special collections cataloging than many people realise. Fifty years ago the Mongolist John Krueger came to Chicago to catalog the Joseph Regenstein Library's Mongolian manuscripts; next year [2013] Uwe Kozok will come from Hawaii to catalog the Joseph Regenstein Library's Batak bark books. Several professors of ancient Semitic languages have left their remarks on the University of Chicago's collection of Ge'ez manuscripts after working with them during the last 40 years, comments which I recently collated and incorporated into our online catalog descriptions. Walking down the street one day I overheard a conversation about Armenian books and after rudely interrupting the conversation I secured the cooperation of a graduate student for the recataloging of one of the University of Chicago's Armenian collections that had been cataloged 100 years ago as "Armenian books volumes one to 73." I was elated to discover that more than 20 of those Armenian books were actually Turkish books printed in Armenian script and that our graduate student was a specialist in this Armeno-Turkic literature. She will be returning for a while this fall with an offer to help with any problems—I mean Armenian books—that have arrived since she was last here.

Admittedly, however, the kinds of materials that most libraries would consider routine, i.e. recent titles in English, present a different set of problems requiring different forms of cooperation than those arising from the cataloging of Ge'ez manuscripts or 19th century Armeno-Turkish imprints. In contrast to such collections, for the past couple of decades when recent titles in English arrive in the library they arrive with an electronic record or there already exists metadata somewhere in electronic format. Sometimes, such as when there is a catalog record in the OCLC database, that metadata is available in a format that requires no alteration to be reused in the library catalog. In other cases the available metadata is in some other format, such as ONYX, a system used by publishers, which must them be "tinkered with" or otherwise adapted for local use. That technical situation will change sooner or later, and the resulting problems, limitations and flexibilities will depend upon the library systems developed as much as upon library policies and the world beyond libraries. Problems do not disappear with technical developments, they just change forms, get more complicated and hide better. The Library of Congress's current cataloging in publication program—ECIP—provides a good look at some of the issues that this form of cooperation brings to the fore.

ECIP data comes from many publishers in a non-MARC format (ONYX I believe) following the publishers' own house style, form and content of metadata. If one desires cataloging information to be standardized in terms of what is presented and how it is presented (i.e. ISBD forms of punctuation, capitalization, MARC coding, LC subject headings, etc.) and available in

OCLC, then the data supplied by the publishers requires a considerable amount of "tinkering" either before or after it is imported into OCLC using the ECIP system. Tinkering means staff time and staff time means money. Get rid of tinkering and one saves time, staff and money. So we are urged to use the data in the form it is recieved, for after all, who could do a better job of providing appropriate and adequate metadata than the publisher and author? If you are nodding your head in agreement, you probably haven't used the ECIP program. But in theory, it is certainly a knock-out argument. Currently, of course, libraries still have to add subject headings and call numbers, but the expectation is that in the near future we can rely on publishers to provide those too, and of course eventually software will do an even better job of this than human catalogers—or so some believe. As a linguist I am highly sceptical of this latter claim; of the former claim, I remind my listeners that publishers want to sell their publications, while catalogers strive to describe as objectively and accurately as possible the subject of the work for a particular readership. Those two activities can produce wholly different descriptions, and the nature of that difference is not something librarians should ever dismiss or forget.

That difference is one of the significant differences between a library and a bookstore and has recently been the topic of an excellent paper by Alberto Salarelli who asks a question that he considers to be of supreme importance:

> up to what point can we modify the forms and activities of the public library before we deprive it of its very nature? Up to what point, in other words, can the meaning of the phrase "public library" be extended before it becomes just a synonym for book store franchise? (Alberto Salarelli, "Barcco, i barbari e la biblioteca pubblica," in *JLIS.it* v.2 nr.1, 2011, p. 9)

The data provided by publishers to the ECIP program are presumably adequate and appropriate for the publishers' purposes.

Yet as a librarian, working with ECIP sometimes drives me insane. I have to add what should easily be automated and to change things that I could have more quickly and easily input directly myself. It is this experience of poorly designed cooperation which leads me not to an argument against cooperation nor even to an argument against bad design, but rather to an argument against those who insist that two kinds of organizations with different needs and desires must reuse each other's metadata even if it entails more work, time and frustration than not reusing it. Why do we have to reuse it? Because in the eyes of the advocates of reuse, differences of purpose should be disregarded in order to take advantage of the potential efficiencies afforded by the technical system they wish to develop. I would point out in argument that it is precisely those differences of purpose that the system needs to be designed to accommodate. Reuse is an acceptable description of what needs to take place *only* when it is the case that there are no differences of purpose —or if one first denies the importance of and even the existence of differences of purpose. If we begin with different purposes as our point of departure then the issue is not reuse at all, but repurposing, and were programmers instructed to design a system on *that* basis we might have a very, very different ECIP program.

Such problems exist, but they do not constitute the whole story, for the result of my travails with ECIP is a record that many librarians and others can use in the familiar MARC format with LC subject headings and classification. As ECIP is expanded to include more publishers and more teams of specialists at numerous institutions the benefits grow. Expanding the participation of specialists (I catalog linguistics and Mongolian studies through ECIP) works well for everyone, although there is a potential problem: the time I spend on ECIP is time I do not spend on the backlog beside my desk. ECIP currently brings many more specialized hands, hearts and minds into the cooperative cataloging of mainstream materials, increasing both the flexibility and responsiblity of participating libraries and the benefits of the involvement of specialists for all others.

Yet irritating difficulties and the enhanced involvement of specialists is not the end of the story, for the future of the program has been proposed to be one that is further automated or left entirely in the hands of the publishers. If and when this happens, then libraries will experience a decrease in both flexibility and responsibility *as well as throwing the specialists out the door*. The big question for the future of library-publisher cooperation is whether the difference realized through the work done in libraries will be valued at all or whether the values of the marketplace—embodied in publishers' metadata—will be the only values underwriting the automated production and exchange of metadata. This latter situation will be the case if and when the decision is made by libraries to accept the information provided as is and allow only automated forms of manipulation and alteration.

Outsourcing and cooperation as these are frequently advocated in the library literature are presented as simple solutions to simple problems. That is a serious misunderstanding or misrepresentation of what is at stake. When recourse to outsourcing and policies for copy cataloging based upon the notion that copy should be used, not evaluated, are accompanied by a reduction in staff it is not just a matter of cataloging that has been outsourced but of responsible people who are no longer working in the library. And when outsourcing and/or cooperation is undertaken as a means for letting someone else do the work, reduction of staff is inevitable. Instead of outsourcing and cooperation adding to the library's range of possible options for achieving some goal, undertaken on this basis they entail a diminution of the library's intellectual capital. And this entails a reduction of flexibility and of possibilities for cooperating within the library as well as among libraries. When the cataloging has been outsourced, who does the bibliographer or the reference librarian go to when there are questions about what is in the catalog? And if the bibliographer is outsourced in favor of an approval plan? And the reference librarian outsourced to Google?

I offer these questions as reminders that just as bibliographers mean more to the library than a PhD with an approval plan and reference librarians are not just algorithms with a floor plan, so too catalogers are not just MARC records with a pension plan. Outsourcing used intelligently will apply to certain materials, certain processes and for certain goals at certain times, and no librarian in my experience could be identified simply and solely with a single task or process in the library. It takes all kinds of librarians working together to serve the varied and changing needs of library users. Outsourcing should be and can be an effective tool for librarians to use in certain situations; it should only be a replacement for librarians if libraries want to cut off their own heads.

No library can support a permanent staff with sufficient knowledge of the world's languages and subject specialisations to find, purchase, catalog and offer reference services for everything from Africa (Asia, ...)—much less the whole world —without drawing on the work of untold numbers of persons outside the organization. It is for that reason that cataloging—like collection development and reference work—has always been a cooperative effort of individuals utilizing printed bibliographies, catalogs and professional contacts, and of course for the last couple decades internet resources and online databases. Institutions that support staff efforts to responsibly provide the best information it is able to provide for the materials collected can utilize all manner of tools and options to successfully achieve the ultimate goal of serving users like my friend Mamadou. The same cannot be said of those library managers who understand their goal as simply moving stock from mailroom to storage facility. It is indeed possible to move an immense amount of materials from the receiving dock to a final destination without ever critically evaluating anything that happens along the way, but just how flexible and responsible can such a system be?

A further question would concern what happens to librarians, libraries and library users when this manner of thinking about libraries determines library policies and practices. Are there no consequences other than speeding along materials processing? The linguist Roy Harris asked a similar question in response to a similar presentation in a book on knowledge management and I will reuse—or rather repurpose—his question for your consideration now. This view of knowledge management, Harris wrote,

> takes knowledge all the way from the laboratory to the market place without ever allowing one crucial question to be raised: has the journey had no effect on the knowledge itself? Is what ends up in the commercial market place any longer knowledge at all? (Roy Harris, *After Epistemology*, p. 122)

In the library we are dealing with information after its trip to the marketplace, and the question remains pertinent. The banality of evil, Hannah Arendt suggested, lies precisely in the fact that no questions were ever asked. The only thing that transpired in Eichmann's office, as in the perfectly efficient library and the knowledge management manual criticized by Roy Harris, was unquestioning obedience to and the efficient accomplishment of policy directives.

I have mentioned my friend Mamadou for a reason. Mamadou is real. He reoriented my life's plans for several years as well as altering the course of Northwestern Library history and African studies worldwide with a single request for information about books in a language most people have never even heard of. And please understand me clearly: Mamadou did that through his request; without his request I would never have begun such a large project. Librarianship for me has a social goal and that goal is to serve library users. Librarianship is about helping Mamadou find books in Pulaar at Northwestern—even though I am at the University of Chicago—and only secondarily about the many techniques and tools eventually used in making that possible.

It is often stated that information wants to be free, but information wants nothing at all. It is people, real people with specific needs and desires who want information, and not just any information but always something specific. Unlike information, however, people do indeed want to be free, and in fact they must be free if they are to be flexible and responsible in responding to specific requests and needs, whether their own or others'. One of the lessons I have found repeated over and over in the literature of ergonomics, cognitive systems engineering, resilience engineering, industrial management and linguistics, is that flexible and responsible people are the single most important factor in making technical systems work. When responsible human beings have been eliminated from a process, whether that is due to policy directives or technical organization, a failure to achieve any social goals is guaranteed to happen down the road.

That should surprise no one who begins on the assumption that social and technical systems should work for us and not the other way around. As another of my mentors—the French anthropologist Victor Scardigli—has pointed out, giving the power of decision making to an automated system is a social organizational revolution and not a technical revolution. Scardigli further argued that the increasing complexity of technical systems requires that they be trusted rather than understood, and in this they require a belief in magic as a condition of their efficacy. And with this critique Scardigli has pinpointed a significant problem with much library science and library management: we are told and we have believed that the system will do it for us, no matter what "it" is. My dear mother insists that we all can and should leave all our burdens and concerns with the Lord, and I find librarians doing exactly the same thing. The library's Lord is, of course, not the same guy that my mother talks about, but an illusion sustained by a lack of critical questioning.

If we reject that social revolution that externalizes all our problems as the responsibility of someone else, whether outsourcing agencies, other libraries or the latest technical systems, and instead assume as the basis for managerial action that our organizational structures and technologies must be adapted to and adequate for our purposes, then the first order of business is to pay attention, and to continue paying attention, to what it is that we want to do, and to develop a varied staff, adaptable workflow, effective tools and flexible policies that will allow us a maximum of flexibility and responsibility in utilizing and evaluating technical systems and organizational structures like outsourcing and cooperative action. These latter offer tremendous possibilities which we will never begin to fully realize unless we approach them in full awareness of what they mean for the social and intellectual life of libraries and the multiple relationships and kinds of communication required to serve those who matter most: those who enter the library to use it.

And of course there has to be someone in the library to pay that attention, and that someone has to be involved in the user practices taking place in the library in order to know how to serve them. The larger the library, the more practices involved, the greater the variety of materials, formats, languages and services encompassed, the more the library needs a diverse community of human beings to deal intelligently and responsibly with that world within the library. A group of librarians who work together within a library, engaging that institution's particular users, are participating in the only context that can and must guide their practices. A group of librarians working together to serve a particular group have the strengths that come from a collegial environment and the numerous webs of relationships that develop among staff and users. A group of librarians have the advantage of the possibilities that open up in debate and the voicing of differences of experience and opinion. In an academic library such a community of librarians embodies one particular form of the old ideal of the university as a community of scholars. As such, it produces the necessary conditions for understanding the very people it is designed to serve, and contrasts sharply with the situation of the outsider hired by an outsourcing agency.

A group of people living and working together everyday within the walls of a library will develop forms of organization, forms of communication and forms of information that differ greatly from what will be produced by a collection of disparate groups working according to a babel of contracts drawn up in contexts that are not apparent or even completely unknown to those undertaking the work. It is under these latter conditions that the solitary outsourcer works. Do library managers ever consider the social and intellectual life of those employed by outsourcing agencies? A difficult task, when the actual workers are unknown and have no direct contact with the library, but a consideration that should be pushed to the forefront of our discussions about outsourcing.

Catalogers who work for outsourcing agencies may do so in addition to having an established position within a library, but in such cases the work performed as an outsourcing cataloger is undertaken more often than not in isolation and largely in ignorance of the institutional culture and the users for whom their work is performed. They negotiate their contracts knowing they must be the lowest bidder but without any access to information relating to the company's and library's expectations, and no standard market price available to base a bid on. They are required to make commitments to complete work on a certain number of materials in a certain amount of time usually with a very limited knowledge of only the most general characteristics of the collection to be catalogued.

The situation can be worse for the cataloger who has no institutional association and working relationships but is simply paid by the item—if he or she is lucky enough to be the lowest bidder—while working alone at home. In most cases the only relationships such catalogers will have is with their employer; there are no relationships with the library requesting the work, nor with that library's users. In *The Origins of Totalitarianism* Hannah Arendt described how isolation of persons through the destruction of horizontal relations led persons to succumb to pressures that they would or at least could have resisted if situated within relations of solidarity. Obedience often trumps responsibility when the only persons to whom you are accountable are those in charge of your wellbeing and they are the ones making demands. And I know from experience that the temptation to do more, faster and not quite so good is almost irresistible when your income depends on the quantity of work finished rather than its quality, and even more powerful when you know no one can even evaluate the quality.

I have heard even worse tales about the situation of catalogers working as hourly employees in outsourcing agencies, both tales of inflexibility and of irresponsibility, but the conditions of such workers differ depending upon the managerial decisions of the company in which they work. Some companies pride themselves on the quality of their work and are very sensitive to the needs of both the libraries served and the catalogers, and I have found this not only evident in the promotional literature from some companies but also in correspondence with employees and in my own dealings when working on special collections for other libraries through an outsourcing agency. We can hope that in the best cases, the same sense of commitment and collegial support in the service of goals freely embraced exists among the employees of outsourcing companies as in libraries.

Yet I suspect that this is not always the case. In some companies the cataloger can be pressured to produce results as quickly and as efficiently as in any other automated industrial process without regard to the effects on the quality of the work performed, much less on the mind and soul of the employee. In a talk at the Joseph Regenstein Library a few years ago a representative of a large vendor of shelf-ready processing of materials boasted of her company's efficiency by stating that no cataloger in her company would be allowed to spend more than 15 minutes cataloging anything. How flexible is that? How responsible is that? Would any of you want to work there? Would your work ethic survive? Would you survive?

Recourse to outsourcing may shield librarians from dealing directly with real people at the same time as it permits and perhaps encourages the growth of an entire class of workers at the mercy of the market rather than supported and exhorted by the values and practices of science and scholarship. As a librarian with only one year of professional experience in a temporary cataloging position I answered an advertisement to work with one of the largest companies then in the business, offering them my considerable experience cataloging in special collections as an unprofessional as well as my limited professional experience and my even greater range of experience with languages, all in exchange for a salary equal to my then current beginning librarian's salary. I received no reply and later found out that the salary they were then offering was only a little more than half what I was making as a librarian. And even had I been offered that position, it would have left me without library priviledges in any academic library and no daily life within a community of users. Much later I was contacted by another company and doing the math realized that in order to match my then current salary I would have to find or create seven or eight bibliographic records per hour, import each record to a local file, convert them to a different format, add local fields, save in a another file, export that file into another database—and I remember no more of the details. Yet in another experience I found myself in a much more acceptable and in fact largely enjoyable relationship.

The main question that needs to be asked in each of these cases—as in all outsourcing—is how much of the working conditions that I learned about and experienced were forced upon the outsourcer by the libraries negotiating the contracts and how much were due to the outsourcing companies' policies and labor practices? Company attitudes and policies can differ radically, but my guess is that libraries negotiating outsourcing contracts are at least as guilty of exploitation as the outsourcing agencies, and perhaps sometimes moreso. After all, a commercial operation asked to produce quick and dirty work and paid accordingly will probably agree to do quick and dirty work to please the customer, and the cataloger who objects to such unprofessional work will find herself unemployed.

Are librarians reconciled to offering their support to sweatshop labor in the information industries? Are we unaware of the glaring social contradictions between our professed ideals of academic freedom, the liberating power of science and our commitment to equality on the one hand, and the fact that many —or is it now most?—of our great libraries are increasingly being built upon the rapidly degenerating economic and social conditions of those who do the work? Do the contracts signed soothe our consciences by making everything appear to be the legal operation of the freedom to sell one's labor in a market economy? Can anyone be allowed—no, let me rephrase that: *should* anyone be forced to serve academic freedom while banished from academic life? Through our advocacy of outsourcing are we once again putting up walls and building ghettoes, this time within the heart of the information society? Do librarians belong within a community that values their cooperative labor or is it acceptable to us that some librarians labor of necessity isolated from those in need of their efforts, under coercive conditions, and the constant threat of unemployment? Are our current practices of cooperative cataloging evidence of an ill-conceived, misunderstood, undertheorized, poorly managed, inadequately evaluated and inefficient utilization of information technologies?

These are the kinds of questions that my experience and my research have led me to ask. And they are genuine questions rather than allegations or answers to questions that you have not asked, because I have lived and worked on both sides of the border in the recognition that outsourcing and cooperation are valuable options for libraries, and in the hope that libraries will approach these options in full awareness of the requirements and obligations each entails of all those involved. I leave these questions with you to ponder along with Norbert Wiener's remark "we shall never receive the *right answers* to our *questions* unless we ask the *right questions.*" (Norbert Wiener, *The Human Use of Human Beings,* 1956, p. 186)

XIX

The Content of Journals Published by Nova Science Publishers, Inc.: *Political History and Culture of Russia* and *Current Politics and Economics of Russia, Eastern and Central Europe*

Abstract
A look at the contents of some journals published by Nova revealed many issues which contained no original materials at all. The journals show a pattern of entire books about Russia from the early 20th century being reprinted chapter by chapter as though they were separately titled articles. Material from US government documents, Congressional Research Service reports, and material excerpted from other recent public-domain sources have been combined, sometimes with one or more original articles to produce journals costing between 700 and 900 US dollars annually.

The Discovery of a Problem

Due to my interest in Mongolian history, I recently picked up an issue of Nova Science Publishers' *Political History and Culture of Russia*. Volume 22, number 2 (2006) begins with J. Maratin Miller's article "Invasion of the Mongol Tartars". The title has an asterisk referring to the following note: "Excerpted from *The Thrilling Stories of the Russian-Japanese War* by J. Maratin Miller, 1904." Consequently the article was of no interest to me. I returned to the table of contents and noticed that the next four articles were by the same author; checking these, I found that they were all also excerpted from the same book. The only other article in this issue was "Alexander II and Russia on the Eve of Great Reforms", but that had a note "Excerpted from *A Thousand Years of Russian History* by Sonia Howe, Philadelphia: J.B. Lippincott Company, London: Williams & Norgate, 1915." I proceeded to look at Volume 22, number 1 (2006). In that issue the first five articles are by J. Maratin Miller and as in the other issue, all were excerpted from the same 1904 publication. These were followed by another article from Sonia Howe's aforementioned history, and the issue concluded with a 12 page essay on Slovenia that appears to be an original submission.

Political History and Culture of Russia claims to publish "scholarly articles dealing with Russian cultural and political developments, personalities and trends" (page 2 of cover). The articles in these issues were all copyright 2006 by the publisher. The subscription price for six issues a year was listed as $795, the first two issues combined containing 155 pages, of which 12 were original scholarship having nothing to do with Russia. How far back does this practice go?

An Investigation of the Problem

The journal was formerly entitled *Political History of Russia*, and the first issue of the journal under the new title was volume 9, number 1, published in 1997. In that first volume there are nine articles by Nicholas V. Feodoroff "excerpted from S*oviet Communists and Russian History* ISBN 1-56072-407-2 by Nova

Science Publishers, Inc." followed by "Bitter memories" by Beloinok and a few poems, all "excerpted from *Forced Repatriation* ISBN 1-56072-447-1 by Nova Science publishers, Inc." The issue concludes with a bibliography "Baltic Occupation by Soviets" (no author/editor) which consists of 40 printouts of records formatted as catalog cards from what looks like the Library of Congress catalog. From that first issue of 1997 through the current issue, most of the issues are of the same nature: excerpts from the publisher's monographs (which are themselves compiled partly or largely from materials in the public domain), excerpts from early 20th century monographs of little scholarly value then or now, and bibliographies which are simply downloaded from the Library of Congress (or elsewhere). And the price, which was 175 US dollars in 1997, is now 875 US dollars (information from the publisher's website, 21 August 2007).

Some of the issues include articles by various authors—all have Russian or Georgian names—and there is no indication that these items have been translated, reprinted or excerpted from elsewhere. For instance, volume 15 number 4 has "The Centralized Russian State: Russia in the Second Half of the Fifteenth and the Sixteenth Century" by N.Y. Nosov, "Feudal Russia in the Seventeenth Century" by A.G. Mankov and I.P. Shaskolsky, and "Early Eighteenth Century: The Formation of the Monarchy" by D.S. Likhochov. Yet suspiciously, such articles in this and other issues are all alike: no bibliographies, no references, and no information of any sort about the authors. The next question was: Is this practice related to the editor or the publisher? The journal offers no information about editors or editorial boards, no affiliation with any academic or governmental body. I checked the publisher's website and found that of the 63 journals published by Nova, 38 have no editors or editorial board listed, while of those with editors, Frank Columbus is the editor for such disparate journals as *Journal of Drug Addiction, Education and Eradication*, the *International Journal of Mathematics, Game Theory and Algebra* and *International Journal of*

Ethics. In the case of the journals related to Russia/former Soviet Union and Eastern Europe, there are only 4: *Current Politics and Economics of Russia, Eastern and Central Europe*; *Caucasus Context*; *Current Politics and Economics of the Caucasus Region*; and *Political History and Culture of Russia*, none of which have any editors mentioned. How do the first three compare to the last one?

Current Politics and Economics of Russia was renamed *Current Politics and Economics of Russia, Eastern and Central Europe* beginning with volume 11 number 1 (1998). In 1998 the price was 200 US dollars per volume with 2 volumes appearing each year in 4 issues per volume. The current price is 975 US dollars per volume with one volume per year and each volume appearing in six issues. The first issue of the journal under the new name contains articles first published in Russian and translated into English, presumably for publication by Nova, as well as one article with no prior publication history mentioned. The second issue of volume 11 includes four original papers and the annexes and bibliography from *Emergency Management in Russia in Practice: case studies on the 1990's* by Boris Porfiriev, "Excerpted from *Disaster Policy and Emergency Management in Russia* ISBN 1-56072-421-8 by Nova Science Publishers, Inc." More recent issues are mixed as well: Volume 18 numbers 5 and 6 consist almost entirely of material reprinted or excerpted from Congressional Research Service reports and other Nova journals. Volume 20 number 1 (2005) has all original articles, while volume 20 number 3 consists entirely of articles reprinted from various other Nova monographs. Volume 20 number 4 is again a mix of original articles (or at least articles that do not indicate any publication history) and articles reprinted from Nova Science Publisher's *Southeast European Security:Threats, Responses, Challenges*, originally published in 2001. It appears in fact that the entirety of that 2001 monograph is reprinted in various issues of volume 20 (2005).

Current Politics and Economics of the Caucasus Region began in 2007 and only volume 1 issue 1 has appeared. According to the information on the publisher's website, it will be a quarterly for 195 US dollars per volume ($55 dollars per issue). The contents of the first issue includes four papers by Jim Nichol, two of which are identified as Congressional Research Service reports, and a paper by Robert C. Rickards and Hochschule Harz "2005: A Year of Corruption, Fraud, Intrigue, Protest, and Some Progress in the Caucasus," which is suspiciously like an article of the same title that appeared in Nova Science Publisher's journal *Caucasus Context*, Vol. 2, No. 2, Nova Science, Spring 2006, pp. 153-168. This latter journal is described on the publisher's website thus: "This new journal brings together important analyses, interviews with key players and cultural background". With the limited information given on the publisher's website and my own lack of familiarity with researchers in this area, it is difficult to ascertain the nature of the contents without access to the full text. Yet the appearance of the Rickards article in both *Caucasus Context* and *Current Politics and Economics of the Caucasus Region* suggests an editorial practice much like the journals examined above.

Responding to the Problem
What is there to say about these Nova journals? First, it is legal to reprint public domain materials and sell them on the market, as it is to repackage and sell under different labels materials for which one owns the copyright. Second, the journals as advertised make no claim to publishing original materials. It was noted above that *Political History and Culture of Russia* makes only the claim that it publishes "scholarly articles dealing with Russian cultural and political developments, personalities and trends." It makes no claim to be publishing either original or current research. *Current Politics and Economics of Russia, Eastern and Central Europe* makes a similar claim: "This scholarly periodical focuses on the rapid changes occurring in Russia, Eastern and Central Europe. The scope of the publication is the entire spectrum of contemporary politics and economics." No mention is made of any other editorial policies

regarding source of materials. It is clear that there is no fraud involved. It is also clear that the lack of information about the nature of the contents and the source of those contents come close to being deceptive even if legal. Furthermore, taking entire books which are in the public domain, publishing them piecemeal under chapter titles in a journal without noting the source in the table of contents and then claiming copyright for the individual chapters appears to be a deliberately deceptive practice aimed at libraries. The question for librarians is then not simply a matter of the value of these journals for collection development, but what the publisher's name means for approval plans, standing orders and subscriptions of any kind.

It has been claimed that in the era of online information and mass digitization, collection development is not just a waste of time but an impossibility.[1] The explosion of information online means that we should reorient ourselves to bibliographic searching rather than collection development and bibliographic description. Publications like those investigated here point to the fallacy of such arguments: these journals are not online and they are expensive. They do contain original materials, but these are of varying kinds: translations, articles first published in these journals, and materials available under different titles in the same publisher's monographic publications. These journals bring together previously published materials that may be scattered about elsewhere and in other languages. But the large amount of duplication makes cost an important consideration. Are these journals worth their price? For which libraries? The fact that a decision has to be made means that collection development is still not only possible but necessary.

Fifty-three libraries are listed in the OCLC database as having the journal *Political History and Culture of Russia*; fifty-seven libraries have *Current Politics and Economics of Russia, Eastern and Central Europe*. Many of those also have the Nova

---

[1] Sheila S. Intner, "Copy Cataloging and the Perfect Record Mentality." *Technicalities*, 10: 7 (July 1990): 12-15.

monographs in which the same content is available, as well as having print and online access to *Congressional Research Service Reports* and the Russian journals in which many of the original articles were published in Russian. While it is true that the multiplication of copies increases the long-term viability of information, these journals and the publisher that issues them present us with some real questions about the importance of collection development and evaluation, as well as the economics and ethics of information provision in libraries today. So long as information costs, we are going to have to make decisions, and those who stand to profit from our decisions cannot always be trusted to present us upfront with all the information we would like to have for making those decisions.

XX

Nullum crimen sine lege[1]

Lawyers insist that there is no crime without a law, and Saint Paul argued similarly that sin is not imputed when there is no law. To speak of transgression then, implies a law that stipulates what is right and what is wrong. And that implies an authority that makes and enforces that law. To speak of transgression in the context of the practice of cataloging one must assume that the practice involves laws and a valid authority that makes them. In a rather trivial sense we can easily identify these: cataloging rules, Library of Congress rule interpretations, the instructions provided for our various tools, local and international organizations such as the RDA steering committee, the Library of Congress, MARC, OCLC and local policy makers/enforcers at individual libaries and consortia. Important as these all are for our day

---

[1] 2017 Association for Slavic, East European, and Eurasian Studies (ASEEES) Annual Convention, Chicago, November 9-12. Paper presented at the session entitled "Transgressions in Library Metadata".

to day work, the validity of these authorities and the rules and regulations they pronounce must be judged at an entirely different level, namely in the experience and opinions of those library users from whom libraries receive their sole justification for existing. Of course I am referring to my listerners here.

If we were to assume that the rules established by the library authorities have been made in full awareness and clear understanding of the practices, needs and desiderata of library users, then we could easily look over our own work and that of others and find a multitude of failures, mistakes and errors as defined by those rules. What then? Shrug our shoulders, repeat the old adage "to err is human" and carry on as before? One may indeed find in the library literature a number of very scientific studies of cataloging quality that find a multitude of mistakes and then declare that the majority are insignificant, giving us all a clean conscience and a green light to proceed with business as usual.

Yet not everyone assumes that the rules have been made with full awareness and understanding; some argue that the practices of readers and researchers have changed so drastically, and are in fact changing so rapidly that the old rules are for past realities, as did the authors of the well known paper "RDA – cataloging rules for the 20th century". Taking this perspective to its extreme some have argued that cataloging is not a practice for the future at all. A decade ago Karen Calhoun famously stated that "the role of catalog records in discovery and retrieval of the world's library collections seems likely to continue for at least a couple of decades and probably longer." Of course that ending "probably longer" is a classic prophetic hedge, and we are still waiting for the death of the catalog or the Messiah, whichever comes first.

I take a different approach. Every new arrival to the library—books and patrons—presents the library and the cataloger with a new situation, a new possibility and a new need. Given a library that has developed over decades or centuries according to the constantly changing and myriad understandings, technologies and practices of librarians and library users, we are all faced each day with the task of integrating our new acquisitions and our new patrons into an existing patchwork structure that will be ever so slightly altered by the new acquisitions and the new needs. Our tools, rules, rule interpretations, vocabularies, attitudes, understandings and habits have to adapt and respond to the new world each book and patron presents us as best as we can. And the cataloger can adapt and respond much more quickly in our work than our tools and rules can. Transgressive practices have a major role to play in that adaptation. That is the good news for transgressors, but it isn't the only news.

I cannot document my statements in a fifteen minute talk. I speak for myself, and from my own experience I offer my conclusions. It is sadly the case that many libraries and library related organizations are not oriented towards the materials acquired by the library nor towards the people who come into the library to use them. The needs of researchers are understood only according to the practices in current library and information science, i.e. only publications of the last decade in English are considered, and that only if they can be obtained electronically. More than by researchers' needs, library policies and practices are guided by budget considerations in light of the promises found in the marketing literature of the information technology industries. Staffing decisions are determined on the basis of ill-informed understandings of sociotechnical systems and dreams of a not-yet-realized but all the more hoped for technologically determined future. Past practices such as citation and bibliography remain vital in any historical research, that is any research that probes the intellectual life of humanity in records created prior to 1990, but these are often dismissed as irrelevant in an online environment. It is oft assumed that all bibliographic description, if indeed it is necessary in systems with fulltext searching capability, will be provided by the producers and distributors of the documents, not by librarians. In this mixture of ignorance, misunderstanding and techno-economic ideology I find the policy origins of the truly heinous transgressions that are destroying cataloging as a practice, the catalogers who do the work and the libraries that accept the work produced under these regimes of ignorance and lies.

The evidence of our own library 'Silent Spring'—Rachel Carson's description of the death of nature resulting from industrial exploitation and its resulting pollution—is abundant but increasingly difficult to identify and interpret because of technical developments such as GLIMMER, the merging and overlaying of records in OCLC and the move to online tools which leave no trace when something is changed. If we want to understand what has happened in a particular instance, that becomes impossible when the history of the record itself and the rules in effect at the time of its creation have been erased or otherwised removed from public inspection. Note that the reproducibility of experiments, methods and results which form the foundation of scientific practice are rendered impossible by these erasures of history in our work, rendering any "library science" impossible.

When working on a project to catalog items from Shaw & Shoemaker's *American Bibliography, 1801-1819* I learned that more than 30% of the items listed in their bibliography were actually duplicates of other items therein. Bibliographic ghosts as they are called, arise when one or more elements in a description are recorded differently and subsequently interpreted as being a different edition or printing. This may be due to error, but also happens when descriptions are correctly produced using different rules for description, for example counting the total number of pages according to the last numbered page or by counting all pages numbered or not. A description which takes the title from the CIP may differ from a description taking the title from the cover, title page, colophon, an added title page in a different language or a summary title. A description which conflates information taken from many different sources within the item may differ considerably from a description based on a rule-defined chief source of information. In short, the surprisingly high number of non-existent/duplicate citations in Shaw & Shoemaker's bibliography was due largely to the irreconcilability of different descriptions produced according to different rules for description. The duplicates were identified only when physical copies of all the items from that bibliography were obtained, examined and compared with the existing citations—as happened when they were microfilmed. We should all realize that there is little chance of eliminating these duplicate but differing descriptions by any automated means precisely because they differ, and the meaning of that difference can only be determined by examining the specific copies that the descriptions represent.

Other problems—mistakes, nonsense, redundancies—appear in OCLC apparently through the operation of deduplicating software itself or record overlays—I cannot determine exactly how these things happen but most of you are probably aware of the problems. Yet technically produced problems are matched and perhaps exceeded by problems that have their origins in policies and workflow. Here is one example.

040 PAU ǂb eng ǂc PAU
020 9785990758179
020 5990758170
090 ǂb
1001 M. Gadas.
24510Obitaemye peizazhi" Garifa Basyrova: katalog vystavki.
260 Moskva GMII im. A.S. Pushkina: Samolet, 2017.

In this example there are fields indicating that the date of publication was 2013 and that the language of the text is English, while in other fields the date of publication is 2017 and the language clearly Russian. What is a cataloger to do? We all know that publishers sometimes use the same ISBN number for different printings and editions, and that there may well be Russian and English editions published simultaneously with the same ISBN or ISBNs in both; is this description incorrect in asserting its publication in 2013 in the English language, or as being a 2017 publication in Russian? The book in the cataloger's hands did not have "katalog vystavki" on the title page, so this record was left alone and a new record created—perhaps exacerbating the problem identified with the Shaw & Shoemaker bibliography. Perhaps the above record was really for the 2017 edition but the 2013/English language fields were populated with default data and the title taken from a distributor's description rather than from the book? A week later I find my own answer in the form of another record with 2013/English data for a 2017 Russian art book, courtesy of the same institution. Apparently a new policy has been put in place at the University of Pennsylvania.

040 PAU ǂb eng ǂc PAU
020 9785906190239
020 5906190236
090 ǂb
049 JPGA
1001 Bogemskaia K.G.
24510Iskusstvo vne norm.
260 M. 2017.

In addition to default data that has nothing to do with the book described, both descriptions also contain missing diacritics, incorrect special characters and coding as well as the improperly entered name, and neither classification number nor subjects are present. At least we have the title! How might such records affect workflows at any other institution that acquires this book? Consider these partial sets of instructions that I have been given for cataloging projects:

A
Accept in either AACR2 or RDA as found.
If no 6xx fields are present, add *one* LCSH.
If no 050 is present, add according to LC hierarchies.
Make **no other changes** to copy records.

B
Copy records aren't expected during the project, but if found accept in either AACR2 or RDA as found. No additional edits are needed. (Note: about 90% of the items had copy in OCLC. Someone was not very good at searching)

Such policies as these not only leave inadequate and incorrect descriptions in the database but reproduce it locally. Yet there is more to this matter than the production and reproduction of poor bibliographical description, there is the additional economic factor of poor—and I mean impoverished—catalogers.

How do such records affect independent catalogers who are paid by the record when working for outsourcing agencies? In the case of records that are not vendor records but which are coded as having been created at a library, the independent contractor gets paid for copy cataloging—perhaps about half what she would get for an original record. That is not all. I do not know for sure, but it seems that many of the same institutions who input such minimal records into OCLC also depend upon outsourcing agencies to provide them with that full catalog record, thereby saving money twice: once by not hiring a cataloger and paying them a decent salary with benefits and an institutional environment, and then again by providing that unknown solitary cataloger with a minimal record that will halve her income. Such a sweet deal for libraries! But is it all that sweet? Are libraries who rely upon outsourcing getting what they think they are getting?

I have worked in several libraries over 35 years, and at one of them the cataloging management team begged and pleaded and cajoled and finally coerced an Armenian book dealer into supplying full electronic catalog records with every item purchased from him. After some time of working with such a splendid arrangement an intelligent copy-cataloger who could read Russian noticed that all the class numbers and all the subject headings were identical -- Armenian literature -- while those bilingual Armenian-Russian books he dealt with were not all on the same topic. Well, well, who would have thought...

Libraries have a long history of eliminating catalogers from their faculty or staff and sending their books (or scans of them) to outsourcing agencies. A test batch is sent to the agency and reviewed upon its return, sometimes by persons familiar with the language and subject of the items cataloged but often the review is performed by someone familiar with library-speak and cataloging rules but who can neither read nor understand the book itself. If the test batch meets with approval, contracts are signed and the library is relieved of its cataloging workload, if not its ultimate responsibility to the library patrons. What happens next? Sometimes the Armenian backlog gets cataloged really, really quickly, and everyone but those who read Armenian are thrilled.

I have been called upon to do test batches for several libraries at some of the largest institutions in the US, but after the work has been reviewed and the contracts signed, I have not received the work—in other words we should all understand that when dealing with outsourced cataloging, someone other than the provider of the test batch may eventually be doing the work. The question is, is anyone then paying attention? Does your library have those smart multilingual acquisitions clerks and copycatalogers who keep an eye on quality for you? From what I see when I trace the history of poor cataloging through the holding institutions' catalogs, I think either not many of our institutions are so lucky or else these intelligent staff are prohibited from "tinkering" with what is deemed to be good enough since it was provided by an agency that passed the test.

It is also widely assumed that authors and publishers will be the producers of metadata, and who could do a better job than the authors, publishers and distributors themselves? Let us examine some of the metadata from a large distributor of East European publications.

Rec stat n	Entered 20051003		Replaced 20051102			
Type a	ELvl M	Srce d	Audn	Ctrl		Lang ukr
BLvl m	Form	Conf 0	Biog	MRec		Ctry un
	Cont	GPub	LitF 0	Indx 0		
Desc a	Ills	Fest 0	DtSt s	Dates 2005 ,		

```
040         EVIEW ǂb eng ǂc EVIEW
020         9994331590 : ǂc USD25.95
029 0       EVIEW ǂb J2001607
090         ǂb
049         CGUA
100 1       Ko<F7>ço, Eno.
245 0 0     Shostakovic dhe Kadare & artikuj, profile, intervista e vrojtime mbi artin mι
            Shostakovich and Kadare & articles, profiles, interviews and observations
            art / ǂc Koço, Eno.
260         Tirana : ǂb Uegen, ǂc 2005.
300         200 p. ; ǂc cm.
546         In Azerbaijani ǂb (roman)
650 0 4     Humanities.
650 0 4     Music.
650 0 4     Albania.
938         East View Publications ǂb EAST ǂn J2001607 ǂc USD25.95
```

Here we see a book that is in Albanian described as a book in Ukrainian (in the language field at the top right) and as in Azerbaijani in a public note.

We find a totally different story when we look into authors providing metadata. One author wrote to the University of Chicago library when I was still there asking for more than 100 subject headings to be added to his book. Like a pornography website, he wanted to make sure that no matter what anyone searched for, his book would always turn up in the search results.

So could it be that the description of a library's materials still need to be provided by someone who works with the library's users and knows their practices and desiderata? Cannot today's technologies do the work for us? Is it not the case that any ignorant student can now type "Russian literature" into a search engine or a library catalog with the right software and get everything they could possibly need? Will not a search for "East European history" bring the PhD candidate all the world's knowledge almost instantly? I haven't the time to argue the point; I will let Ms Langer provide a commentary. My assumption is that an intelligent researcher and an intelligent librarian working together can utilize information technologies more or less successfully if both understand what is needed. Bibliographers and reference librarians probably have a more intimate connection to the library's users than most catalogers, but they often object to being involved in the actual technical aspects of cataloging. Thus some librarians become catalogers and it is the quality of their work that needs to be understood. Is their work an aid to research or an unfulfilled promise and a waste of money?

      It is fairly safe to speak of the poor quality of work performed by some unknown outsourcer or even of paraprofessional staff who may be doing the original cataloging at some of our institutions, even in languages they cannot read. We can snicker at the excesses of authors and the ignorance of booksellers as well as the salesmanship of publishers. It is not so comfortable to inquire into the quality of the work produced by library professionals who are fluent in one or more of the languages with which they are expected to work. The problems that are uncovered by a little investigation into the cataloging produced by multilingual professionals are not few and insignificant. They arise as often as not from being expected or commanded to work with languages "within our area of specialty" as Slavic-Eastern European-Central Asian librarians, for these are languages that we often do not know at all. At one time at least I found Romanian cataloging to be the worst of all cataloging produced in this area; today Hungarian seems to suffer greatly. How many catalogers know Albanian or Estonian? And how many libraries collect materials in these languages without having anyone employed in their library that knows these languages at all?

Language is not, however, the whole story, and inadequate knowledge of the meaning, scope and usage of Library of Congress subject headings is a problem, as is relating these intelligently to a classification scheme. Related to that but at an even deeper and more problematic level is the expectation that we should be cataloging books in subjects that we do not understand at all. In order to keep my talk honest and my criticisms of the work of others in proper perspective, I offer as an example one of my own mistakes.

In spite of knowing nothing about the law when I took my first cataloging job – it was in a law library—and not knowing much more about it 35 years later, I am often asked to catalog law books—even if only for the test batches. I find cataloging law difficult enough, but to catalog it in Amharic, Indonesian, Polish and Ukrainian often leaves me embarrassed. How can I honestly accept such work? On the whole it isn't impossible but it takes a lot of research trying to find the proper English translation for legal terms that I do not understand in English, much less in Russian or other languages. So, to make an embarrasing story short, I misinterpreted a phrase meaning an accused's "right to legal counsel" to mean a judge's "right to judicial assistance". I discovered my mistake when asked to catalog the same book for another library and found not my original record but a Library of Congress record that had replaced it.

That anecdote, painful as it is for me, was a necessary prelude to a discussion of mistakes made by others. We should understand and forgive ignorance. However cataloging a book about the right to legal counsel as anything other than just that right is not acceptable to me nor should it be acceptable to anyone. When we find such mistakes we need to consider how it happens that such misleading cataloging exists. Such mistakes are common and not always trivial as we shall soon see in some examples.[2] Who made the mistakes in the records to be discus-

---

[2] The 20 pages of examples used in my presentation have not been reproduced here, as the discussion was not recorded.

sed next, why they were made, how they acquired their present form in OCLC, these are all questions that I cannot answer precisely because I cannot tell when the work has been created by a specialist, a copy-cataloger, an outsourcing agency, upgraded or overlain by another institution or copied from elsewhere. The cataloging we find in OCLC now comes from many sources, gets altered and corrected and mangled and destroyed by many persons and automated processes, and is rarely the same when you go back to take a second look. Yet without trying to evaluate what we find in our catalogs and trying to understand why we find what we find, we will continue to work on the basis of misinformation and ignorance, which in fact remain the foundations of library cataloging policies nationwide since hardly anyone seems to be paying attention to the quality of our databases.

Upon finding a record that seems incorrect, we might simply fix the record and go on. We could scowl and look down upon the lowly cataloger, perhaps that moron David Bade. But in order to understand what is happening, that is not how we should work. Sometimes I do indeed find bibliographical records that at first glance strike me as ludicrous, but instead of snarling in contempt I have learned to always assume that my first impression led me astray and that I need to look carefully at what the other cataloger has done and try to understand why. I learn much that way. A title may be ambiguous to a reader who has not looked within, and the assumptions we make about language and world may lead us far away from the book's contents. Nor does the language of our subject terminology and anglo-american perspective always match the language of authors elsewhere and at other times.

The question that we must ask is: who are we asking to do our cataloging? Whose cataloging are we accepting without review? Why does the results of our work of describing library materials so often provide evidence that the person doing the work does not know the language or cannot understand the topic? And that is a question about library staffing, workflows, database sharing, interinstitutional relationships and economic relationships with publishers, distributors and for-profit library services. I am **NOT** assuming that I and a select few do cataloging right while others get it wrong; the profound problems that face us all are the limits of library budgets and the limits of each individual cataloger in a situation where a handful of catalogers are expected to do everything for everyone else who, according to other libraries' policies, need only copy our work without evaluation or correction.

Because of my own work responsibilities, a majority of the records that I find problematic come from the great libraries with the finest Slavic/East European/Central Asian collections. These are the institutions who do much of the work, do it quickly and sometimes get it wrong. Without knowing what goes on in these institutions or who does their cataloging, I have to assume that the prevalence of error in these cases is not simply the result of a few incompetent catalogers somewhere who could be identified and disemployed, but that the problems can be directly connected to policies in effect and workflows, including the use of anonymous catalogers like myself who get paid the same for our work whether we do it correctly or not. Why do we find such disturbing misunderstandings so frequently signed with the institutional signatures of our most illustrious libraries? That is a question to which we must find an answer and a response.

XXI

I Know Where I'm Going, Do You?[1]

I must begin with the caveat that although I have many years experience creating, using and searching serials information in bibliographies, card catalogs, OPACs and online databases, I have never been involved in any activities involving serials cataloging and control other than the initial creation of a bibliographic record for a serial. In other words, in my cataloging work I have focussed entirely on title level access issues, never on article level access issues.

With that caveat, I gave these remarks the title "I know Where I Am Going, Do You?" in part as a humorous response to the title of this forum, but also for a serious reason: I really do know what I want from a bibliographic record, and I know that without any references to standards and metadata communities.

---

[1] Remarks at the ALCTS Serials Section, Continuing Resources Cataloging Committee, Update Forum "Continuing Resources Cataloging: Where in the World Are We Going?" ALA Annual Meeting, Washington, DC, June 25, 2007.

I know where I am going when I create a record because of my engagement in searching various bibliographic information sources for both serials at article and title level, as well as by author and subject. I do that both as a librarian with an item in hand and as a researcher with a topic in mind or a citation in hand. My orientation towards cataloging continuing resources is rooted in that wider experience, and leads me first of all to comment on a few issues that underlie all of the questions we have been asked to address, issues that we need to keep in our minds as we think about these questions.

First, serials are neither simple to describe nor to use. They have always been maddeningly complex and unpredictable objects, and online/Internet journals have compounded the problems rather than making them simpler. Barbara Tillett's desire to "Catalog it once and for all" cannot be extended to continuing resources. Attempts to simplify our treatment of such complex objects must not be undertaken on the assumption that simpler means easier or better. Recent work in joint cognitive systems theory has concluded that designing for simplicity is impractical, that instead we should design for whatever level of complexity exists. We need to develop transparent tools that give users control over their tasks rather than prosthetic devices that interpret the world for the user, simplifying that world but thereby depriving the user of control. Doing everything behind the scenes makes things much easier for the user so long as everything works, but it leaves the user powerless when anything fails for whatever reason.

Second, information technologies require not just any standards, but unambiguously defined data elements. For any task that one wishes to automate, all interpretation must be done by human beings at some point beforehand, because information technologies deal with information in only 2 ways: rigorously defined data elements, and algorithmic treatment of probabilities. Whenever accuracy is a goal, probabilities are not good enough.

Third, we cannot forget the reasons for and importance of citation, not only for the user of the library, but for the crucial scientific practice of reproducibility of results. What reproducibility of results is for the experimental sciences, checking the sources is for library based research. With the digitization, repackaging, reformatting, relabeling and revising that are rampant in the creation of electronic resources, these practices may eventually be rendered impossible *for electronic documents*. On the one hand, a digital object identifier is useless for citation purposes if the object lacks stability over time. On the other, a system which gives us a resource and a resource identifier that does not inform the reader/user of the provenance—original source and/or reproduction history—makes citation and research into context problematic. One example: Sarah Thomas' article "Quality in Bibliographic Control" is available in Cornell University's institutional repository. But the article as I found it (via a Google keyword search) had no indication of the author or publication details. I only knew what it was because I had read it previously. Someone who had not read that article previously would have no idea who wrote it when and published it where based on the item from the Cornell Repository document. That article is also available via findarticles.com, but without indication of volume, issue and pagination. I had to go find the publication details from a third search in an EBSCO database, get it again, and compare the three versions to make sure that what I had from EBSCO, the institutional repository and findarticles.com were in fact all the same item. Even then, I did not compare every word to determine if there were differences somewhere in the text. Because the first 2 versions found had incomplete metadata about who, when and where, it was impossible for me to determine whether those three versions were identical reproductions of a single paper or multiple versions without metadata distinguishing them and identifying them chronologically or otherwise. An article level service must have that metadata completely and accurately.

Fourth, any discussion of cooperation and interoperability must take seriously the diversity of purposes. Libraries cannot expect other organizations engaged in other practices in pursuit of other goals to do what we want them to do, even if we bend over backward to make it possible for them to fit into our plans. Technical systems tend to develop autonomously as possibilities reveal themselves; like markets, governments and criminals, technical developments do not follow what users of existing technologies imagine, hope for and plan for.

Fifth, implicit in all the questions is that the practices involved will all be automated processes. This means that the multiple imagined uses of cataloging/metadata are assumed to have no importance for the creation of the metadata. Given the proper packaging—whether Dublin Core, MARC, ONYX, XML or DHL—everyone can use the same data so it need only be created once. While it may seem evident enough that there is only one way to describe such things as pagination in a book (in fact there are many ways to record even that), the key issue is rather that both what information one includes or excludes (e.g. pagination) and the form in which that information is recorded are always dependent upon the purposes for which it is recorded. In an environment of automated data exchange, either we have to be satisfied with whatever we do and do not get, no matter for whom or for what purposes it was created, or we have to have a human being examine, evaluate and adapt that information to our particular purposes.

With the above assumptions and orientations, let me now tackle the three questions.

Question 1. Do libraries need to change their cataloging/metadata practices to accomodate the needs of other communities?

I felt it necessary to answer this question by changing it. A better question, one which I feel comfortable answering, would be: How do libraries need to change their cataloging/metadata practices to accomodate their own needs? The reason I rephrase it is that it seems clear to me that we need to change practices, but not at all clear how far we must accomodate the purposes of other organizations doing other things for other purposes. The motivation for the original question is that we want organizations external to the library to do certain things for us, i.e. we want to outsource certain operations.

We can outsource certain operations either because we do not want to do them or because a service appears which could enable us to do things that we would not otherwise be able to do. Altering the ways we do things to accomodate newly available services or to take advantage of enhancements that may come along is something we should not shy away from, but we need to look carefully at what this will mean for all other aspects of our work—and our patrons practices—before inadvertantly crippling practices in one area in our eagerness to enable something else.

Our current systems, structures and standards have been developed to enable us to do what WE need to do, and they are therefore not necessarily suited to other users with other tasks and goals. For example, MARC was designed for libraries in order to enable users to discriminate between data elements so these could be searched individually or in combinations. The production of a complete MARC record therefore requires the creator of that record to interpret the document described in terms of those defined elements and to code them properly. It is that labor of interpretation and detailed encoding that gives databases such as OCLC their extraordinary powers of refinement in searching. That labor costs and costs dearly, but without it we would have records which humans could interpret but machines could only treat probabilistically. That difference is evident when we compare the results we get in Google versus the results in GoogleBooks, since the latter uses metadata, not simply probabilistic juggling of the universe of information available.

It is obvious that other metadata communities can and already do use MARC metadata, but it is just as obvious that there is no reason that they need to or will continue to do so if they find or develop some system that serves *their* needs more cheaply or better. And this will continue to be the case, no matter what cataloging/metadata systems we develop or adopt in the future. We need standards that serve our purposes and techniques and organizational structures to deal with other metadata communities with their purposes, practices, structures and standards, as they come and go, and insofar as we can efficiently and effectively benefit from that orientation of our efforts.

Finally, there are many pathways to failure. One sure way is to forget about what it is we are trying to do and try to satisfy the needs of someone or everyone else. Cooperation works when those cooperating have a clear understanding of a common goal. Hafter mentioned the observation made by two Canadian librarians in 1979 that the original objective of library automation was "to harness technology for the benefit of the user" but that this "was soon replaced by the substitute and less complex objective to apply technological innovation to the manipulation of bibliographical records." Our cataloging/metadata practices must serve our purposes, and whatever changes we make in our practices, they must continue to serve all OUR needs, for all our materials in all formats. If we need the discriminative power of a MARC record, then we should abandon it only if something more useful comes along, and in any case we should be very reluctant to alter our practices to incorporate metadata that lacks that power of discrimination. If we do not need that—and some libraries clearly do not—then simpler, cheaper systems will be adequate *for those libraries.*

Question 2. Should continuing resources cataloging standards change to accommodate greater use of non-library data?

Again, the wrong question. Let us ask instead: What is the best way in which we can use non-library data to accomplish our goals? The problem with the original question is that the assumption is that non-library data fits the library's needs and purposes and it is the library that needs to change, not the data. There is a lot of non-library created metadata which I use daily. I regularly search online bookstores and databases (as well as print materials) for information on past or current issues of serials in attempts to interpret numbering (does 3 mean that it is the 3rd year of an annual and this one is for the year 1996, or is it the 3rd issue of the year 1996, following 1996 numbers 1 and 2?), dates, title changes and all sorts of other information. One thing I find is that the information is often not there, not encoded or not disambiguated, often it differs in different sources, and consequently is sometimes simply wrong. Those sources are important for me whether as confirmations or disconfirmations of my own interpretations, clear indications that insufficient information is available, or additions to my knowledge, but in every case I have to interpret what I find and evaluate it, as well as copy and paste or rekey it into my own MARC record in OCLC. In this respect the only thing that has changed from the days of print only information sources is the possibility of entering the information into the record in ways other than simply typing it all myself. To suppose that we could rely on metadata harvesting if only our metadata schemes were compatible is to assume that both interpretation and evaluation are unnecessary. That is only possible in an operation in which something, anything, is good enough, that is, in certain acquisitions, warehousing or circulation processes in which merely filling in the blanks permits the performance of the desired activity.

There certainly are and in the future will be even more ways in which we can use externally generated metadata for our purposes. But for any automated use of such metadata for our purposes, we must first guarantee that the content—not just the metadata scheme—is fit for our purposes.

Question 3. I am in a somewhat better position to comment on the CONSER Standard Record since I was a participant in the pilot project when it was called the Access Level Record. Some of you may have read my brief but harsh criticism of that pilot in which I stated that I was very positively disposed to any standard that focussed on access, but that such an approach would necessarily focus on exactly those elements that require the greatest degree of interpretation and therefore the most costly activities. I find the standard viewed in itself, apart from all issues of implementation, to be laudable. In particular the insistance in the documentation that the cataloger is free at any point to intelligently adapt the guidelines to the specific resource being cataloged. There are not that many non-required fields identified, and the guidelines state that if the patrons would indeed benefit from the addition of a non-required field, catalogers should feel free to add that information. I myself intend to create and add more 130, 245 and 246 information than either the current or former standards suggested, for the simple reason that more information in those fields is not only helpful, but often crucial for me when searching and interpreting the records that I find.

One problem apparent in the standard itself is the conflict between the two goals indicated in this third question: the standard is intended to reduce redundancy and create less cluttered, easier to read public display records. There is actually very little redundancy in a MARC record. There are text based display fields that communicate to the human users, and there are coded and controlled fields for machine manipulation. That is not redundancy, they are in each case information created for different users. Most of the elements relegated to Not Required status in the standard are either there for machine manipulation and the patron display element is retained, or vice versa. Any time we delete the controlled, structured elements that the software reads, we are in for trouble in all future technical enhancements. Any time we delete the information available to the patron, we leave the patron in a state of ignorance. We can do either or both, and if indeed neither the machine nor the patron needs a particular element, let's forget it. But in every case let us be very clear about what we are doing and the consequences.

Unfortunately, standards can never be understood in and by themselves. They will be implemented as matters of policy. They will be implemented in an environment in which cost is a factor, and in the minds of many administrators, that is the factor which overrides all others. It was precisely in that environment and primarily for that reason that the CONSER Standard was proposed and implemented. From that origin, we can predict with a considerable degree of certainty the kinds of problems which the implementation of this standard will entail.

I doubt very much that in practice any standard focussing on subject and other access points will save time since these are the very elements of each record which require the most thought and take the most time to determine and create authorized headings for. If catalogers really do focus on access, then there will be an insignificant savings of time and money on the whole. Any reduction in the descriptive information will likely make the initial activities of searching for copy more time consuming in the long run anyway. My real fear, however, is that the CONSER Standard Record has been implemented solely in the interests of saving time and money with all the reference to access being simply propaganda. Very clear indications of that were evident in the report of the pilot project. Abandoning the name "Access Level" also strongly suggests that access was emphasized in order to market the standard, not in order to guide its use.

One common theme in the literature of high reliability organizations is that quality assurance programs are often adopted and implemented for reasons other than a concern with quality. Usually those other reasons—prestige, following the trend, increasing managerial control over employees, public relations moves in the face of failure—guarantee that the program will fail in its ostensible purpose. If the CONSER Standard is implemented in institutions in the same manner as PCC was implemented in some places—as a managerial demand rather than an option available for the cataloger's discretionary use—then we can expect short term savings of time and money and long term reduction in access.

A policy implemented for reasons of cost will predictably enforce the least costly manner of implementation. In the creation of these records, the lowest allowable level of interpretation and information creation will become the maximum allowed. Not Required will become Not Allowed. At least one subject heading required will become Only one subject heading allowed. In the reuse of these records by institutions other than the creators, the policy will be "It is a CONSER Standard Record" so accept it as it is. Instead of being a record guaranteeing a certain minimum it will be treated as a record that must not be touched. The technical operations of exporting and importing will be matched organizationally by policies that insist that the cataloger see no evil and do no good.

If we maintain a dedication to serving the needs of the principal users of our bibliographic data, we can create metadata that others can harvest should they choose to do so, we can use metadata created elsewhere, adapting it to fit our purposes, and we can use the CONSER Standard Record, interpreted, modified, adapted and sometimes ignored, in our efforts to provide library users with the tools they need to perform the tasks in which they are engaged. If on the other hand, we get confused about what we are doing, for whom, and why, we may end up creating metadata that no one anywhere finds useful, and upon discovering that, we will once again be asking ourselves "Where in the world are we going?"

www.ingramcontent.com/pod-product-compliance
Lightning Source LLC
Chambersburg PA
CBHW071230290426
44108CB00013B/1356